My Marian Year

by
Robert Philip Bolton

Also by Robert Philip Bolton

The Artist as an Old Man (Self Portrait)
It's What Eddie Did
The Fable of Flitcroft Point
Jacko. One Bloke. One Year.
The Boys and Men of Auckland's Mickey Rooney Gang
The Fine Art of Kindness
Six Murders?
Underneath The Arclight
To The White Gate
The Boltons of The Little Boltons
The Tapu Garden of Eden
For Viktor. The story of Mussorgsky's 'Pictures at an Exhibition'
The Collected Short Stories
(in which is combined *Nana's Special Day and other stories*, *The Dolphin and other stories*, and *Quickies*)

Robert Philip Bolton was born in New Zealand in 1945. He has been writing most of his adult life. Most of his work is about New Zealand and New Zealanders. He lives in Auckland.

MY MARIAN YEAR
Copyright © Robert Philip Bolton (v4 11/25)
www.bolton.co.nz

ISBN: 978-0-473-15083-9

Cover from a photograph of Three Lamps Corner, Ponsonby, taken in 1951 by Graham Stewart and used with his permission.
Cover design by Craig Ross.

For Stephen, Kelly and Daniel

My Marian Year

by
Robert Philip Bolton

January

ON THE FIRST DAY OF JANUARY, AT THE VERY beginning of the Christian calendar, the Baby Jesus had his foreskin cut off. Evidently it was done on January the first because that's what Jews did to their baby boys seven days after they were born.

I didn't know that at the beginning of nineteen fifty-four, my Marian year. All I knew was that we — Mum and Dad, my Aunty Irene, me, and my little sister Tessa — had to get up and go to mass early on January the first because it was the feast of the circumcision, a holy day of obligation. I knew what a holy day of obligation was but I didn't know anything about circumcision. Nobody told me and I never heard it discussed even though every Catholic in the world — including every Catholic in our little parish of Saint Michael's — was obliged to go to mass to celebrate the mysterious event. If we didn't go to mass on a holy day of obligation Father Yeates and all the sisters at Saint Michael's said we would commit a Mortal Sin and go to hell.

So that's how my Marian year started: going to mass on the feast of the circumcision, a holy day of obligation, and worrying about going to hell if I didn't.

There were I think six other holy days of obligation. I used to know them all off by heart but now I'm not so sure. I know the other important ones, after the feast of the circumcision, were Good Friday, Christmas Day and the feast of the Assumption on August the fifteenth. Mum knew them all too plus she had a special Catholics-only calendar hanging on the wall by the safe in the kitchen to remind her of them, and of all the saints' days. Mum liked her Catholic calendar, especially at the beginning of a new month when she took it down, turned it over to a new page, immediately and superstitiously said 'white rabbits' three times for luck, and then spent a few minutes studying that month's holy picture. Then she checked the month for her notes about birthdays and appointments and of course to remind herself about any holy days of obligation so she could make sure we all went to mass properly to avoid going to hell.

There were of course many other ways to go to hell, a place to which I really didn't want to go. 'Close your eyes now and imagine how much it hurts when you put just the tip of your finger into the flame of a candle,' said Sister Ursula during catechism which we had every day in the hungry half hour before lunch. 'Now,' she said, and she seemed to enjoy saying it, 'imagine your whole body being burned by a huge fire. The flames licking up your naked body and burning your tender young skin.' And I, who possessed a vivid imagination, imagined, and shuddered with genuine fear; and I noticed that some of the girls were sniffing and wiping their eyes.

'Imagine joining all the other evil sinners in hell and hearing all their horrible screams of pain for ever and ever without end,' she ended joyfully, failing to explain how a loving god could be so unforgiving and downright cruel to little kids. Then she crossed herself quickly. We all did.

I'm not sure why but we were always crossing ourselves then although, like genuflecting, I don't remember learning how to do it nor being taught. I just knew it. Perhaps I was born knowing it. And because I found both crossing and genuflecting easy and natural I always thought it was funny to see protestants, grown-ups and kids, make such a mess of them both. I also thought they, protestants, shouldn't even have tried to do the sign of the cross or to genuflect; that for them to do those Catholic-only things must have been a sin. I suppose there was a touch of sinful pride in this as there was in my secret pleasure of knowing when to sit, stand and kneel at mass, and when to bob my head for Jesus, when protestants, who I thought shouldn't even be at mass anyway, were obviously confused by the whole special ritual.

Of course there was more to my life than being a Catholic. But because the church's teachings and dogma were big influences on my family, especially on Mum, and because they frequently weighed heavily on my mind, they are the backdrop to the stage upon which I played out my Marian year.

So here's how we made the sign of the cross. First, the simple words: *In the name of the father, and of the son, and of the holy ghost, amen.* Not so simple were the hand actions. While you said the first bit, *In the name of...* you held your left hand limply against your tummy, somewhere out of the way, while you sent your right hand — fingers together and slightly bent, the thumb held and hidden behind them — travelling smoothly upwards timed in such a way that when you said ...*the father...* it gently and briefly touched your forehead. Then you sent it south while saying ...*and of the...* to ensure that it touched your lower chest region just as you said ...*son...* then it went flying up and across towards your left (never your right) shoulder while you said ...*and of the...* ensuring that you said ...*holy...* just as you touched that shoulder; then it, your right hand, had to go rather awkwardly back across your chest to touch your right shoulder for the saying of ...*ghost.* Finally you sent it back to the centre of your chest where your fingers should have straightened, your thumb should have emerged from its hiding place, and your entire right hand should have come together with its opposite number which in the meantime should have stiffened and risen to its final position in anticipation of the meeting, for the saying of ...*amen.* Then your two hands should have been held stiffly together in the standard praying arrangement. For a less formal and more comfortable look you might have arranged your fingers so they were loosely bent and clasped together for the duration of whatever prayer might have followed the sign of the cross.

Once, later in the year when we were all saying the rosary, I made the sign of the cross by saying what Roger Machynlleth — one of the big boys from Milton Street — had taught me. 'Spectacles, testicles, wallet and watch,' I said as I put my right hand through its ritual paces. Dad laughed out loud but Mum clipped my ear with her fingers and said 'Fraser!' to Dad.

'It's an old joke, Leen,' said Dad.

'It's blasphemy and I don't like. And I don't like you encouraging him.'

Dad didn't say anything more but he gave me a secret wink and I was glad even though my ear was hot and sore.

Crossing was frequently done silently. I knew I always had to cross myself silently whenever I entered or left church by first dipping the tips of my fingers into one of the shell-shaped holy water fonts that were screwed to the wall at each side of the main church door and to the side of the two side doors. The water they contained was 'holy' because it had been blessed by Fat Pat but why I had to dip my fingers in it I didn't know and was never told. Mum had a little glass holy water font screwed to the wall beside the kitchen door although where she got her holy water from I didn't know. She used it frequently but Dad and I didn't and Tessa couldn't reach it.

Genuflecting, the other common, everyday but really important personal ritual, was performed in church whenever you moved, for whatever reason, across an invisible line drawn from the locked tabernacle, which held the communion hosts — Our Lord's body — and stood in the very centre of the altar at the front of the church, to the very centre of the back of the church. So most genuflections were made in the central aisle before you entered your pew, or as you left it before you turned your back on Our Lord to leave the church.

Like riding a bicycle, genuflecting was easy once you knew how, and once you knew how you never forgot. Here's how it worked. You placed your left foot forward of your upright body while you put the toe of your right foot behind you. Then you bent both knees and so lowered yourself until the right knee touched the floor at which time you raised yourself again bringing your right foot forward beside your left.

It sounds simple but in practice genuflecting at Saint Michael's came in an infinite variety of speeds and styles. Some people genuflected slowly, resting momentarily on their bended knee, adopting a deeply pious look, some even managing to cross themselves at the same time which I always thought was skiting. Kids naturally genuflected quickly and easily but the old, and even middle-aged people like Mum and Dad, often found it put demands on their legs and knees, their back and balance, which they were ill-equipped to meet, and so they used one hand or the other to steady themselves on the end of an adjacent pew.

Genuflection was meant to be a sort of curtsey, a mark of servility, of pious respect for Jesus who apparently lived in the tiny locked and dark tabernacle (actually a wooden cupboard with a brass knob) on the altar. But in practice, and like the sign of the cross, genuflecting was performed only casually by all but the most godly people at Saint Michael's most of whom were old ladies.

But let us return to January the first, the first day of the year and the first holy day of obligation of the year, the feast of the circumcision. Being obliged to attend mass early in the morning of January the first that year was especially hard for Dad because he and Mum had gone to a new year's eve party at Uncle Cliff and Aunty May's and got home real late. I was asleep then but Aunty Irene, that's Mum's sister who wasn't married, who stayed with me and Tessa, said that Dad got home a bit under the weather. Dad liked parties, and was often under the weather, and going to a party was always more important to him than going to mass. But he went to mass that day because he said he was more afraid of Mum than he was of the fires of hell. 'Your mother would kill me if I missed mass, Johnny Boy,' he said to me once. But he wasn't really afraid of Mum, he was just respectful and considerate of her much greater holiness. 'She's a bloody saint your mother, sometimes,' said Dad sometimes. 'You gotta thank your lucky stars for her.'

Dad was only nine years back from the war — where and when god only knows what he saw and did — so I knew he wasn't afraid of anything. He sure as hell didn't worry about hell or care even a bit about Fat Pat — that's what he called Father Yeates, or sometimes The Dork from Cork — or his opinion and he certainly wasn't afraid of him. Nor was he afraid, as I was, of Sister Ursula (who was about to become my Marian year teacher) whom he called Sister Worse-ula; once, later in the year, I even heard him call her The Old Bitch.

And so we walked to mass together that January the first morning all dressed in our Sunday best. Mum had on her best hat and Tessa and Aunty Irene wore berets because it was a sin for women and girls to go to church without something on their head. Just about anything would do and if a woman forgot to wear a hat, or had popped into church to pray on a day she wasn't wearing a hat, she might simply open her handkerchief —providing it wasn't snotty — and spread it over the top of her hair-do. Dad, too, was wearing a hat but he would have to remove it before he went into the church because while women *had* to wear a hat in church men mustn't. Indeed it was sinful for a man to enter church with his head covered so the church porch was furnished with rows and rows of coat- and hat hooks. Woman must wear a hat. Men must not wear a hat. Like the god of Jews, Muslims and Sikhs, and no doubt the gods of many other small and obscure races, nations and sects, the Catholic god was evidently obsessed with what humans did to their hair and wore on their head.

As well as his new brown summer hat Dad was dressed in his Sunday-best brown double-breasted suit, pinstriped shirt, paisley tie and his best shiny brown shoes. He looked young and dashing, walking to church with us that sunny morning, but he was in fact far from well, his quiet submissiveness due in part to his thumping headache. For while Mum could shame him into going to mass on this holy day of obligation she couldn't stop him eating and drinking after midnight the night before. We knew — Tessa and I — from when we were coached by Fat Pat for our first holy communion, that if you wanted to take holy communion at mass you had to fast — no eating or drinking — from midnight the night before otherwise you'd commit a Mortal Sin and go to hell if you died before you went to confession.

It was also a Mortal Sin to go to communion when your soul was stained with any other sins, Venial or Mortal, although sins of either kind could be washed away by going to confession. But eating and drinking after midnight, and committing other sins, which I'm sure Dad did at Uncle Cliff's new year's eve party, meant there was no chance for him to go to confession before early mass which meant he couldn't go to communion that morning which meant Mum was mad at him; and ashamed. She knew — as I and everyone else did — that those people who didn't take communion at mass on new year's day, but remained in their seats for the duration, must have done something really bad the night before and were therefore silently judged by all present.

'Why hasn't Fraser Little gone up to take communion?' 'He must have committed a terrible, terrible sin at that party last night.' 'She's a martyr though.' 'I wonder what he did.' 'I bet it was drink.' 'He's a devil around women.' 'How does she put up with it?' 'It's disgraceful how he carries on.' 'Never knows when to stop.'

'You're a disgrace, Fraser,' said Mum as the five of us walked quickly to mass in the heat of the early morning sun. 'You make me feel ashamed.'

Dad said nothing but I felt him tighten his grip on my hand. It felt clammy and I wanted to pull it away but I didn't.

Fat Pat said mass. He was the only priest at Saint Michael's and so said all the masses that needed saying as well as conducting all the baptisms, funerals, weddings, and confirmations. Mass was said in Latin and he did the whole thing facing the altar, his back to us, turning only to walk to the pulpit for the sermon and, later, to the communion rail to serve communion.

Mum went up to the altar rail of course, and so did we, Tessa and I, even though I couldn't see the point and didn't believe the story that Fat Pat could change bits of bread — it wasn't even real bread but funny little, hard, flat white round things called hosts — and a little jug of port wine into the body and blood of Our Lord. But I knew what I had to do so I did it; I lined up in the aisle to take my turn kneeling at the altar rail beside Mum, tipping back my head and sticking out my tongue so the mumbling Fat Pat could put one of the white wafers on it with his sweaty and chubby finger and thumb. A bit of Jesus's body for me to eat — that's what they said — but only Fat Pat got to drink the blood. Then I returned to my place with my hands joined, my head bowed, looking serious and sombre and holy but noticing that Dad wasn't the only man who didn't go to communion. Like the others he was sitting patiently in the pew, staring into space. He stood up to let me in and gave me a smile and a secret wink and I wondered what he was thinking about. I kneeled on the hard wooden kneelers, crossed myself and pretended like mad to pray and meditate until the silly little watery wafer had dissolved away and my stomach cramped slightly and made a gurgly noise. I was hungry.

Fat Pat said the mass but there were lots of important answering bits in Latin which were said on cue by the two attending altar boys; boys older than I who were in form two at Marist.

'They'll be priests, those boys, god willing,' Mum said. 'And won't their mothers be proud.' She said she hoped they wouldn't be brothers because brothers were only second-class priests who couldn't say mass or hear confessions.

They, the altar boys at work, wore black cassocks and white lacy surplices while Fat Pat wore ornate robes of pure white over which he hung his chasuble, a brightly coloured poncho-thing made of just one large piece of heavy fabric, intricately embroidered with silver and gold thread, with a hole in the middle for his fat, red, head which was bald but for his white hairy horseshoe. The chasuble's colour was a creamy-white that Friday but the colour changed according to the church calendar. Its colour, design and style were matched by the other altar bits and pieces of which there were many. I don't know how they decided on the mass colours but I knew from experience that purple was used during lent, black on Good Friday and for funerals, white on

Christmas Day, Easter Sunday and for weddings, and green on the all-important Saint Patrick's day.

Mass that first day of the year was like all masses: an hour-long bore that made me yawn. I couldn't understand the Latin but I knew some of what was being said and done because not only did I learn all about it at school but like all Catholic kids I had my own missal. A missal was a floppy book in which the whole mass was printed out in Latin and English with descriptions of what Fat Pat should be doing, and other notes about the scriptural readings, which varied according to the season, printed in red. Missals were important. Mine had a limp, black, leather-looking cover with a dull gold cross stamped on the front. The pages were very thin, the thinnest pages I had ever seen or felt, and the edges were coloured red. Tessa's missal was made especially for girls with a rigid plastic cover that looked as if it were made from mother-of-pearl. It had a simple cross embossed into the front and a tiny and elaborately engraved gold lock on the side. But the inside pages of Tessa's missal were exactly the same as mine — as far as I could see all missals were the same inside — and although she was especially proud of her hard-covered version I thought it was awfully sissy and could hardly bear to look at it or touch it.

I knew that people in protestant churches didn't use a missal, or even have their own version of a missal, but instead took a bible to church. Apart from what was taught from the bible at school — mostly the Christmas story, the Easter story, the parables, the beatitudes and the ten commandments — I didn't know much about the bible and it didn't seem very important. We didn't have one at home and I didn't know any Catholics who did.

Another thing that was different about Catholics at mass: unlike the protestants at their services, we didn't sing. But we did have singing at Sunday night benediction which Mum sometimes made me go to. The favourite hymn at benediction was called *Faith Of Our Fathers,* an Irish song of protest against the Church of England. Miss Fitzpatrick, Fat Pat's housekeeper, pressed out its rebellious notes and chords on a wheezy old organ and men especially seemed to enjoy singing lustily about their faith and being '…true to thee till death'. I don't know what benediction was all about; I hated having to go although I always liked the smell of the burning incense.

Anyway, early mass for the feast of the circumcision, on the morning of new year's day, a Friday, in nineteen fifty-four when I was nine and a half years old, was the start of my Marian year. Two days later, on Sunday, I had to go to early mass again. As usual on Sunday mornings I missed the first half of the kids' request session on the radio which was another thing I didn't like about being a Catholic.

During that first week of my Marian year, after having gone to mass on the Friday, for the feast of the circumcision, and the following Sunday, Mum and Dad took us to the beach for a picnic. Until then it didn't really feel like the summer holidays at all. School had finished a week before Christmas but Mum and Dad had been too busy getting ready for Christmas to take us to the beach. But once Christmas was over and the new year had started they relaxed properly to enjoy their own brief summer holiday and that included joining our aunts, uncles and cousins for an all-day picnic at the beach. My aunts, uncles and cousins from Mum's side of the family were all separately and together central to my life. Without their knowing it they brought mostly happiness to me; fun, laughter and innocent joy from simple and shared sources common to all happy families. Little did I know then that a perfect and happy family is an illusion; that the grown-ups of my family, whom I loved, respected and admired so much, were, like the grown-ups of all families, less than perfect and deserving. They had their own share of human frailties, their own faults and vanities, fears and anxieties, worries and doubts, feuds and jealousies, all of which they concealed successfully from their children. Meanwhile I'm sure they enjoyed the family get-together at the beach that day as much as I did.

It was a perfect picnic. A long and perfect day during which the tide came and went and came again while my cousins and I played endlessly in warm shallow water, on the damp sand with our new long wooden spades and tin buckets printed with bright English-looking seaside scenes. We clambered over exposed rocks to explore the clear pools left by the ebbing tide, teasing and catching small crabs and imprisoning them in our slippery-sided buckets, closing the anemones with our wrinkled fingers, collecting hard starfish and catching slippery rock cods in our open hands.

The only drawback to me was that Mum made me wear a horrible hard sun hat because she and everybody then thought that kids who got too much hot sun on the head would get polio.

'Johnny Boy,' she said when I protested. 'You don't want to be like

Michael.'

She didn't know, and could never guess, that lots of kids, including me, secretly envied Michael Sturgess for the attention and special treatment he received from grown-ups just because he had polio in one leg.

'I wouldn't mind,' I said.

'You wear your hat and be done with it,' said Mum sternly. 'You're not getting polio and that's that.'

Hat wearing didn't usually bother me but that summer there was a new hat fashion, the safari hat, and I had received one for Christmas. The safari hat was a hard, military-styled thing, somewhat like a policeman's helmet, moulded in the shape worn by nineteenth-century British soldiers in India and Africa, with a sloping brim, longer at the back than the front and sides, and coloured in a pale khaki. Safari hats — for men and boys — were made of cork, or some rigid cork-like material, and were heavy, hard, uncomfortable, and utterly impractical for playing in so we — my boy cousins and I — took them off whenever we could. And anyway they looked ridiculous and made our girl cousins laugh.

As we played on the beach, often with Dad and the uncles, Mum and my aunts sat on fringed tartan rugs spread out together under a tree on the grass, or on the sand itself against the stone wall, smoking, chatting about nothing I could imagine, laughing often, feeding the babies, changing nappies, or getting up to dangle babies, squealing and naked, in the shallows. There was plenty of food to be shared laid out on the middle of the rugs: cakes and biscuits for morning and afternoon tea; sandwiches, cold sausage rolls and mince pies, custard tarts and fruit for lunch; ham and luncheon sausage for tea with a simple salad of lettuce and tomatoes, celery, grated cheese and hard-boiled eggs covered with an easily-made salad cream. I often helped Mum prepare this family favourite dressing; it was made with a tin of *Highlander* brand sweetened condensed milk to which was added a big teaspoonful of powdered mustard, about half a cup of strong malt vinegar and some salt. The condensed milk — a standard item in every pantry — was especially sweet and sugary, yellow and sticky, and so condensed to be more viscous than engine oil, but the vinegar reduced it a more pourable consistency while the vinegar and mustard together served to counteract the sticky sweetness and so deliver a classic sweet and sour finish. I still think it's delicious.

An infinite supply of orange or lime cordial was on hand for us children. Mum made up ours at home, adding water to a sweet and sticky concentrate, and took it to the beach in bottles sealed with a cork wrapped in grease-proof paper. The men brought tall long-necked bottles of DB draught beer which they drank from plastic mugs during the course of the afternoon. Essential to the women's comfort especially was strong, hot tea and although they all took a thermos of hot water to the beach — making the tea properly with real tea leaves in a cheap and dented camping teapot — together with small bottles of milk that soon became warm and sour in the heat, and screw-top jars of sugar, they soon needed more hot water than they could ever have carried to make a pot of tea every couple of hours or so, or perhaps to heat up a baby's bottle. Then they sent off the older kids — including me — with a couple of the largest teapots, empty, to the beach tea rooms where boiling water was supplied free from a Zip water heater fixed to the wall.

As a reward we were given a few pennies to buy an ice cream from the little green kiosk under the trees. We stood together there, between the gnarled pine tree roots, littered with brown and slippery pine needles, and in the cool shade, in a long line of scantily-clad kids just like us, pushing and shoving, waiting impatiently to be served.

Then, at last, when the still-hot sun was going down but the sea was still warm and the air still humid, we joined the hundreds of other families going home by car or tram or on foot. We didn't have a car so we split up to be taken home in separate cars. Tessa and I got in the back seat of Uncle Harry and Aunty Doreen's Vauxhall with our cousins Robert and Peter. We sat on wet towels in cold togs, our bottoms full of damp sand. We were cold and wet and tired and hardly able to talk or say goodbye when we got dropped off at forty-three. It was dark by then and Mum made us have a quick bath before bed to warm us up and wash away the salt and sand.

I loved it at the beach and had had a wonderful day there. And even though, before long, Dad and my uncles had to go back to work Mum managed to arrange other picnics with her sisters — my aunties — to help make the most of every day of the summer holidays. But I knew, even then, that nothing would last forever, that the big summer holidays would come to an end and that I'd have to go back to school and face the whole of my Marian year with nasty Sister Ursula.

Grandad Little had a big black American car, a Chevrolet, and on some Sundays that summer he and Gramma Little picked us up after lunch and took us for a Sunday drive. A Sunday drive was a popular way of filling empty hours at a time when the words Sunday and entertainment were never seen or heard together. But I thought a Sunday drive was boring; a waste of time. It seemed to me something that promised much but delivered nothing. I suppose Grandad Little meant well, and Mum and Dad seemed to enjoy themselves, but I didn't. I sat in the big back seat with Tessa and Mum on long and tedious journeys, feeling vaguely sick, to a series of places beyond the boundaries of my familiar world. I knew that a Sunday drive was a way for the grown-ups to fill an empty day but I resented it because, once mass was over, I planned Sundays that were far from empty.

The Scenic Drive through the Waitakeres was a favourite destination of the grown-ups although I thought it was strange to be on a road made dark and cool, even on a hot sunny summer's day, by the thick and overhanging bush. And when we stopped at a high lookout, to look down at Auckland so far away, and Dad pointed out where we lived, and the great landmarks of Mount Eden and One Tree Hill, Mount Albert and the lava flow from there that was the Meola reef, I was never quite sure what I was looking at although I said I did. I always recognised Rangitoto.

We went to Cornwall Park, the domain and up Mount Eden because they all had 'nice tea rooms' with a 'nice outlook'. Such were the boring things that were important to grown-ups on a Sunday drive. I liked the domain best because there was a duck pond beside the tea rooms.

'They've always got lovely lamingtons here,' said Mum.

'We don't want to go in there,' I said with Tessa standing beside me in solidarity. 'It's boring.'

'Yes. Can we have an ice cream instead?' asked Tessa so nicely.

'I'll get them an ice cream,' said Grandad Little and he did.

And so we were allowed to sit with our ice creams on a cold hard scoria rock beside the brown pond watching people feeding the ducks while in the tea rooms our grown-ups watched us watch the ducks while they enjoyed their own tea and cakes and talk.

I liked the yachts around Tamaki Drive — long and sleek with deep keels and tall masts — standing in wooden cradles on the hard, many with men working on or under them, sanding and painting, with

Rangitoto in the background. And as the big Chevrolet glided swiftly and smoothly around the curves I was fascinated by the flickering effect of bright light and dark shade on the road caused by the tall and overhanging pohutukawa. We went up to Bastion Point, to the grave of Michael Joseph Savage, where Mum and Dad stopped and looked and bowed their heads, and Mum crossed herself and said a silent prayer, although I didn't know why, while Gramma and Grandad stood back a little with Tessa and me. And then, below, the remnants of the Ngati Whatua marae and the Orakei village at Okahu Bay, so close to downtown Auckland. There was a small, decrepit church there with a rusty corrugated iron roof, a graveyard, and a number of old and tumble-down houses. And there were Maori kids playing everywhere, even running unsupervised across the road and onto the beach.

'They let them run wild,' said Mum indignantly. 'They act like they own the place.'

For some reason grown-ups found a Sunday drive — which amounted to nothing more than sitting in a comfortable car for hours doing nothing at all — awfully tiring which meant that soon after Grandad and Gramma dropped us home, our tea, which is what we called our evening meal, was always simple and easy. Soft boiled eggs perhaps, with buttered toast cut into thin strips called soldiers; or Wattie's tinned spaghetti or baked beans on toast. Something simple and easy for Mum's sake.

But that summer, whether returning from a long and tiring day at the beach or a long and boring drive in Grandad Little's big Chevrolet, I remember nothing of day's end but falling into a deep, long and dreamless sleep in a cool bed, secure in my own home with my own family in my own little world. I was only vaguely aware that no summer lasts forever, that all holidays must come to an end, that it would soon be February when I would be back at school for my last year at Saint Michael's, and that every carefree day spent in my own little world, whether winter or summer, at school, at the beach or in the big Chevrolet, with my family, my cousins or on my own, when added all together would one day be seen, only faintly and from a great distance in time, as the best years of my life.

Nor was I aware that, for my anxious mother, our family Sunday together was only a brief respite from the worry and fear that haunted her for the rest of the week. As I was being overcome by sleep she was sitting in the breakfast room with Dad, smoking a cigarette, silently worrying about money while he, apparently without a care in the world, smoked a cigarette — a *Grey's* — and finished the *8 o'clock,* the Saturday night sports edition of *The Auckland Star.*

Was Mum right to worry? Were we poor?

Like most young couples then and now the hardest times for Mum and Dad came at the beginning of family life when their children were young. But although they didn't have much money they had their health, plenty of energy, and optimism about the future, and we kids had our own natural health, strength and resilience. So we may have been poor but not desperately so; not like the families who lived in the states, the nearby colony of state houses. True, our standard of living was low compared with standards taken for granted later that century but at the time it was more a matter of being 'hard up' as they said, plain financial hardship of the type and degree then being experienced by all working class families in post-war New Zealand.

We were a bit poor, but we were not alone, and the tight-fisted, penny-pinching stinginess that came naturally to Mum was essential to our little family's survival. Dad was only recently returned from war, had no savings and earned only low wages, but he shared his circumstances with thousands of other men of his generation. Indeed it took many years of shortages and struggle before New Zealand and its frugal working people recovered from the dreadful war that had come so soon after the economic depression referred to universally as The Slump. And the fear that The Slump would return, like a plague, as silently and mysteriously as it had arrived in nineteen-twenty-nine — when Mum and Dad were themselves children — and bring with it more unemployment, hunger and degradation, haunted working class people in a way that made them more cautious than the times required and left them insecure, frightened, wary and unreasonably parsimonious for the rest of their lives.

And so were we poor? Not really. And should Mum have worried? Probably not. But she couldn't help it. Like all mothers she worried because she thought of nothing but the welfare of her children. She made economies in many ways and must have scrimped, saved and worked hard to provide nourishing meals. And she must have protected me and Tessa in ways that I will now never know. And if she *was* worried — and she must often have worried about the shortness of money, the health and welfare of her family, and her heavy responsibilities — then she mostly kept it to herself. But sometimes, often, during that year, usually at the end of the week, Tessa and I waited with her after school, watching helplessly, as she stood outside Easts' Four Square, her fingers groping hopelessly into an open but empty purse, unable to find the few coins she needed for some harmless little luxury.

'Mum. What's the matter?'

'Oh, it's nothing, Johnny Boy,' she said, wiping her eyes with her fingers. 'A wee bar of Cadbury's would be nice, wouldn't it.'

How could a ten-year-old boy comfort a weeping mother?

Despite my awareness of our general but not desperate neediness I personally never felt poor or disadvantaged. No doubt due to Mum's personal sacrifices, her cleverness and care, Tessa and I never experienced the hunger which she herself had experienced as a child of The Slump. But while I was aware of Mum's trials — because she was always at home, day and night, before and after school, when I was ill, and during the holidays — I didn't know what sacrifices if any Dad made to help his young, harassed and worried wife make ends meet. Perhaps he thought, as many men then did, that being the wage earner was sufficient a contribution to the family economics. Certainly he worked hard — working overtime twice a week and most Saturday mornings — but so did Mum work hard, physically hard, with two small children to care for, not enough money, a household to manage on her own, and no help from the machines and appliances which later generations took for granted.

Despite Mum's fears and worries we were in fact quite lucky. We lived in our own house in Winstone Street which was bought, during the war, by Grandad Little who seemed to me to be rich but was probably what was then called 'well off'. And although Dad was repaying him by way of a mortgage, and the regular mortgage payments must sometimes have been hard to find, I knew that our house, number forty-three in a long street of privately-owned quality bungalows built in the nineteen-twenties and –thirties, not only provided a place to live but made us feel secure and somewhat superior to the more obviously poor rent-paying tenants in the drab streets of the states on the other side of the main road.

Grandad Little often helped out by buying little things — and sometimes not-so-little things — for me and Tessa. One Sunday in the summer holidays he and Gramma arrived for a Sunday drive with two brand new scooters. Tessa's was a standard little-girl thing, painted red with cream-coloured wheels, two at the back for the sake of stability, but mine was a much more modern and streamlined model, smarter than any I had seen before, with chromium trim, pneumatic tyres, sprung wheels and a better-than-normal brake which worked like a lever to press on the back tyre when pushed by the heel of the scooting foot. I don't know how or where Grandad Little found such a beautifully-styled scooter — I had never seen, nor ever saw, another like it except in American pictures — but I became especially proud of it and the way it attracted a lot of attention and envy from other kids. School was to start at the beginning of February and I think Grandad expected us to ride our scooters to school every day. Although many kids rode their bikes to school, and Saint Michael's had a spacious bike shed to shelter them, no one rode a scooter to school and I was not going to be the first.

While Mum was always grateful to Grandad Little for his help she was also vaguely uncomfortable about it. I wasn't told about all the things he bought, nor how else he contributed to our welfare, but I know he paid for many things Dad could never have afforded including the installation and rental of our telephone ostensibly so he and Gramma Little could more easily keep in touch with us. It turned out later that he had a dark and ulterior motive but Mum didn't know that then and she wept openly, with joy, when the new telephone — so big and black, hard and heavy, with a braided cord, a shiny chrome dial, and a loud ring from real bells — was installed at the end of January, just before school was due to start. I had often seen her weep quietly, but from sadness, outside the red phone box at the end of Winstone Street when she couldn't manage the two pennies she needed to telephone her mother, my Gramma Fahey. She tried to telephone Gramma Fahey whenever she went to the shops which was almost every day. If I were there, waiting outside the phone box, bored and restless, chipping away idly at the brittle putty around the many windows of the little wooden building, I found these long phone calls tedious in the extreme. The one-sided conversation — which I could hardly hear anyway through the closed and soundproof door of the phone box — was of no interest to me yet there was nothing to be done but wait. Sometimes it seemed the talking would never end and I often had reason to silently thank a stranger whose arrival at the phone box, especially if he showed signs of impatience — foot tapping and sighing and pointedly looking at his wrist watch — obliged Mum to end her call. I therefore had my own reason to be grateful to Grandad Little for providing us with our own telephone.

Dear Gramma Little helped too. She was an expert tailor-dressmaker. She owned a Singer treadle sewing machine upon which she had, during The Slump, made clothes for her own two boys — Dad and Uncle Cliff — and was therefore, unlike most dressmakers, accustomed to making boys' clothes. And so she made me many handsome shirts and shorts when Mum could afford nothing more than my standard school uniform, as well as many frocks for the growing Tessa in a frilly and feminine style, which my tomboyish sister secretly despised, and many complicated pleated skirts and dresses of a more mature style for cousin Sandra, all of a style and quality which our respective parents would never have been able to afford.

Gramma Fahey too was skilled with her hands although not at sewing or anything else especially practical that could contribute to the welfare of her grandchildren. Her special skill was crochet for which she was widely admired. I was always amazed at how she could take a ball of white or brown string, manipulating it around a simple hooked needle, using crooked fingers on hands bent and crippled by arthritis, sometimes hardly looking, and quickly turn it into a delicately patterned and lacy round thing whose charm and daintiness varied only according to the coarseness of the chosen thread. The problem was that everything she made was round or was made of sewn-together separate pieces which were themselves round. I assumed that crocheted products had to be round by definition and thought that despite her skill and prodigality there must have been a natural limit to how many round things could be absorbed into even her large circle of family and friends. There was hardly a flat surface at forty-three which didn't sport a round doily — white in the bedrooms and brown elsewhere — once produced by Gramma Fahey with her crooked hands and hooked needle. But her products weren't all dainty and delicate. Everyone she knew, including Mum, had one or two of her cleverly designed white string shopping bags which seemed capable of being stretched infinitely in every possible direction to accommodate more shopping by volume than anyone could ever possibly carry by weight.

Mum didn't sew or crochet but she was a good knitter. Unlike sewing and crochet, which both required concentration, knitting could be done almost anywhere at any time. And while wool — which was widely available in a vast variety of colours and weights — wasn't cheap it was a lot cheaper than buying the equivalent in a finished garment. It was bought in loose coils called skeins which had to be rolled by hand into a ball, about the size of a cricket ball, before it could be used.

I hated it when Mum drafted me to help her with perhaps the most boring task a boy could ever be asked to do: to stand in front of her — she was seated — and hold my flat hands vertically inside each end of the new skein, applying a gentle outward pressure to keep the skein reasonably taut, while she quickly and deftly drew off the yarn and rolled it into a few soft round balls with which to begin her knitting.

'Come on, Johnny Boy, keep your hands still,' she said, but it was hard for me to stand in one place for five minutes without moving my hands. And suddenly I developed unbearable itches in awkward places which I simply wasn't allowed to relieve with a scratch.

Mum could knit almost anything in the interest of producing warm if not particularly stylish clothes for herself and us. She went nowhere without her knitting kit, an old leather bag containing all her knitting accoutrements including the current printed pattern, a partly finished garment, a skein or two of wool and a soft partly-used ball with the two long knitting needles pushed through one of which held the current project by the last knitted row. So equipped she could sit anywhere — in the tram, in Grandad's big Chevrolet, by the fire, listening to the radio, at the beach, in a soft or hard chair at home or away — and seemingly engage in long and meaningful conversations while paying almost no attention to her handiwork. There may have been a brief pause at the end of each row, while she switched the knitting-on and knitting-off needles between hands, or if the yarn, emerging jerkily from the open top of her knitting kit, became snagged on something and had to be freed, but otherwise her knitting continued smoothly, without interruption, without effort and apparently without thought.

The pressure of home economics forced Mum to be more practical with her knitting than she may have liked. Most of her time and effort went into the creation of bulky warm jumpers, cardigans, scarves and gloves for us all, and even my vain father didn't mind wearing one of her bulky warm sweaters on his winter bike rides to and from work.

But she was less serious and sensible when she knitted numerous gaily-coloured pixie hats — woollen hats with a pointed top and a buttoned chin strap — which were then popular with small girls, and layettes of beautiful designs, with frivolous touches of pink and blue, and perhaps white, pink or blue satin ribbon, for the numberless nieces and nephews being produced by her five sisters.

While she enjoyed knitting, finding it pleasurable and therapeutic as well as productive, she definitely didn't enjoy darning. But because so many clothing items were made of wool darning was an essential homemaking skill as it was the only way to repair the wear-and-tear holes in the toes and heels of socks and the elbows of jumpers and cardigans. She was a good and tidy darner but it was a chore she always postponed, putting the holey garments aside in the darning basket — in fact a small and lidded wicker basket — until she could put off a darning session no longer. By then she would require two or three evenings of two or more hours each to painstakingly stretch each holed piece over a special piece of smooth wood with a handle below — a tool called, I think, a darning mushroom — and while she held the holey piece in place with her left hand, by gathering it tight around the handle below, she used a thick and slightly curved darning needle to bridge the hole with a matching thread of wool, backwards and forwards, and then again at right angles, alternately going over and under the crossed thread, basket-weave style, gradually filling the hole as neatly and smoothly as possible.

Despite her money-saving efforts there were still plenty of worries for Mum, and not only about money. Our health was a constant concern. Children's health was first judged by everyone, including teachers, doctors and nurses, by their physical appearance. So a fat baby was considered healthy and bonny, his weight signifying family affluence and excellent motherhood. But pale and thin children — like the Worboys twins, a boy and girl, who lived in Milton Street, went to the local primary school, and were naturally pale and thin — were considered the victims of anaemia, malnutrition and rickets, and therefore of poverty and neglect. They were taken from their parents for a few weeks and sent to Pigeon Mountain, a government health camp established for the health of the country's post-war children, to receive the nourishment, fresh air and exercise they were deemed to need. I had heard about Pigeon Mountain from kids who had been there and dreaded being made to leave my own home and my own little world for even a few days in such a place. But many children — including the Worboys twins — sent to Pigeon Mountain for their own benefit were in fact naturally thin and actually became ill from being with genuinely sick children, and from chronic homesickness, and so were sent home early from the so-called health camp in worse condition than when they arrived.

It must have been hard for mothers who had their frail little ones compulsorily taken away to a health camp to have to admit to themselves, their family and friends, and to the authorities, that they couldn't afford to give their dear children the care and nourishment they needed as a foundation for a healthy life. And so Mum lived in fear that we were looking thin or pale or that our health would fail due to one of the many infectious diseases which were then common and to which children in particular were especially vulnerable. German measles (rubella), English measles, chicken pox, mumps and whooping cough were commonplace and could be dangerous. However most mothers were not exactly happy but somewhat relieved if their little girls contracted rubella, or their boys mumps, knowing that mild infections in childhood would provide valuable immunity in later life. Poliomyelitis, diphtheria and scarlet fever though were the greatest worries and mothers lived in constant dread of these diseases and their children's survival.

I had reasonably good health, and thought myself to be generally well, although I was plagued in the winter by tonsillitis and the painful earaches that came with it. Those earaches sometimes kept me awake for hours and left me — and Mum who stayed awake with me, fretting — exhausted, and unable to go to school. But happily, and almost certainly thanks to a careful and conscientious mother, I never came to the attention of the authorities for looking pale, thin or rickety.

Good food is the foundation of good health and children know from the moment they are born, when their tummies are first tweaked by hunger, that food is essential to their survival. They seek it instinctively, bawl if they don't get it, and when they do get it they soon want and need more.

I never knew real hunger, and if money were short, as it often was, Mum made sure we were never short of good food. There had been some food rationing in New Zealand during and after the war but it was an artificial shortage due only to sending so much of our abundant output 'home' to Britain where post-war food shortages were real and the human suffering genuine. New Zealand was a remarkably efficient producer of quality food grown naturally. Meat — especially that from beef and sheep — was plentiful and cheap as were the vast quantities of butter, milk and cheese that came from our little country's hugely efficient dairy farms. Vegetables and fruit were also plentiful and cheap and produced naturally entirely in accordance with the seasons. The range and variety of available food — whether meat, dairy, vegetables or fruit — were limited not by the inadequacies of New Zealand production but by the very plain demands of the British market which bought most of our food production and therefore benignly dictated what should be produced. Happily and coincidentally the tastes and desires of New Zealand's people — largely British immigrants or the descendants of British immigrants — coincided exactly with those of their British customers. Inevitably Mum and Dad, more especially Mum, had inherited the simple tastes and plain-cooking recipes of Britain although in New Zealand the recipes had evolved a little to suit the circumstances, lifestyles and climate which were so different from those which ruled where and when the British preferences naturally arose.

So the foods and tastes with which I was familiar were plain and simple — and, it must be said now, bland and uninteresting — meaning that anything different or foreign, especially foods with strong or unfamiliar flavours, were spurned, not without a disparaging comment.

Mum's face assumed a look of utter disgust when for some reason she had been given some pickled herrings by Mrs Jansen, a Dutch immigrant neighbour.

'In Holland these we like very much, Mrs Little,' she said. 'You must try.'

'Oh, ta,' said Mum. 'I will. Later.'

And later, at home, she put one of the rolled up little grey things on a plate, picked it up tentatively with a fork and put it nervously to her mouth. Actually she never got past the smell of the brine to even taste the herring itself. She pulled her head away, made a horrid face at me, and dropped it fork and all to the plate before rushing to the toilet to make retching noises I could hear from the breakfast room.

She came back looking weak and pale.

'Do me a favour, Johnny Boy,' she said, wiping her screwed up mouth with her apron. 'Chuck 'em all in the rubbish bin.'

'Let me try,' I said but I was forbidden even a tiny taste on the grounds that pickled herrings, enjoyed for hundreds of years by millions of Dutch people, were not only foreign and foul tasting but probably poisonous.

It was the same whenever she sampled or accidentally tasted something foreign including such harmless and common foods and tastes as garlic, capsicum, chilli, gherkins, olives, strong black coffee, dry wine, yoghurt, pasta sauce and lasagne, and salty liquorice. I don't know how or why these remarkably strange and exotic foodstuffs were even allowed over the threshold at forty-three but out they all went to add even more foulness to the large and always-foul rubbish bin — dented and misshapen, with an ill-fitting lid — which stood at the back of the house until Dad put it out for collection on Thursday mornings before he went to work.

And so our diet, while good and healthful, was plain and unadventurous. I started my day with a breakfast cereal. In the summer it was usually a plate of cornflakes or rice bubbles with milk and sugar. In the winter it was hot porridge. Mum used to use naturally coarse rolled oats for the porridge, which she had to soak overnight prior to cooking in the morning, but she had recently discovered a prepared and processed brand — the packet had a picture of a saluting boy scout signifying, I suppose, being prepared — which didn't need overnight soaking and produced a smoother porridge. I liked that porridge. I liked to put a big spoonful of butter in the middle of my serving which would melt, yellow and runny as an egg yolk, from the porridge's heat, before adding milk — preferably top-milk, the name used for the cream which always rose to the top of the milk bottle — fetched fresh from the gate that morning, and sprinkling heaps of brown sugar over the whole big dish.

Winter also brought ripe grapefruit to the table. A not-large tree stood at the end of our back yard together with a lemon tree. Despite its modest size its winter branches were laden and bent with bunches of the juicy but tart fruits, waxy, shiny and yellow, some almost as big as bowling balls. Just one half of one of these monstrous fruits was enough for me and it was best prepared the night before. Mum cut two grapefruits in half through the equator, sprinkled the exposed surfaces with white sugar, and left them overnight. By morning the pale and cool flesh, comprised of millions of tiny fibrous and transparent bags of juice, had absorbed the sugar's sweetness while the sugar itself had joined together to make two or three large and crunchy crystals. I ate the sugar first and then used a teaspoon to scoop out the cold, sweet and juicy flesh, one segment at a time, taking pride in the neatness of my work and the symmetry of the empty case and its unbroken membranous walls.

There was always hot buttered toast for breakfast, winter or summer, made only with white bread cut by hand into thick slices directly from the loaf. Mum bought our bread fresh every day from the local bakery. It was always white, unwrapped and uncut. No one bought brown bread while the coarse, grainy and truly wholemeal breads of later years, or bread that was pre-cut and wrapped, simply didn't exist. Only two loaves were available from the bread shop: the Sydney flat, which made square slices, and a bread called a chub which Tessa and I secretly called bum bread because the top was divided into two rounded and raised humps quite like a pair of large and sunburned buttocks. Both these standard loaves were segmented in the middle meaning the baker could easily break the loaf in half by hand for customers who didn't need a full loaf. Having collected a loaf of fresh bread from the baker the temptation to break it in half and tear away layers of the warm, soft, white bread was more than could be resisted and caused many kids, including me, to get in for it with an angry mother. There was also a loaf called a Vienna which was also rounded on top but in one continuous end-to-end form, and the barracuda which was like a short and thick *baguette*, neither of which was segmented and so couldn't be broken in half. This should have made them proof against childish pilfering of their insides but many kids couldn't resist picking away, like hungry birds, at the crusts of any loaf. But Mum didn't buy the Vienna and barracuda loaves because they were more expensive.

'They're all made from the same dough anyway,' she said. 'I can't see the point.'

She was probably right.

Bakeries were small privately-owned local businesses. Our bakery, on the main road near the bottom of Winstone Street, stood in the middle of a large block of land and had a small stand-alone shop fronting the main road from which it supplied most of the neighbourhood. I went into the shop often enough, sometimes on my own, but what happened in the big windowless bakery behind the shop

— with its tall and tapering chimney — was a mystery.

'There's a baker who spits in the dough,' said Anthony Hughes once. 'There are big machines kneading the dough for ages and ages and he gets bored and spits into the dough which gets mixed up by the machines.'

Anthony Hughes was a big boy who lived in Milton Street. We Winstone Street kids didn't believe him about the spitting — or perhaps we didn't want to believe him — but we knew it might be true because his father really did work at the bakery.

Sometimes while walking past the bakery on the way to school I caught a distant glimpse of Mr Hughes and the other bakers standing smoking at an open door, dressed all in white, sometimes shirtless but in a white singlet, dusted with flour, and I wondered which of them was the spitter. I could see the big machines behind them, cream and pale green and chrome, and the hint of black and smoky ovens, but as all the baking was done at night, so that fresh bread would be available in the shop by morning, the men must have been at the end of their shift. I didn't tell Mum what Anthony Hughes said but I thought about the spit every time I had a sandwich.

Like most people we had a regular bread order which had to be collected each day. As Mum walked past the shop every day on her way to and from the shops — food shopping had to be done every day — it was easy enough to pick up the bread order on the way home. The unwrapped loaves stood, end out, on deep cream-painted shelves behind the counter. Bread reserved by regular order was labelled with the customer's name printed on a white card which was held in the grip of a small tight spiral of steel wire the other sharp end of which was stuck into the end of the reserved loaf. Spare bread, as it was called, was set aside from the ordered bread so that casual customers passing by, or customers who needed more than their regular order, could see at a glance what if any spare bread was available. 'Pop in and see if there's any spare bread, Johnny,' was an instruction I received when more bread was required at short notice and this arrangement saved the man in the shop having to answer the same question, 'Any spare bread?', from me and so many other customers.

The unwrapped bread was handed over, unceremoniously, by a bare hand, with no attempt to wrap or otherwise protect the loaf. Mum would take it and add it, unprotected, to her bag or trundler. If I were collecting it I'd simply carry it home in my hands or under my arm working hard at every step to resist the temptation to break it open or pick at the crust.

Bread was baked and available fresh only five days a week meaning that for the weekend we had to double our bread order on Fridays. But there was no way to keep bread fresh so a loaf or two of extra bread bought fresh on Friday became dry and stale over the weekend, awful for sandwiches and suitable only for toasting. Perhaps its only merit was that, compared with soft fresh loaves, it was easy to slice accurately and thinly without losing its shape. This state of weekend bread affairs, even worse over a long holiday weekend, was accepted without question by passive and uncomplaining housewives like Mum who were conditioned to believe that everyone, including bakers, was entitled to a weekend without work. Later though some bakeries began baking on Saturday nights to provide hot, fresh bread on Sunday mornings although at a premium price. Fresh bread on a Sunday was such a luxurious novelty that people happily paid the few pennies more it cost and the term 'Sunday bread' was coined to denote warm, fresh, white bread that was somehow better than that available during the week.

But whether the bread was fresh or stale, week-days or weekends, it was always toasted and buttered while hot as a breakfast standard. Like most people I liked nothing better than the salty taste of Vegemite and melty butter on my hot breakfast toast. Some people preferred Marmite, an almost identical product but made by the Seventh Day Adventist church whose *Sanitarium* brand vegetarian products were avoided by my Catholic mother; she considered Adventists, and Mormans equally, to be nothing but evil devil-worshipping cultists.

'I open the door and make the sign of the cross to them and they always go away,' she said.

And they always did.

Marmalade was also popular at our breakfast table, especially if it were home made with plenty of coarse grapefruit and lemon peelings from Dad's own trees, although Mum preferred home-made sweet jams like strawberry, raspberry and plum.

At a time when refrigerators were a luxury and home freezers unknown many housewives were necessarily highly skilled at the traditional, demanding and time-consuming home-crafts of making jams and jellies and preserving fruits and vegetables in jars. And although Mum possessed the skills, and would have appreciated the savings and the luxury of being able to draw from a full larder, she lacked the necessary time and so depended on the generosity of friends and family for the wonderful home-made marmalade, jams and jellies she and we so enjoyed at the breakfast table. But at least she, or rather Dad, was able to contribute to the home economics by providing the makers with copious grapefruit, lemons, figs, apples, grapes and passion fruit from his back yard orchard.

Sunday breakfast was different. On Sundays, and only on Sundays, Mum prepared a big cooked breakfast when we got home from mass. Perhaps because it was the only day Dad never went to work, or perhaps because having fasted for communion since midnight Saturday they were especially hungry, perhaps as a reward for their fasting, or perhaps because breakfast didn't have to be rushed and there was time to both prepare it and enjoy it, a cooked breakfast was a Sunday morning ritual. Mum started making it as soon as we returned from mass and she had changed out of her Sunday best. Dad, meanwhile, relaxed at the table with his *8 o'clock*. It was a predictable and standard cooked breakfast, one that would now be called an English breakfast, of fried eggs, thick rashers of bacon with plenty of lean meat edged with fat and a crisp rind, delicious black pudding — made by Pellows, our butchers, to be dry and peppery with plenty of barley — tomatoes, and sometimes split bananas, all fried in a pan deep with dripping, and served with hot buttered toast. Sometimes the bread was fried instead of toasted and sometimes tinned baked beans or spaghetti was added to the side of the fried food. And sometimes there would even be liver or lamb chops. There was tea of course, and a second brew was inevitable. Meanwhile I chewed the fat from the bacon rinds left on other plates while Mum read the *Zealandia,* the Catholic newspaper which she bought from a stand in the church porch after mass every Sunday. Dad resumed his reading of the tabloid *8 o'clock* which was an essential read for all men as all sports were played on a Saturday, and only during the day, never at night, and there were no Sunday newspapers to report the racing and sports results. The *8 o'clock* filled a large gap in a man's weekend leisure.

Mum and Dad had plenty of time to read their papers because weekends were legally and officially set aside for family life. No shops except dairies were allowed to open on Saturday and Sunday while the law discouraged all but essential Saturday work by forcing employers to pay overtime rates. Saturday was the day for kids' and grown-ups' participation in and watching sports while the only spectator sport held at night was the noisy but exciting summer speedway at Western Springs.

While there was plenty of other grown-up entertainment available on Saturday nights, including picture theatres and dance halls, Sunday was an enforced day of rest; nothing was open and nothing happened. Commercial activities of any sort were not just frowned upon but were forbidden by law. The only people allowed to work on Sundays were those whose job was considered essential including — and this was necessarily spelled out in detail at school because working on Sundays, the Lord's day and a day of rest, was considered a sin — workers on trams, trains and buses, doctors and nurses, firemen and ambulance men. Advertising was banned and some of Saint Michael's high-minded Catholic tradesmen, who used their van to go to mass, had canvas blinds, weighted at the bottom, fixed to the side panels of their vans which they could drop down on Sundays to cover the van's advertising sign which usually announced nothing more wicked than the owner's name and phone number.

The Auckland anniversary day holiday at the end of January brought me an unexpected treat. Aunty Irene had acquired a new boyfriend called Dennis who decided — or perhaps it was decided for him — that I should go with him and Aunty Irene to the carnival at Western Springs. Dennis was a lot of fun; he liked me and I liked him although I realise now that I was probably sent along as a chaperone. If that were the case then he showed no resentment but treated me kindly, generously and somewhat like a little brother. He was prepared to take Tessa too but Mum said no, it would be too much excitement for Tessa, and her little legs wouldn't be able to keep up, and I was secretly glad.

It was early evening when we got to the Springs. Dennis had his own car which he parked at the top of the Bullock Track and I noticed, as we made the steep descent to the Great North Road, looking down on the colourful circus, the grazing elephants and donkeys, the lions' cages, and all the lit up rides, blinking and flashing brightly in the dusk, and the shabby sideshow tents down one side, that Aunty Irene walked between me and Dennis, holding his hand as well as mine. And they walked around the fair together holding hands whenever they could.

'I even saw them kissing,' I told Tessa later.

Tessa grimaced. 'I wouldn't want to kiss him,' she said in disgust. She was nearly eight.

Dennis said I could have anything I wanted to eat and we could all have two rides and one side-show together, and I could choose. I had been to the carnival only once before, with Mum and Dad, but that time I was allowed only one ride, one candy floss and no side-shows. Now, unbelievably, thanks to Dennis, and no doubt his desire to impress Aunty Irene, I had an almost unlimited choice. My excitement must have shown because Dennis laughed and so did Aunty Irene and I felt special and spoiled. I had candy floss again, a big serving this time, pink and white mixed, and two battered sausage hot dogs dripping in tomato sauce, one when we got there and one when we were leaving, and I dripped tomato sauce on my school shirt and Aunty Irene said it didn't matter. For my rides I had *two* goes on the dodgems, one after the other. The first time I went to the carnival with Dad, and had a go on the dodgems, Dad did all the steering and the fairgrounds man had to keep jumping on the back of our car, holding on to the power pole with one hand and steering with the other, to get us out of a traffic jam. But both times with Dennis he let *me* do all the steering and the fairgrounds man hardly ever jumped on the back.

It was hard to choose a sideshow from all those available. But Dennis said it was up to me so I had to make a decision by looking at the signs. Most of the sideshows featured a misfortunate man or woman with some sort of physical handicap or deformity. There were even grown-up Siamese twins.

'It's awful,' said Aunty Irene.

I thought it was neat.

'They're freaks,' said Dennis. 'It's the only way they can earn a living, going around the fairs and carnivals, letting people pay to look at them.'

It was amazing. Dennis was shouting and I was free to choose some strange freakish person to really and truly stare at as much as I liked. I looked at all the signs and murals that decorated the sideshow tents and advertised their strange performances, and Dennis, strolling around holding hands with Aunty Irene, gave me plenty of time to make up my mind. There was a bearded lady, a fat man, a hairy man, a strong man who could blow up hot water bottles, a tall man and a midget together, grown-up Siamese twins and the Half Man as well as a fortune teller, a hypnotist and a magician. Finally, after walking up and down the saw-dusty grass avenue of sideshow tents, with Aunty Irene and Dennis happily trailing along behind, I made my choice.

Dennis laughed.

'Right,' he said, 'The Half Man it is.'

Inside the dimly-lighted tent we joined a small hushed audience seated on folding wooden chairs arranged on the saw-dust and grass around a small stage. In the middle of the stage, above our eye level, was a man — the Half Man — whose body ended a bit above where I thought his tummy button should be. He was there, his arms folded, his eyes closed. Silent. As still as a statue.

'Is that him?' I whispered to Aunty Irene.

'Yes, Johnny. Shhh.'

'But what's happening? Why isn't he moving?'

'He'll wait until there's enough people.'

'But how will he know?'

'How will he know what?'

'When there's enough people.'

'What?'

Grown-ups can be so dumb.

'He's got his eyes closed so *how* will he know when there's enough people.'

'I don't know, Johnny,' she said impatiently. She sounded just like Mum. 'Just shush and wait and watch.'

And so I waited. And I stared. I stared at the still, silent Half Man with his eyes closed. I stared at his dark skin, his thick black hair and his black goatee beard. I stared at his red fez and his gold jacket; it was decorated with elaborate red and green brocade, threaded with beads and diamantes, and had fringed epaulettes on the shoulders like a soldier or something.

It was nearly dark in there and the underneath of the stage was covered in with a painted canvas skirt, dirty and crushed. It was my belief, shared by others I think, that we were being tricked; that the Half Man was simply a whole man standing in a hole in the stage, hiding the lower half of his body below stage level. Consequently there was a collective gasp — Aunty Irene even put her hand up to her mouth in shock — when someone behind the stage banged a tinny gong and the Half Man suddenly opened his eyes and looked about the tent at us; he stared at us staring at him. Then he put his long-fingered flat hands to the stage surface and lifted his half-body so that it hung between his long straight arms. And when he swung his little body forward I could see that his gold jacket ended underneath with a soft green velvet pad held in place by a gold draw string and that it was on this pad that he rested while talking.

The show lasted about twenty minutes during which time the Half Man talked to us in a strange accent about his life, being born a Half Boy in Turkey and working as a child in circuses all over Europe. He was, he said, even in a Hollywood picture. And while he spoke he showed us how he could walk around on his hands, up and down the steps of the stage. He could even run. It was amazing. The show ended with the Half Man answering questions from the audience — he sounded bored — although nobody asked him what I longed to know. So when we came out of the tent I plucked up the courage to ask Dennis. I never could have asked Aunty Irene.

'You know what I wanted to know?'

'What's that, Johnny?'

I stopped and beckoned Dennis to bend to my level so I could whisper in his ear.

'How does he go to the toilet?'

'What?'

'You know. Does he have a proper willy or what? And what about number twos?'

Dennis laughed.

'You know, mate,' he said. 'I wondered that too.'

'Well?'

'I don't s'pose we'll ever know,' he said.

'And where's Turkey?'

'What?'

'Where's Turkey?' I asked again.

'Why?'

'That's where he said he comes from.'

'Did he?' said Dennis.

'Yes. That's what he said,' said Aunty Irene.

'Oh,' said Dennis. 'I missed that.'

'Well where is it?' I asked yet again.

'In Asia somewhere,' said Dennis. 'Near India I think.'

But I could tell he didn't really know.

When, later, I told Dad and Mum and Tessa about the Half Man I was surprised that Mum seemed annoyed and somewhat disappointed that Aunty Irene had let Dennis take me to see such a thing and even more annoyed that I had spilled tomato sauce on my new school shirt. But Dad just laughed.

'The poor bloke actually paid good money for that Half Man?' he said. 'Must be love.'

Tessa was just plain jealous.

It must have been an expensive outing for Dennis but evidently in vain as I never saw or heard of him again.

February

THE START OF SCHOOL AT THE BEGINNING OF
February, the hottest month of the summer, marked the real beginning
of the Marian year. Until then I didn't know anything about it. Fat Pat
must have known about it since September the previous year when the
pope told Bishop Liston and the bishop told him. But he didn't tell us
until the beginning of February when he knew all the grown-ups would
be back from their summer holidays.

Fat Pat was a large, mostly bald, round-headed, round-bodied,
round-faced and red-faced old Irishman, somewhat dull, who smoked
heavily and never declined the offer of a drink, especially whisky, from
Dad or any parishioner. He tried to be jolly with kids, manly with men
and charming with women but he failed in all respects. But no one
could accuse him of failure as a parish priest; he was passionate about
his job in the church and utterly dogmatic about the church's teachings
and authority. And so when the time came, at the beginning of
February, to introduce the Marian year to his flock he didn't just
announce it but thundered it out from the pulpit with such a passion
that his red face turned redder and his stiff white collar looked as
though it would strangle him.

Evidently the pope had declared that nineteen fifty-four would be
dedicated to Our Lady, the Marian year, during which 'da holy farter'
(that's what Fat Pat called him) demanded that the faithful should pay
particular attention to the veneration of the Virgin Mary. It was
therefore the duty of each wife and mother in the parish, as Our Lady's
representative, to show her devotion to Our Lady by having her entire
family say the entire rosary every day for the entire year. 'The family
that prays together, stays together,' he thundered, somewhat
unoriginally, bringing his podgy pink fist down hard on edge of the
cheap pine pulpit and sending the parish notices flying in the process.
The Children of Mary girls, who were sitting below him at the front,
had to rush to collect them and hand them up to him in a disordered
pile.

Tessa and I set off together the next morning for the first day of
the new school year blissfully unaware that Fat Pat's Sunday sermon
about the rosary and the Marian year had changed Mum suddenly,
dramatically and irreversibly. All I knew that day was that the summer

holiday, which in December had seemed to promise so much, including the excitement of Christmas followed by endless days at the beach, now seemed to have been nothing but a brief interlude. I realised glumly that in fact my life was dominated by school and the sisters of Saint Michael's.

Saint Michael's school was part of the large church complex. There were the school buildings themselves, one playing field, two asphalt playgrounds marked out for girls' basketball (these days called netball), the large convent house in which the sisters lived, the humble parish church, and the presbytery in which Father Yeates lived with his housekeeper Miss Fitzpatrick. Miss Fitzpatrick, who doubled as the church organist, was an unpleasant and mean-spirited old woman who looked remarkably like the Wicked Witch of the West only with blue hair which was matched by the thick blue veins that stood out on the mottled and wrinkled tops of her organ-playing hands. Miss Fitzpatrick showed no interest whatsoever in the affairs of the school or its children. She studiously avoided the school grounds although sometimes she had to cross the playground during play time or lunch time to find Fat Pat; we kids scattered out of her way whenever we saw her striding across the playground. Grown-ups considered her a spinsterish and anti-social old busy-body.

From my first day at school I had to wear the Saint Michael's uniform of matching navy-blue almost-black shorts and shirt, cotton in the summer, serge in the winter. Tessa's uniform was a dark blue cotton pinafore in the summer and a heavily pleated navy gym dress in the winter. Buying our school uniforms — one set for summer and another for winter — and regularly, to keep up with our growth, must have been an awful expense for Mum and Dad, and all working-class Catholic families, especially when kids attending the public primary school required no such uniform or expense. But school uniform garments were sturdy, well made and long lasting which meant they were economical. And so I had to wear my uniform shorts, shirts, jumper, socks and shoes, or sandals, not only after school and at weekends but even on special occasions throughout the year, as if they were the best clothes in my limited wardrobe, which in fact they were; Mum wanted and needed to extract every possible minute of wear from a set of expensive clothes she knew I would soon outgrow.

For the start of the year, in the summer, Mum took me to Mr Nicholls's shoe shop and bought me a pair of inexpensive brown

Roman sandals. In the winter I was supposed to wear a standard pair of cheap black leather lace-up shoes of a simple flat-looking style finished on the bottom with a cream-coloured crepe rubber that was slippery on wet paths and grass. Like the rest of the uniform both sandals and shoes needed to be replaced regularly because I outgrew them before they wore out. In practice sandals and shoes rarely wore out for the simple reason they were rarely worn. I and all the kids I knew, Catholic or protestant, rich or poor, young or old, except the prissy standard six girls, frequently — more often than not — went entirely without footwear even in the winter. It was a uniquely New Zealand habit, common to the point of being normal, which newcomers to the country mistook for a sign of poverty and neglect. But although it must have saved on footwear wear and tear it was not due to poverty or parsimony but to a preference for bare feet so deep-seated that if I were made to wear shoes or sandals to school I would simply remove them as soon as I was out of Mum's sight and stow them in my schoolbag where they remained for the rest of the day. I felt — as most kids did — although I couldn't explain it then, that life was more simple when I could feel the earth, including the concrete and bitumen of street, footpath or playground, beneath my naked feet. The only exception was the extreme heat of the bitumen footpaths and playgrounds in summer which was often enough to burn even our leather-like toughened soles. The sight of kids on the playground hopping from one bare foot to the other, or walking quickly and awkwardly on their heels from one shady spot to another, or seeking the grass verge in preference to the footpath, was common in summer when the sun's heat was enough to reduce the tar of the streets, footpaths and playgrounds to a black, shiny, runny and sticky mess, best avoided by bare feet. As a result of that stickiness I often had to take the time at the end of the day to sit on the ground, holding one foot at a time in one hand, sole upwards — in a manner grown-ups would find impossible — to pick off lumps of black and sticky tar, complete with the small stones, gravel, grass and twigs that my feet had acquired in the course of a day of running and playing barefoot over field and playground.

From his meagre stock of 'family footwear' Mr Nicholls managed to satisfy our family's footwear needs. Mr Nicholls was a tall, heavily built man with a large head and a large jaw across which he rubbed a large hand whenever he was thinking about his stock. He knew his stock well and could easily reach it, stretching up to reach even the upper shelves, although he seemed to groan and grimace whenever he had to bend or kneel to fit a shoe to my foot, resting on the sloping footstool, or raise himself up again. He wore a heavy grey overall, more like a coat, that was always shiny and smeared with what I assumed to be red, tan, brown and black polish from the shoes he repaired in the workshop at the back of the shop behind a torn and threadbare wine-coloured velvet curtain. He had only a limited range of shoes but it was sufficient to meet the simple fashion demands of the times and place and anyway anything more fashionable would have been too expensive for Mum, and most mothers, who had to shoe themselves and their children on a limited budget.

An unfortunate side effect of having to wear the Saint Michael's uniform was the way it identified us as convent kids and so made us an easy target for the teasing and bullying of the primary kids heading to their school in the opposite direction. At best they would chant insults at the Catholics and at worst would throw stones or even a punch. We were accustomed to these insults — all convent school kids were — and usually gave as good as we got including the popular chant, screamed by as many Catholic kids as possible, as loudly as possible, in perfect unison: 'Catholics, Catholics, ring the bell, publics, publics, go to hell'.

Some of the primary kids, especially the older ones, could be quite vicious in their attacks, with hurtful anti-religious insults that were far too clever to have been invented by children. And sometimes those from the states exercised and demonstrated their superior toughness with pushing and shoving, even punching, that was pure bullying with religion being nothing but an excuse.

This was a revelation to me when I started school, as an innocent and naïve five-year-old, in the middle of nineteen forty-nine. Until then I had met and mixed with few kids outside Winstone Street except my own cousins. Only when I started school was I exposed to kids from the states who were obviously poor and scruffy and sometimes even unclean. They seemed to have dirty hands, unkempt hair and snotty noses. But they were strong and tough, unafraid of fighting each other or anyone else, and unimpressed by grown-up authority, and so I envied them.

Sometimes on our Sunday drives with Gramma and Grandad Little we'd go through the streets of the states, on the way to somewhere or other. Mum rarely said anything during the short journey, trying, I supposed, to be charitable, but I was acutely aware of her discomfort. So many new-looking but dilapidated state houses with broken and dirty windows, bare sections devoid of flowers, shrubs or trees but littered with broken toys and bicycles, unmown lawns with long grass and weeds growing rank through and around the hulks of rusting cars. And I knew she hated seeing so many grimy and tough-looking kids playing outside, on the street, without apparent supervision.

'Why do we have to go this way, Grandad?' she asked.

There was always some tension between Mum and Grandad Little, and she could never call him anything but Grandad which I thought was funny because he wasn't *her* grandfather.

But it was Dad — not Grandad — who replied. 'The kids should thank their lucky stars, Leen,' he said. 'They don't know how lucky they are.'

He meant us, Tessa and me, but driving through the streets of the states I knew well enough how lucky we were. One Sunday Dad drove us through Napier Street in Freeman's Bay, what he called the worst street in Auckland. He said his cousin had once worked as a volunteer for the city mission.

'It wasn't right,' Mum said. 'Ruth working for an Anglican mission.'

'She was a volunteer, Leen,' said Dad, sounding annoyed.

There was a school in Napier Street.

'Worst school in Auckland,' said Dad although I don't know how he knew that. 'You two can thank your lucky stars you don't go there.'

The houses there were dirty and derelict with grimy and broken windows, limp curtains tied in a knot. 'I hate that look,' Mum said, even of our own state houses. There were dozens of poor-looking Maori kids with thick, black, dull hair, and dirty faces, hands and feet, wearing torn and ragged clothes, playing in the street but moving sullenly to the side to make way for the car, and staring into it, some of them directly at me, as we drove through.

'Just so you know how lucky you are,' said Dad again.

I didn't need such a reminder but I knew that Dad was also trying to find new ways to fill a dull Sunday while I would much rather have been at home. Mum wasn't alone in her unchristian contempt for the people of the states. Most of her family, friends and neighbours shared her opinion. And while most of the states kids went to the local primary school a few went to Saint Michael's where even the sisters were unkind to them perhaps because they weren't used to unruly and independent-minded kids who were not easily intimidated by threats of sisterly discipline.

I envied the free-and-easy ways of the states kids — at least the ones I knew at school — and often wished I could be more like them, although they were generally shunned by the other kids, whether instinctively or under instructions from their parents. I liked it that they played only with each other and didn't care what anyone else thought. Whether they were aware of the mild odium they aroused in other kids I didn't know but if they did they showed no sign of caring. That appealed to me and in the first weeks of school that year I felt myself softening towards them. I wanted to know them better; perhaps I was hoping to learn from their self-confidence and so be more like them. Whatever the reason, and using the power of the smile, which I had mastered and they had not, I easily befriended Rangi and Tommy Cronk, cousins, who were in Sister Ursula's class with me. And then a miracle happened: as soon as Rangi and Tommy accepted me I was immediately and automatically considered a friend by all the states kids, Catholic and protestant. Suddenly Tessa and I were permanently freed from the worst of the before- and after-school teasing and bullying. It was wonderful.

I started playing regularly with Rangi and Tommy and their friends after school, in their streets, and so for a while became one of the unruly kids, apparently running wild and unsupervised, whom Mum so abhorred. They taught me how to do a charlie — the name given to kicking another kid in the side of the thigh with your knee — which hurt so much when they did it on me I never did it to anyone else, a really hard horse bite (gripping and squeezing another kid above the knee with your thumb and middle finger) and a Chinese burn (in which you gripped another kid by the wrist with both hands and then turned the gripping hands in opposition as if wringing out a wet rag). They also let me smoke their cigarettes, in fact cylinders of white candy, tipped with red colouring, about the size of a real cigarette. They used these fakes to imitate their fathers and older brothers nonchalantly going about their business with a lolly fag hanging out of their mouths. I tried to imitate them but the temptation to eat the sweet thing usually overcame the desire to practise my tough look.

I also went to their houses and met their mothers and fathers, brothers and sisters. I could see that their houses were untidy, inside and out — I knew that my fussy mother would be appalled — but they weren't dirty. And I could see that their furniture was old, broken and worn not because they didn't care about nice things but because they were poor. There were empty beer bottles stacked on their sides at the back door which would have appalled my mother even more but I knew that Dad too had such a pile but it was kept out of sight under the house. When I went inside their houses the mothers, who all seemed older than Mum, and tired looking, were almost always cooking — it was always after school when I was there, late in the afternoon, so they must have been getting tea ready — and so there was always the lingering smell of coal gas which I had been taught by Mum to associate with poverty but which they didn't seem to notice. They, the mothers, were more kind and tolerant of me, and all kids, than I had expected, speaking to me as if I were more grown-up and more experienced than I was or felt, without the slightest hint of insincerity or sentimentality.

The first time I went to Rangi's house I waited in the porch, at the kitchen door, while he went to get his marble bag.

'Come in, boy,' said his mother who was peeling potatoes at the kitchen sink.

I went in; I was shy and reluctant but comforted by a small glass holy water font hanging beside the door, a Catholic feast day calendar like Mum's hanging on the wall at the end of the bench, and, on the opposite wall, a gold-framed picture of Our Lord holding open his blue shirt to show us his heart wrapped in thorns with a little fire and a cross on the top and rays of sunshine coming out. Mum had the same holy picture in her bedroom.

'You Johnny Little?' she asked.

'Yes.'

'Fraser Little's boy?' she asked me over her shoulder.

'Yes.'

She stopped peeling and turned around, wiping her hands on her house coat.

'Where do you stay?'

'Winstone Street, that's over the…'

'I know where Winstone Street is, boy.' She sounded a bit annoyed. 'You know Roly Little?'

She was looking at me hard. Pushing up her sleeves. Why did she want to know?

'He's my Granddad,' I answered.

'Lives over in Sandringham, right?'

'Yes.'

She tossed her head back almost imperceptibly, and looked up at the ceiling, but I didn't miss either gesture; together they seemed to say 'Oh, no, not him,' or something like that.

Then, after a few moments pause, staring out the window, she turned and smiled at me.

'That's all right,' she said, cuffing me lightly on the head with a damp hand, friendly. 'Not your fault.'

Rangi came back into the kitchen then and his mother turned back to the sink.

'You fullahs go and play now,' she said over her shoulder, her hands in the sink again. 'But, Rangi, tea'll be ready soon, when your father gets home, and then you better get home too, Johnny Little, before your Mum starts worrying.'

'What was she asking you?' asked Rangi when we were in the back yard heading for the alley patch.

'About my granddad.'

'Why?'

'Dunno.'

'What about him?'

'Dunno.'

Rangi Cronk's father was a wharfie, as were many of the states men, which I knew condemned him and them to shame in the explicit judgement of my family and all the other grown-ups I knew although I didn't know why. Taken altogether though I could see why Mum thought that the people of the states were a bit rough and ready. But I knew — from experience, and was glad to know — that they were not dirty, dishonest or frightening. And I could see no reason to dislike them, or shun them, as many non-states people did.

I also began to see myself through the eyes of the states kids, and I didn't like what I saw. Compared with them I was small and weak, with only flaccid muscles in my chest, shoulders, arms and legs, where theirs were hard, swollen and bursting with strength. I couldn't run as fast as they and couldn't beat them at wrestling. My hair was too short and too tidy and my uniform was new and clean and ironed and altogether too neat. And compared with their bravado and strutting self confidence, especially in the company of grown-ups, I was and appeared nervous and shy; where they were quick, clever and crafty — not necessarily dishonest — I was slow, innocent and guileless, perhaps altogether too honest and trusting for my own good.

Rangi and Tommy Cronk, and many but not all the states kids, were Maori, or part Maori, although more parts than Grandad Little, Dad or me and Tessa. But while I knew the people from the states were judged harshly, and even somewhat feared — unnecessarily as I now knew — by most of the grown-ups in my world, I knew for sure that none of the judgement or fear was based on their Maoriness as it had been when Dad was a kid. And anyway, apart from the states kids, who lived in their own area, there were very few real Maori people around us and fewer still from the islands. Those thousands of Maori who migrated to Auckland from the country after the second world war had settled in faraway Freeman's Bay and Ponsonby while the Polynesian migration to New Zealand, which would replace them there, had only just begun. There was just one Maori family in Winstone Street, a Catholic family with kids at Saint Michael's, with whom Mum was well acquainted. I think the lady was in the Legion of Mary with Mum. There was also a Polynesian but non-Catholic family in the street for whom my ukulele- and guitar-playing father had the deepest admiration: the man of the house played the steel-guitar in a dance band that specialised in the Hawaiian music Dad loved.

My friendship with Rangi and Tommy Cronk was not well grounded. And although Mum didn't like it, and probably wished she could forbid it — although she had no grounds — she had only to wait knowing that I didn't really have much in common with the Cronk cousins and their friends. And so we soon and naturally drifted apart. But Rangi and Tommy, their family, friends and neighbours, never forgot our brief familiarity and were forever friendly and protective. And the general knowledge of their loyalty was enough to stop the teasing and intimidation formerly directed at me, Tessa and my friends by protestant bullies from the states and elsewhere. But whenever we drove through the states streets in Grandad's big Chevrolet — as we did more and more as the year went on — I shrank down in my big seat, below the level of the windows, hoping not to be recognised.

School started at nine o'clock although Tessa and I arrived more than an hour before that to maximise our play time. Dad, who biked to work in all but the worst winter weather, left home at seven-thirty. We had breakfast with him and once we had said goodbye there was no reason not to go to school. It was only a short walk but we took our time — especially in the summer — dawdling along barefoot at our own pace, joining up with friends on the way, talking idly.

Playing with my school friends — the friends I saw only at school — was the most enjoyable thing, the *only* enjoyable thing, about school so getting there early was important. I wasn't alone; by a quarter to eight, when Tessa and I arrived, the playgrounds were full of uniformed but unsupervised kids, their schoolbags lying in brown lumpy clusters against fences and walls and under trees and hedges. Before long two or three of the sisters emerged mysteriously from their convent, adjacent to the playgrounds, to open the classrooms, perhaps to do some preparatory work or undertake some token supervision. But having come through the tall gate from their private and secret garden, into which children were never admitted, they didn't get far across the playground before they were surrounded by sycophantic older girls, from standards five and six, for whom I and all boys had nothing but contempt.

At this time, before school started, the usually stern and disciplinarian sisters seemed relaxed and approachable and their morning mood — which was short-lived on even the best days — was shamelessly exploited by the toadying girls. But the sisters were not blameless; they seemed to enjoy the adulation of the girls who clustered around them, pushing and shoving and jumping and competing for their attention by calling out 'Sister, Sister, Sister,' with their arms raised and punching the air. I listened to their conversations from a distance but it was limited to a series of closed questions from the sister: 'Have you been good girls?', 'Did you go to mass on Sunday?', 'You haven't disobeyed your parents, have you?' or 'You didn't eat meat on Friday did you?' all of which were answered earnestly if mechanically with a group chant of 'Yes, Sister,' or 'No, Sister,' as appropriate, from the circle of adoring girls. Or there may have been a series of questions that required only a raised arm in response: 'Who went to benediction last night?'; 'Who's been saying the rosary every night with their mother and father?'; 'Who's been studying their catechism?'; to which most of the simpering girls raised their hands and called out 'Me, Sister, me,' with what even the sisters must have seen as sinful vanity and pride not to mention sloppy grammar. But they appeared to be oblivious to the girls' fawning servility and would simply smile benignly with innocent joy happy to believe that their young female charges were being properly trained to become good and devout Catholic women, some of them, god willing, even finding a holy vocation in the convent.

Eventually the sisters hurried away to go about their pre-school duties and the girls went off to play their games. I never took much notice of what girls played before school except their clever skipping. Sometimes they used one long rope — thick and heavy — with a girl at each end, the two of them holding and turning it together, but more often two ropes of matching length were employed with the girls holding the ends one in each hand and turning them rhythmically in big, lazy circles, in opposite directions, in such a way that the bottom of one rope would just skim the ground on the way up as the other was reaching the top of its circle and beginning its downward journey. Into this blurred confusion of ropes, turning in opposition to each other, one passing under the feet while the other passed over the head, the older girls would glide easily being able to immediately adapt to the speed of the swinging ropes. They held their arms down straight at their sides, to modestly restrain their bouncing gym frocks — the sisters insisted on that — skipping at first with two feet together but then, as they got into their rhythm, with clever variations, much as you'd see from the Irish dancers they so resembled, all timed to allow the ropes to slip under the shiny black strapped shoes which the older girls wore. It would not stop there: girls would enter and leave the skipping centre smoothly and effortlessly, without ever breaking the constancy and rhythm of the turning ropes, and without seeming to signal their intentions to the others. Or the girls doing the rope turning would, intuitively, or at some invisible signal, speed up or slow down the speed of their churning arms or even seamlessly hand over the ropes to another girl so they could join the skippers in the middle. There were special songs and chants which were sung, in high-pitched little-girl voices, by all the participants together, obviously designed to help them maintain their swing and rhythm.

Rangi and Tommy Cronk and some of their friends often terrorised the skipping girls by running past them, chasing each other in a mock game, and pretending to accidentally bump into one of the rope-turning girls or even run through the turning ropes knocking over some of the skipping girls. Of course the girls were furious — 'We *hate* you horrible little boys,' they said, brushing themselves down and collecting up their ropes — but there was little they could do as the boys were too cunning to be seen and caught by a supervising sister. But the boys' fun ended one day when they knocked down Michelle Keating, a standard six girl and a favourite of Sister Olivia, the head sister of Saint Michael's, and broke her right arm. Nobody saw exactly who was responsible and none of the pranksters admitted his guilt and so no one was punished. But the guilty boys knew they had gone too far when Sister Olivia told them — by telling the whole class in no uncertain terms — that Mr Keating had reported the matter to Mr Thomsette, the local policeman, and that he was also considering legal action, whatever that meant. As far as I knew nothing else happened but at least the girls were left alone for the rest of the year to enjoy their skipping without interference. Meanwhile Michelle Keating became somewhat famous amongst the other big girls and evidently enjoyed the six weeks of attention she received while wearing her white L-shaped plaster cast.

Hop scotch was another popular game, especially with the younger girls. Some girls played basketball although without much enthusiasm, competing at goal shooting more than actually playing the game. Some older girls didn't play games at all but stood about listlessly in small whispering groups, their heads down, looking sullen and moody, being careful not to mix with the younger girls while glowering at the boys and generally trying to look older than their eleven or twelve years. Meanwhile we ingenuous boys, absorbed in our own games, ran and played noisily and boisterously, oblivious to the younger girls and their games and utterly unaware of the silent scorn being aimed at us by the haughty senior girls.

It was now, before school started, that we boys began games which were frequently picked up again, as though without interruption, at play time and lunch time that day, the next day and even beyond. New games seemed to start in the morning spontaneously — although there must have been a leader — with two or three boys linking arms over each others' shoulders and marching around the school in a wide rank chanting an invitation. 'Who wants to play (pause) cowboys and Indians?' was a perennial favourite but it was a theme with many variations and the 'Who wants to play...?' call could be followed by the name of any game made to fit the rhythm of the monotonous chant. Those who wanted to join the game joined it physically by linking an arm over the shoulder of the boy at one end or the other of the crooked rank until someone decided there were enough people to make the game worthwhile, or the line became too long and unwieldy and would divide into two parts, spontaneously, like a living cell, making two sets of players where there had been only one, and so two separate games each of which went about its own business happily independent of the other.

I joined but never began such game lines and realised later that the act of starting or joining a line, marching around school linked at the shoulders, and chanting the invitation to play, was a ritual that was often more fun than the intended game. Sometimes a game starting line would form in the morning, reconnect at lunch time and would still be moving and growing and dividing when the bell went to signal the end of the break. Sometimes but not always the game proper would begin the next morning but more often the participants found that they had enjoyed the recruitment process so much, with the marching and chanting, that they had now no desire to start the game proper even if they remembered what it was meant to be and who were to be the players.

Meanwhile, at home, Mum had changed. Until Fat Pat's sermon about the Marian year and the importance of saying the rosary every day, she and we, her little family, were considered good Catholics, not especially devout but no better or worse than any other person or family in the parish. But now Mum began following the pope's enjoinment, as relayed by Fat Pat, with a remarkable but not infectious enthusiasm and so became one of the most devout women in the parish. After tea on that Sunday evening at the beginning of February, and then every night for the rest of the year, Mum tried to make Dad, me and Tessa kneel down with her in front of a small glazed statue of Our Lady, which stood in the middle of one of Gramma Fahey's crocheted string doilies on a low table in the breakfast room, to recite the rosary.

The rosary was a long and tedious process of repetition that took fifteen or twenty minutes or more although it always seemed longer to me. I would have rushed through it and Dad would have skipped it altogether, and often did, but I was purposely slowed down by my newly pious mother. Tessa though seemed to enjoy the evening ritual;

she easily assumed a look of devotion with her head bowed and her little brow furrowed in concentration.

All Catholics, children as well as grown-ups, had their own set of rosary beads and although they all had the same number of beads, in the same configuration, there was an infinite variety of styles, materials and value. I had a simple and cheap set of wooden beads strung on a light chain; Dad's were black, chunky and masculine looking while Mum's were made of pink glass. Many people, especially women, were inordinately and inappropriately proud of owning flashy and expensive-looking rosary beads. They carried them in their purse, or wore them around their neck with more or less ostentation, wherever they went.

But for complete and obscene ostentation no rosary beads could beat the weighty and oversized chain that the sisters of Saint Michael's wore hanging from their waists. Each brown wooden oval bead was as big as a cherry while the metal figure of Jesus — their beloved saviour — almost naked, with nails though his hands and feet and a crown of thorns on his head, looking skinny and tortured and unhappy on his shiny wooden cross, was carried at the waist, thrust through their thick leather belt like a dagger, wherever the sisters should go. I should have been embarrassed to wear such a big crucifix around the shops or on the tram, or to be Jesus and to be seen, naked, bony and ugly, in public, but they didn't care. On the contrary they seemed immensely proud of their strange brown clothes and the oversized rosary beads that swung, rattled and clattered at their sides.

Whatever their size or style a set of rosary beads was always made of a circle containing five sets of ten beads. Each set was called a decade and was separated from the next decade by a single bead. Attached to this circle was a short chain upon which was set a sequence of one bead, three beads, and one bead, and on the end of which was the crucifix of more or less elaborate design but always depicting the same gruesome sight of a near-naked Jesus wearing a crown of thorns and nailed to a cross through his hands and crossed feet. It was the contemplation of this dreadful figure — we were required to hold the crucifix in our hands and look at it and imagine the pain that Jesus must have endured for our sake — that marked the start of the rosary. Mum kissed Jesus at the beginning and end of each rosary session and Tessa copied her but I didn't and nor did Dad. After a minute or so of this contemplation Mum would say an Our Father on the first bead of the short chain followed by a Hail Mary on each of the three beads which followed, ending with a Glory Be on the last bead of the short chain. Then, moving into the main circle of beads, the rosary proper began.

While saying the rosary, kneeling on the floor in the breakfast room in front of Mum's little shrine, I had to hold each bead, one at a time, between the crook of my first finger, counting them off with my thumb while the rest of the circle and its short chain hung from my hands. Each decade was introduced by an Our Father and ended with a Glory Be. Protestants called the Our Father the Lord's Prayer, which seemed fair enough to me, and gave it a different ending —

'...for thine is the kingdom, the power and the glory, for ever and ever, Amen.'
— which Mum said was blasphemous and not in the bible.

The Hail Mary, which protestants never said, had two parts. Mum said the first part:

'Hail, Mary, full of grace, the lord is with thee, blessed art thou amongst women, and blessed is the fruit of thy womb, Jesus'.

As usual at the mention of the name Jesus in the Hail Mary, or for that matter in any prayer or even in simple conversation, all Catholics had to nod their head. It may have been — it was — a sign of respect but it always looked funny to see all the people in church bobbing their heads in unison like so many nodding idiots. Like most rituals it was usually done more from habit than piety or any conscious awareness of its meaning.

And then we all said the second part of the Hail Mary together:

'Holy Mary, mother of God, pray for us sinners now and at the hour of our death, amen'.

So the Hail Mary was recited ten times (a decade) with five decades in a rosary. Each decade was assigned a mystery of the church upon which we were meant to meditate as we prayed. There were fifteen of these mysteries each of which had its turn at being meditated upon; they were categorised as the joyful mysteries, the sorrowful mysteries and the glorious mysteries but the individual name of each mystery was and remains a complete mystery to me.

And then each decade ended with the so-thankfully-short Glory Be:

'Glory be to the father, and to the son, and to the holy ghost, as it was in the beginning, is now, and ever shall be, world without end, amen.'

And so, ever-so-slowly, the circle of beads moved through my fingers, one bead at a time, until five decades had been recited and we were back at the junction of the short chain where we had started so long ago.

Saying the rosary was supposed to be a regular after-tea ritual for the whole family — 'The family that prays together, stays together,' said Fat Pat — but to me it was merely another form of Catholic punishment. All I wanted to do after tea, especially in the summer, was go out and play, not stay in and pray. Even though there was no daylight saving then the summer evenings of my Marian year were long and light and warm and it was horrible that after tea in the summer, while I was having to say the rosary, I could hear the shouts, squeals and laughter of the other kids in the street who always gathered together to play until dark. But as soon as it was over, as soon as we had made the last sign of the cross together, I chucked my rosary beads on the little table, stood up and rushed outside, with Tessa following, as Mum, trying hard to look calm and serene, stayed on her knees and called out 'You're a good boy, Johnny,' to my back.

But to me the nightly ritual resulted only in an unvarnished contempt for the rosary and for the chain of beads that were used in the process. I was, after all, not quite ten years old at the beginning of the Marian year and saying the rosary was just an awful, time-consuming, boring and meaningless chore.

After tea — the time assigned for rosary saying — was in the summer the most sociable time for the neighbourhood kids; two or three continuous hours when the grown-ups of our world, doing dishes, reading the paper, smoking, listening to the radio, and simply relaxing after tea at the end of a busy day, made no demands on us and we were free to do whatever we chose until it got dark and we were called inside. We congregated here or there, naturally, as kids do, without planning, two or three, a dozen, or sometimes even twenty or more, boys and girls, old and young, big and small.

Sometimes our evening amusements were remarkably simple. We picked the long flat leaves of some prickly plant, whose hooks clung to fabric like Velcro before Velcro was invented, and made patterns on our clothes. Or we snapped off the hooked and vicious thorns of rose bushes and stuck them to our nose or face, using spit as a glue, competing for who could apply the most thorns in the most elaborate and scary pattern. Plants were always at hand: I liked the way the brightly-coloured flowers of big summer snapdragons could be squeezed gently between the fingers to open and close like a mouth. The big boys showed me how to hold the stiff leaves of some grasses between the inside edges of my thumbs and then, bringing my hands together as if to pray, up to my mouth, and blowing hard across the grass through the narrow gap between my thumbs, to make a piercing, screaming noise. A similar noise could be made by taking a length of hollow dandelion stem, flattening it at one end and blowing through the reed-like tube from the flattened end with just the right amount of pressure. We called the dead dandelion flowers fairies because the whole flower, fluffy and white in its maturity, could be held by the stem and blown apart in such a way that perhaps hundreds of fairies — each one a tiny seed hanging from its own delicate filament — flew off into the air to be wafted away by the wind, high and out of sight. I was always charmed by the sight of those tiny fairies drifting effortlessly away, over fences, hedges and houses, on even the lightest zephyr.

Playing with those yellow flowers in their full golden bloom was for some reason thought or half-believed to lead to a night of bed-wetting; it was an interesting superstition not without some foundation as dandelions are still used as a herbal diuretic. Meanwhile it was thought that if another golden flower, the shiny buttercup — like dandelions, mere weeds in the lawn — showed a yellow reflection in the skin if held under the chin then that person must like butter. That seemed a silly notion to me as everyone's skin seemed to reflect the yellow flower and everyone I knew liked butter anyway. Another grown-up superstition, largely ignored by all but the most timid kids, was that the fennel plant, which grown-ups called devil's weed and which grew taller than a tall man on a vacant section at the end of Winstone Street near Andersons' paddocks, was deadly poisonous. This belief of the grown-ups is thought to have been based on the idea that fennel had once been used in the preparation of absinthe but we — all the kids in Winstone Street — simply didn't believe it; no one we knew had ever died or had become even slightly unwell from playing in and with fennel and some of the braver kids had even eaten it. Even the grown-ups, the unquestioning inheritors of this and many other superstitions, seemed to doubt their own belief although they seemed reluctant to surrender entirely to the obvious. And although they only weakly discouraged us from playing and hiding in the fennel forests they would have ridiculed the idea that such and ugly and smelly plant might be considered a beautiful, delicate and aromatic herb by millions of foreigners.

Many other common plants, growing wild on vacant land, were introduced naturally into our summer evening games. They included cutty grass — that's what we called it — which was used for no particular game but which fascinated us because we knew from experience that its sharply serrated edges really could cut the skin; *toi toi*, the long flowering stems which Mum, perennially unaware of or stubbornly unwilling to use well established Maori words and names, called Prince of Wales feathers, which we cut down to make tall pennants much like those carried by the knights we had seen at the pictures in *Ivanhoe;* and flax whose leaves the big boys taught us to cut and fashion into pointed darts which we launched by peeling back almost all of the leaf's strong orange-coloured spine, tying it to the end of a stiff piece of wood, and launching it in the fashion of an Aboriginal throwing stick.

The cambered but smoothly-paved surface of Winstone Street was an ideal playground in the early evening when there were few cars about and kids happily and safely rode their tricycles, bicycles and scooters on the road. Roller skates too were popular. Mostly they were cheap and simple one-size-fits-all affairs with four hollow tin wheels each, two on each side, which made an awful metallic din on the road, raised edges to hold the skater's shoe in place, an adjustable central shank to shorten or lengthen each skate as required, and thin leather buckled straps around the ankle and across the toes. Many of the older kids were especially skilled and graceful skaters. They had expensive skates and proper skating boots, and they told me about a magical place called the Deluxe.

'Where's that?' I asked a big girl skater called Betty Blamire who stopped to help me when I fell over and grazed my knee. Betty had long blonde hair that streamed out behind her like yellow ribbons when she skated, even on the street.

'It's in Khyber Pass, Johnny Boy,' she said kindly, helping me up.

I didn't know where Khyber Pass was and I didn't like to ask.

'Get your father to take you there,' she said.

I liked skating and was reasonably accomplished on my cheap, strap-on skates, and vowed secretly to go to the Deluxe one day, when I was old enough, to do proper skating. But I knew I couldn't go without proper skating boots and I didn't think Dad would ever take me on his bike or on the tram.

Even big kid skaters like Betty were once small and awkward and so now willingly took the time to coach and encourage us, their smaller neighbours, during those long summer evenings. There were many more knees and elbows to be grazed, ankles to be twisted and bottoms to be sat upon hard before we learned to skate with confidence and grace. But before long we learned to gain speed without effort, to stop quickly on a turn, to glide and sweep in wide curves, on one foot or two, even backwards or squatting down, just as we had been so cleverly and patiently taught by Betty and her friends, some as old as fourteen or fifteen, who sometimes joined us on the street before dusk.

Beyond forty-three, Winstone Street fell away towards Andersons' paddocks in a long and gentle slope ideal for trolleys and so in the evenings attracted big boys well beyond the immediate neighbourhood. There were trolleys of all shapes and sizes but they were all built — by fathers — to the same basic plan based on a central chassis of a strong, thick and rigid plank of wood at one end of which was fixed a wooden box as a cabin, open at the front, or some other suitable seating arrangement, and under which was fixed the back axle and wheels. The front end was home to the steering business; the front axle, with a wheel and one end of the steering rope at each end, was bolted loosely to the chassis at its centre with a single large and thoroughly greased bolt and washer. The trolley rider sat in his seat, legs bent at the knees, his hands gripping the steering rope much as a horseman holds his reins, and steered his vehicle by pulling his steering rope, and so turning the front wheels, to the left or right as required.

Most trolleys were equipped with small cast-iron, flat-faced wheels about twelve centimetres in diameter which may have been made for some industrial purpose but which, because I had seen them used for nothing else, I assumed were made especially for boys' trolleys. Whatever their real purpose they made ideal trolley wheels because at the end of a high-speed down-hill journey the trolley driver could make a sharp turn, one way or the other, and, leaning into the turn, send the whole trolley into a long, majestic and thoroughly exciting sideways slide that left shiny skid marks on the road which were viewed with admiration by the driver and, inevitably, a small audience. Of course other wheels could be and were used; the spoked and rubber-tyred wheels from old and unwanted prams and pushchairs, which came with ready-made steel axles, were popular because they ran so quickly, smoothly and quietly but their rubber grip on the road meant they couldn't be ridden broadside; any trolley driver attempting such a move on rubber wheels would soon find himself on the hard road, with grazed elbows and knees and a sore head, watching his trolley tumbling down the hill ahead of him. Despite their better manoeuvrability the iron wheeled trolleys created a dreadful din on the street and three or four trolleys together, racing down the Winstone Street hill and sliding to a stop at the end, must have filled the air with a loud and horrible noise. But there were no complaints from the grown ups in the street who were remarkably tolerant of the younger generation. I didn't have a trolley but Roger Machynlleth often let me sit between his legs for a fast run all the way down to Andersons' paddocks if I promised to haul his trolley back to the top of the hill for him. I did, and the thrill of the ride and the iron-wheeled broadside made it worth it.

Although he was thirteen or fourteen years old Roger Machynlleth often joined our games or even organised them in a way that we couldn't have done on our own. I suppose he was a natural leader. If there were enough of us playing together he would organise a game of French cricket which he had once shown us all how to play. I don't know why it was called *French* cricket but it was an ideal game; it could be played by anyone, boy or girl, of any age, anywhere, on any surface and in only a small space if necessary. French cricket required nothing more than a bat of sorts — a tennis racquet or even a stout stick would do — and a soft ball, both of which were always at hand somewhere. The rules were simple and adaptable: the player who was in protected his wickets, which were in fact his legs, with his bat. The bowler bowled underarm attempting to hit the batter's legs. The batter could send the ball off in any direction. The fielders, that is all the other players, placed themselves in a rough circle around the batter, and the successful fielder, having taken the ball, could aim it at the batter's legs in another attempt at stumping. If the fielder chose not to attempt a stumping, or attempted and failed, he became the next bowler having to bowl from where he took the ball. Catching the ball on the full put the batter out as did a real stumping on the batter's legs, the batter then changing positions and roles with whomever had put him out. Rounders — something like softball — was also a popular game but it had rules that were more formal and required us to divide into proper teams. Roger and one of the other big boys took turns to choose their players from the kids available. As a result it was played less often and, because it was taken somewhat seriously by the older players, it usually excluded me and the younger ones.

These then were only a few of the ways that we — Tessa and I and as many of the neighbourhood kids who were out at any time, boys and girls, young and old — passed our free time on a summer's evening, alone or together, with our dogs, our trikes and bikes and scooters, our skates and trolleys, bats and balls, in our yards or on the street, with an uninhibited and unconscious pleasure in life and in each others' company, until the street lights came on, the windows of our homes glowed with a yellow light, and grown-ups began calling through the dark. Then, reluctantly, I said hurray to everyone and trudged home through what had suddenly became night into a house that seemed suddenly bright, feeling suddenly tired but inordinately happy about the way my day had ended.

'Don't forget to say your prayers, Johnny Boy,' were the last words I heard from Mum each night. But what prayers? Mum encouraged me rather than required me to kneel beside my bed each night to say a prayer although there were no standard Catholic prayers for bedtime. Perhaps she assumed I had learned my bed-time prayers at school but I hadn't; perhaps the sisters left that part of my religious education to Mum. Sometimes though I did kneel to silently repeat a small and somewhat old-fashioned prayer I had learned from some unremembered source.

> *Now I lay me down to sleep,*
> *I pray the Lord my soul to keep;*
> *But if I die before I wake,*
> *I pray the Lord my soul to take.*

But it was always hurried and insincere, meant to please Mum more than anything, and the idea that I might die in the night seemed plain silly. And now it seemed to me that any end-of-day prayers had been made completely redundant by the saying of an entire rosary.

March

HISTORY AND LITERATURE REMIND US THAT SMALL boys have never liked school and unless something changes, which I doubt, they never will. I used to wonder why grown-ups, who were once children, didn't remember their own dislike of school and why, now that they were in charge, they didn't do something about it. Blake remembered well enough:

> *But to go to school in a summer morn,*
> *O! it drives all joy away;*
> *Under a cruel eye outworn.*
> *The little ones spend the day.*
> *In sighing and dismay.*

The sighing and dismay — and there was plenty of it — started at Saint Michael's at nine o'clock. There was a quarter of an hour play time at ten o'clock, an hour for lunch at noon, and then school again from one o'clock until two, another short play time which was a waste of time because there was nothing to eat, no afternoon play lunch, and then school again from ten past two until three.

That amounted to about five hours a day of dreary schooling, twenty-five hours a week, one hundred hours a month. How did we survive all those hours?

> *How can the bird that is born for joy*
> *Sit in a cage and sing?*
> *How can a child, when fears annoy,*
> *But droop his tender wing,*
> *And forget his youthful spring?*

There was no escape from our classroom cage and we were doomed to spend the largest part of our year indoors. We started school when we turned five, a little earlier or later to conveniently coincide with the start of a new term, joining the infant class. Gradually, over the next two years, more or less, we moved through primers one to four in such a way that we were ready for entry into standard one at the beginning of a new year graduating to a higher standard each year. At the end of standard four we — the boys of Saint Michael's — left primary school, about age eleven, for what was called Vermont Street, the intermediate school in Ponsonby run by the Marist Brothers, where we would spent two years, in forms one and two, before moving on to high school, usually Saint Paul's in Richmond Road, beginning in form three. Meanwhile the girls stayed at Saint Michael's for their two years of intermediate schooling — forms one and two but at Saint Michael's called standards five and six — before moving directly to high school, usually Saint Mary's in Ponsonby, for form three onwards.

My first day as an infant at Saint Michael's, immediately after the May school holidays of nineteen forty-nine, was a much more daunting experience for Mum than it was for me. A month or so earlier I had met 'sweet' Sister Rhian — that's what Mum called her — and spent an introductory hour or so in her classroom wondering mostly why blackboards were called blackboards when they were green. The classroom interior was new territory to me but I was familiar enough with the school itself and its grounds as they were part of the Saint Michael's parish complex which I visited when I went to mass on Sundays. For the same reason I saw nothing strange about the brown-robed and -hooded sisters who engendered mild fear, expressed as scorn and ridicule, in most protestant kids. So I was comfortable in my new surroundings, my new classroom, with my new teacher, and with what was expected of me, and began my schooling full of confidence, quiet excitement, high expectations, and a sense of growing up at last.

While on that first day Mum waited outside in the cold, chatting idly with Sister Rhian, I went boldly to the cloakroom adjacent to my new classroom where I hung my new sticky raincoat and my new, stiff, brown leather schoolbag, which contained nothing but my play lunch and lunch, on one of the hooks. I had worn my new schoolbag on my back, from home to school, walking with Mum but wishing I were alone, having previously got Roger Machynlleth — who was in standard three then — to show me how to arrange the bag's strap under my arms and across the back of my neck like a knapsack. He had shown me how to do it and how to adjust the buckle to lengthen or shorten the strap so the bag sat high on my back; if it were set too low it would jump and bounce about when I ran. I had practised, sometimes in the front of the mirror in my room — putting on the bag and taking it off smoothly so as not to look dumb in front of my new but more experienced classmates — for what seemed like long weeks before at last the real day came.

When I came out of the cloakroom Mum and Sister Rhian were

waiting for me. Mum, looking cold and worried, with a restless little Tessa in her pushchair, was on the wet concrete apron at the bottom of the two or three steps up to the porch of the primers' cloakroom and classroom, looking up; a melancholy scene. By now Sister Rhian was standing patiently on the porch itself, looking saintly and benign, her arms folded so that each was hidden in the opposite deep sleeve of her brown habit, looking down at Mum. I didn't know why Mum looked worried but Sister Rhian merely smiled down at me and offered me her hand. And when I took it — cool and smooth — somewhat reluctantly, on that cold and misty May morning in nineteen-forty-nine, without even glancing again at my unhappy mother below, I began my five and a half years of Saint Michael's schooling, formative primary school years that were not always happy, ending in Sister Ursula's standard four class for my Marian year, nineteen-fifty-four, my last year at Saint Michael's.

But on that first day, in May nineteen-forty-nine, once inside the primer classroom, nothing impressed me more than the low green-coloured blackboards which were obviously designed and positioned for kids. I liked the way that unlike the cheap and shiny toy blackboard at home, which was no more than a thin piece of board, painted black, resting insecurely on a flimsy easel, the classroom blackboards were painted in same dull green as real school green blackboards and were fixed to the wall, or were in fact the wall, which meant they presented a hard, unyielding surface onto which I could press firmly, or fill in a block of colour as fast and hard as I wished, without the surface yielding, wobbling or falling off its easel. And there was an unlimited supply of chalk of every imaginable colour, and a wide double-grooved shelf at the bottom of the blackboard from which the chalk never fell. And although for weeks I had dreamed and day-dreamed about the luxurious green blackboards, and the limitless supply of coloured chalks, I was disappointed to find that when given the tools and materials I had always wanted my talent for drawing fell far short of my ambitious dreams.

There was a large green blackboard at the front of the room in front of which stood Sister's desk. Across the top was a frieze of the alphabet, large and small letters, in a *sans serif* and juvenile printed style. We kids sat on our own miniature chairs at our own miniature tables, facing the front. Tall folding windows, of the type which could be concertinaed together to open the whole room to fresh air, took up the entire left and northern side of the room while fixed to the entire length of the opposite wall, and to the one at the back — into which was set the door to and from the sheltered porch and cloakroom — was our continuous green blackboard divided vertically at intervals with white painted lines to define the individual's working area. On the wall above these continuous strips of green blackboard were more examples of the printed alphabet, in upper- and lower-case, as well as another narrow frieze carrying a repetitive set of numbers from nought to nine.

I enjoyed reading, and was naturally good at it, and before long Sister Rhian secretly gave me my own complete set of Janet and John reading books. 'You take them home and read them to Mum,' she said. It was from these small soft-covered books I learned to read. I suppose they were cleverly written although I found their short, simple and repetitive sentences, supported by rather plain drawings of a rather dopey girl and boy — Janet and John — who looked, acted and said nothing remotely like any girl or boy I knew, to be a meagre diet from which to satisfy my hunger for words. But I took them home and rattled them off somewhat pompously to my adoring mother.

She said Sister had given me my own books because I was ahead of the other kids. 'She doesn't want them to hold you back, Johnny Boy,' she said proudly.

She didn't seem to know, and I forgot to mention, that I was holding back the rest of the class in sums and was getting special attention from Sister in that department. It's true: I was good at reading but plain dumb at sums. My precocity with words took even me by surprise but it was a natural aptitude for which I could claim no personal credit. It astonished and impressed my mother but was dismissed somewhat contemptuously by Dad who was more annoyed than pleased by my cleverness.

'What does *that* say?' he said once, pointing to a headline in the *Star*. I easily read the words about Berlin, the Soviet Union and the Reds but I had no idea what they meant.

'Skite,' he said.

He thought I was skiting to get his approval, which in fact I was, and he didn't test me again.

By my Marian year I enjoyed leafing through the *Star* regularly, trying to read stories with interesting headlines, and did so, alone, whenever I could, picking my way through long sentences and trying to pronounce and understand words that were new to me. The meaning of world news in particular was a mystery but if I didn't know the places mentioned in the headlines, or understand the notions they stated so plainly, I did at least remember the words and phrases which remained engraved on my mind as clearly as they were printed so blackly on the page; *Ike* and *K, Churchill* and *Eden, Menzies, Holland* and *Nash,* were names that were always in the *Star.* There was a war in Korea, and Formosa was mentioned a lot, as were the acronyms U.K., S.E.A.T.O. and U.S., which I knew meant the United States, while words like *Reds, H-bomb, A-bomb, Crisis* and *Summit,* all of which I recognised as important, conveyed nothing to me. Sometimes I asked Dad for an explanation of the news but if I received an answer it was rarely satisfactory.

I knew that Easter was on the way when at the beginning of March I had to go to mass on Ash Wednesday. Ash Wednesday marked the beginning of the forty days of lent. It was not a holy day of obligation but Tessa and I had to go to mass that morning with Mum anyway. We lined up with her to go to the communion rail where Fat Pat mumbled something I couldn't understand and made a small cross on our foreheads using his thick thumb dipped in a tray of damp black ashes. These ashes were made by burning the so-called palm leaves which had been used in church on the Palm Sunday of the year before.

'But, Mum,' I whispered in protest as we stood in the aisle together waiting for our turn to be daubed with damp ashes. 'Those aren't real palm tree ashes.'

'Shh.'

'But they're not. They're from the tree in Father's front yard.'

'If you don't be quiet…'

'But they are. They are. Aren't they, Tess. Everyone knows.'

We — Mum, Tessa and I — were shuffling up the aisle together. Mum had her eyes closed and her pink glass rosary beads draped over her joined hands. But she unclosed her eyes and unjoined her hands long enough to give me an unholy glare with her eyes and a sharp pinch on my ear.

'Be qui-ette,' she whispered loudly.

'Ow. That hurt.' And it did.

But it hurt more to know that my knowledge was not acknowledged. Because I knew — really knew — that the so-called palms used in Saint Michael's on Palm Sunday, and burned a year later to make Ash Wednesday ashes, were in fact merely coarse leaves and branches cut from the huge tree — a New Zealand *macrocarpa* — which grew in the centre of Fat Pat's front lawn.

I hated that black smudgy Ash Wednesday cross on my forehead. I wore it home from mass that morning, and kept it on at home while I had breakfast, but on the way to school I rubbed it off with spit as vigorously as I could.

'Is it all gone?' I asked Tessa.

She nodded but I wasn't sure.

'Fair go?'

'Yes,' she said unconvincingly.

I spat on my fingers again, rubbed my forehead vigorously, and checked my fingers for evidence. All gone? I hoped so.

But Tessa's was still there and I didn't like the curious looks it attracted from passers-by and especially the taunting which ash-cross wearers received from the protestant kids. But Tessa, and many other Catholic kids, especially girls, wore their smudgy, dirty cross with pride, trying to preserve it all day, in a public display of piety designed I thought to attract the attention and approval of the sisters.

Lent was supposed to be a time of sacrifice and we were encouraged, at home and school, to give up something for lent, although there was no coercion. 'What are you giving up for lent?' was a common question to kids, from parents, other grown-ups and teachers, although I didn't give up anything and was never checked for my success or failure. There was always plenty of talk about grown-ups giving up beer or cakes or sugar or smoking or the pictures but as far as I could see lent wasn't taken very seriously by any of the grown-ups I knew including Mum.

Despite the importance of lent Saint Patrick's day was even more important in March, at least at Saint Michael's. After all the cathedral in Wyndham Street — near the Farmers' — was called Saint Patrick's and Fat Pat — the dork from Cork — came from Ireland and spoke with an Irish accent. That meant that Saint Michael's had a school holiday on Saint Patrick's day — a Wednesday — so we could go to the big Saint Patrick's day picnic at Coyle Park.

It was a huge social occasion — complete with three-legged races, sack races, egg and spoon races, and what was said to be the biggest lolly scramble in the world — organised and managed by the Irish-run waterside workers' union for its members and their families. That meant the Auckland waterfront was closed for the entire day which said a lot about the power of the new union which had emerged from the chaos of the nineteen fifty-one waterfront strike.

Mum and Dad knew lots of people in the 'fifty-one strike including Uncle Harry, Aunty Doreen's husband. He had been a member of the old union, deregistered, and so was never allowed to work on the wharves again. Now he worked for a nurseryman in Greenlane. Dad said it served him right. 'Now he has to work all day for his money like the rest of us,' he said.

Tessa and I weren't allowed to go to the picnic because Dad said that the new watersiders were the same bloody communists as before and how come Catholics are supposed to hate bloody communists because the bloody communists in Russia persecute the church don't they and yet it's all right if they're Irish Catholic communists? Mum didn't mind if Dad said bloody about communists.

'It doesn't make sense,' he said to Mum. He was trying to make a big thing of it but Mum didn't seem to care one way or the other. 'They're not bloody going, Leen, and that's that.'

'Fraser!'

'What?'

'Don't speak like that in front of the children.'

I didn't know what communists were, nor what they did that was so wrong, but I knew they were important because we had to pray for them at the end of every mass. Except for the sermon it was the only bit of the mass in English. Fat Pat turned to us and asked us to join him in praying for the conversion of Russia. Then he kneeled on the carpeted steps below the altar and we all said a prayer for the Russians. Evidently the Russians were communists, heathens who had turned away from god and the church, and it was every Catholic's holy duty to pray for their return to the true religion, their conversion.

I know now that the pope cared less about Russian communists than the fact that the huge Russian church had split from Rome in the great schism nine hundred years earlier. If the church of nineteen fifty-four was praying for the downfall of the communist regime of the Soviet Union and the return of Russia to Christianity then its prayers were answered in nineteen eighty-seven, but if it wanted the Russian church to again recognise the power of Rome and the supremacy of the Roman pope then it was to be sadly disappointed. Anyway, because of the bloody communists and the Irish communist wharfies Tessa and I didn't go to the great Saint Patrick's Day picnic of nineteen-fifty-four but had a holiday at home.

'You should've seen the lolly scramble,' said Roger Machynlleth when I saw him at school the next day. 'I reckon it must really have been the biggest lolly scramble in the world.'

To the three standard Rs — as they were illiterately labelled — of reading, writing and arithmetic, which were then considered the only essential parts of a child's education, the sisters of Saint Michael's added a fourth R for religion. Other things, such as music and sport, were considered, at least by the sisters, as unnecessary, frivolous, perhaps even sinful, and were undertaken only when required by the official syllabus of the education department, and then only grudgingly, without enthusiasm, in a way that rubbed off on me and I assume many others.

Our formal religious instruction was called catechism and was undertaken religiously every day in the half hour before noon. The catechism was contained in a small, blue, soft-covered book prepared and printed especially for New Zealand Catholic kids in Catholic schools. It set out, in simple language, the dogma and doctrines — then considered immutable — of the Catholic church. There was no religious debate or discussion during catechism, and no attempt to help us understand what we were learning. We were required only to memorise — not question — the contents of the catechism and to demonstrate our memorisation with word-perfect answers to random questions posed by Sister or sometimes, on an apparently random visit to the classroom, by Fat Pat.

One of the most important lessons concerned our duty to remember the holy days of obligation. On these days, said Sister, quoting the catechism, we were obliged to attend mass as if it were a Sunday. Failure to properly observe these special and holy days was a Mortal Sin which made attending mass something more than a simple obligation.

There were many other things to be learned and memorised from the catechism.

'What must we do to save our souls?' asked Sister Ursula to which we had to answer from memory: *To save our souls we must worship God by faith, hope, and charity; we must believe in him, hope in him, and love him with all* our heart.'

'And how shall we know the things which we are to believe?'

We shall know the things which we are to believe from the Catholic church, through which God speaks to us.'

'Where shall we find the chief truths which the church teaches?'

We shall find the chief truths which the church teaches in the Apostles' Creed.'

And then, led by Sister, we would say the Apostles' Creed together without referring to the book.

I believe in God, the father almighty, creator of heaven and earth; and in Jesus Christ, his only son, our lord; who was conceived by the holy ghost, born of the virgin Mary, suffered under Pontius Pilate, was crucified: died, and was buried. He descended into hell: the third day he arose again from the dead: he ascended into heaven, sitteth at the right hand of God, the father almighty; from thence he shall come to judge the living and the dead. I believe in the holy ghost, the holy Catholic church, the communion of saints, the forgiveness of sins, the resurrection of the body, and life everlasting. Amen.

Although I did my best to learn my catechism, and to correctly answer Sister's questions when asked, I noticed that girls were consistently better at catechism than boys and I didn't know why. The end of catechism came with the ringing of the noon *Angelus* bell when Sister stopped whatever she was saying and signalled us to stand up; she then led us in the *Angelus* which, like drinking our milk before play time, was something horrible and boring we had to do before we could go to lunch and play.

First we all crossed ourselves together. Then the *Angelus* proceeded; Sister led, we responded:

Sister: *'The angel of the lord declared unto Mary.'*

Kids: *'And she conceived of the holy ghost.'*

Then Sister said the first part of the Hail Mary which was to be said twice more before the *Angelus* was complete: *'Hail, Mary, full of grace, the lord is with thee, blessed art thou amongst women, and blessed is the fruit of thy womb, Jesus'.*

Of course, at the mention of the name Jesus we all gave our little head a little nod.

Kids: *'Holy Mary, mother of God, pray for us sinners now and at the hour of our death, amen'.*

Sister: *'Behold, the handmaid of the lord.'*

Kids: *'Be it done unto me according to thy word.'*

Although I said the words I didn't really know what 'Be it done unto me' meant.

Then we all recited the Hail Mary again.

Sister: *'And the word was made flesh.'*

Kids: *'And dwelt among us.'*

And then, led by Sister, we said the Hail Mary for the third and last time before crossing ourselves and rushing out to lunch.

By way of Angelus explanation, and as part of our religious instruction in that half hour before lunch, we were told that that an archangel, not just an ordinary angel but a real archangel — the Archangel Gabriel — had come down from heaven to tell Our Lady that she would be having a baby. There was indeed a lovely coloured picture on the wall showing a beautiful, tall, winged angel in pure white floor-length robes — although I could never see how angels could fit their robes over their wings or get their wings through their robes — speaking to Mary who was kneeling and praying on a little prayer stool in front of a long maroon drape and a stained glass window in her living room; she had a perfect golden and glowing halo hovering over her holy head. It all meant, said Sister, that because Mary was a virgin it would be a virgin birth and that the Baby Jesus would be the son of god.

We were told rather than taught these things. I had no idea of the meaning of so many coded words and phrases including 'handmaid of the lord', 'conceived', 'and she conceived of the holy ghost', 'be it done unto me', 'virgin' and 'virgin birth', 'the lord is with thee', 'the fruit of thy womb' and '...the word was made flesh'. Sister Ursula — old and no doubt inexperienced and virginal — was happy to have technically done her missionary duty by the church while in fact leaving us in complete ignorance.

The crabby old sister wasn't alone in her prudishness; birth, whether virgin or otherwise, and the intimate and presumably odious details that preceded and followed it, were touchy subjects for most if not all grown-ups. If they discussed such things amongst themselves — and surely they must have — they never discussed them with or in the presence of kids. It was obvious that the discomfort felt and shown by grown-ups — including especially the sisters at school — was somewhat at odds with the mysterious conception and virgin birth of the Baby Jesus when we were asked to imagine Mary's discomfort at giving birth in a cold stable, in the company of animals, and having to lie her new baby in a manger. Apart from not knowing what a manger was, and not being told, it was of course impossible for us to imagine such things. How could it be otherwise when we — the kids in my world — were denied the most simple explanations about the conception and birth of even their own baby brothers, sisters and cousins.

I was only two years old when Tessa was born so to me she had always been there. But Mum's family was a major contributor to the New Zealand baby boom which meant there was a steady stream of new baby cousins. I was never officially told that I had a new baby cousin or two. It would just happen that I would be at a family gathering and notice that one of my aunts was carrying one of those soft white bundles I knew from experience must have been a new baby and that the other aunts, grandmothers, great aunts and other women who might be there were gathered around. 'Johnny Boy,' they said, 'come and say hello to your new wee cousin.' And so I was pressed forward while my aunt or mother or someone else used their fingers to draw back the knitted swaddling so I and others could better see the tiny red, screwed up and spotty face that looked no different, better or worse, than the last red, screwed up and spotty little face I had been made to inspect under precisely the same circumstances. But my aunts clucked and fussed and said how much he or she looked like him or her. Uncles came forward awkwardly, a cigarette between their fingers, perhaps a glass of beer or scotch in their hands, to touch an unbelievably soft and tender cheek with a gnarled knuckle or a nicotine-stained finger, and, having made a silly noise, or whistled a short jingle, something ridiculous which they thought appropriate, they withdrew, relieved, to the temporary bar and the company of their male relatives.

There was in fact an underlying unease about the arrival of a new baby. I knew — because I had been taught so at school — that the soul of all beautiful new babies was stained by the original sin that humans had inherited from Adam and Eve. And I knew that all the members of my family knew. And I and they knew that until that awful stain was removed by the sacrament of baptism this new member of the family, regardless of how beautiful and perfect it looked now, was far from beautiful and perfect in the eyes of god but was horribly stained by original sin and was doomed to spend eternity in limbo if it died before it was baptised into the holy Catholic church.

The logic was that because an infant wasn't capable of understanding his inherited unworthiness, and couldn't be expected to choose to be baptised and so join the holy Catholic church, good Catholic grown-ups called godparents could be appointed to speak for him, consent on his behalf to being baptised, and then be responsible for his religious upbringing should his own parents die or otherwise fail in their religious duty. But if the baby should die before being baptised he wouldn't be sent to hell or purgatory — that wouldn't be fair — but nor, unbaptised, could he expect to enter the paradise called the kingdom of heaven. And so he would be doomed to spend forever in that awful half-way house called limbo.

So it was that all the new babies in my family were baptised only a few days after coming home, much to the relief of every family member who each seemed until then to be incapable of loving the new baby wholly. Rather they lived in constant fear of baby's premature death as if they would be personally blamed by god, their family and the church for not having had it baptised quickly enough.

The noon bell brought the Angelus, the end of the daily catechism lesson, and the break for lunch. The eating of lunch was supposed to be an orderly affair. We were supposed to sit quietly together on the unshaded forms which ran along the front of each class building or, if it were raining, in the big wooden shelter shed at the back of the bike shed. Then, after ten minutes or so, when we had finished eating, it was time for play interrupted only by drinks of fresh water gulped from the stainless steel drinking fountains which were set at a suitable height outside every classroom.

I took sandwiches to school every day although many kids were allowed to buy a pie from the dairy on Mondays — which we called pie day — because by Monday morning there was rarely any bread left for sandwiches and if there were it would be stale and dry. But Mum always made sandwiches, using stale bread on Mondays if she had to, or if there were no bread at all using water crackers which I preferred anyway. She made my sandwiches each morning, wrapped them in a waxed lunch paper — which was supposed to be moisture proof but wasn't — and put them, together with my play lunch, a snack to be eaten at play time, and inevitably a piece of fruit, into a paper bag drawn from the vast supply of used brown paper bags with pinked tops which she had flattened and saved from her shopping.

But whether the bread was fresh or stale I rarely enjoyed Mum's sandwiches. In this I was conforming with the kids' school lunch law which states that everyone else's sandwiches are more interesting than one's own. I suppose Mum did her best but I was always disappointed with my sandwiches and ate them only because by lunch time I was hungry. There was always something wrong: although I liked the taste of sardines in my sandwiches I didn't like their oiliness mixed with butter and disliked dealing with their soft bones. Tomatoes carried so much wetness that by lunch time my sandwiches were no more than soggy lumps of buttery white bread which caused the lunch paper to disintegrate and which were impossible to hold. Mashed banana sandwiches also broke through the paper and the bananas not only made the sandwich bread wet, soggy and unmanageable but they turned brown and looked awful. Peanut butter, a yummy favourite at home, was dry and unpalatable by lunch time, and the jam in jam sandwiches also became dry and unappealing after a few hours in my schoolbag. I always looked enviously at the lunches of other kids, thinking that their sandwiches looked nicer, held their shape better, and had more interesting and tasty fillings. Meanwhile, and despite my own disappointment, most kids thought my sandwiches much more appealing than their own. As a result lunch time began with sandwich trading. To be fair, Mum's sandwiches weren't always disappointing; I especially liked her luncheon sausage and tomato sauce sandwiches, and the tinned spaghetti sandwiches, but my favourite by far was the Vegemite, cheese, lettuce and chopped celery sandwiches although I had to squash them flat to embed the pieces of celery into the bread and butter so they didn't fall out.

I never complained to Mum about my lunch. For one thing I was aware that she, often short of money, had to make my sandwiches from whatever was available. For another I simply didn't know how to explain why I thought sandwiches made by other mothers appeared to be nicer and neater, seeming to be less soggy and to hold their shape better, and even seemed to taste better. And so, not knowing how to explain, I said nothing.

Whatever the source of the sandwiches and the rest of the school lunch the fact was that all kids at school ate only healthful, wholesome and nutritious food made at home by caring and conscientious mothers. So-called fast food, or junk food, was unknown then and I never knew of a primary school with a tuck shop. But while our salt and sugar intake must have been remarkably low our intake of animal fats — from meat and butter, milk and cream, and the use of dripping and lard in cooking — must have been disproportionately high. But there really was no alternative. Cooking oil was unknown, and margarine was available only when prescribed by a doctor; and, anyway, margarine was thought to be a dreadful and inferior substitute invented in England, for the English poor, as a cheap alternative.

'The poor old poms can't make real butter anyway,' said Dad one morning at breakfast. 'And when they do it's as white as milk. Yanks too. I seen it in the army.'

'Why?' I asked.

'Why what?'

'Why can't they make real butter?'

'It's obvious, boy,' he said. 'It's so cold there in Pomerania, and America for that matter, that the cows live inside all year otherwise they'd freeze to death. And they eat dry hay not real fresh grass. So the butter's white not yellow.

'Look at that,' he added, holding up a fresh pound of golden New Zealand butter and showing me the label. 'Pure New Zealand creamery butter. You should thank your lucky stars, Johnny Boy.'

I did too. I was thoroughly glad to live in New Zealand where the cows ate real grass and their butter was pure and golden yellow.

And so, despite the rich, yellow butter and all the other animal fats in our diet, we — my generation — were remarkably fit. In a world with few diversions and artificial entertainments, especially no television, we were never idle but romped and played constantly outdoors, unsupervised, in the street, on the beach, at parks and playgrounds, even in our own back yards, in the course of our own games at home and at school, to the point of healthy exhaustion. And so we went to bed early and spent the night in the deep, uninterrupted and therapeutic sleep which falls naturally on young bodies after hours of vigorous exercise in the open air.

Despite the church and the sisters' squeamishness about things to do with sex, birth and babies there was no such discomfort about death. On the contrary, the church and the sisters wallowed in death and so made the human demise — and what might follow — the focus of our training. That we were born unworthy, stained by original sin, and were constant evil sinners, and that because the moment of inevitable death could never be known in advance, we must always be prepared for heavenly judgement. And so, while the details of virginity, conception, the fruit of the womb, a virgin birth, and even circumcision, even those connected with the founder of our religion, were glossed over by the sisters, the inevitability of death and its eternal consequences were drilled into us with a passionate conviction illustrated by real examples that were meant to frighten us, and did. And the daily lessons from Sister Ursula were constantly reinforced by Fat Pat when he sometimes took catechism, especially the dreadful fate awaiting us if we died with unconfessed Mortal Sins.

'You must confess all your sins,' he said, 'or you'll never pass into paradise to join god, his son, his arch-angels and angels, cherubim and seraphim, all the blessed apostles and saints. And,' he added ominously, 'you'll never see your mother and father, your brothers and sisters, again because you'll be spending eternity burning down there in the fires of hell.'

They were dreadful and frightening lessons and thoughts which haunted my dreams as they no doubt haunted the dreams of many other young, sensitive and impressionable kids, as they were surely meant to.

Although nobody in my family died during my Marian year we, the Saint Michael's innocents, were given regular if unplanned lessons that made us thoroughly familiar with death and the dreadful misery and grief that followed it. They weren't part of the school curriculum but occasional and unexpected breaks from routine that came with the randomness of death itself. And when death came to the parish — as it did once or twice a month — we, all the kids of the entire parish school except the infants, were taken from class to sit at the front of one side of the church to attend the requiem mass.

Even at the best of times I found the arcane, hour-long, Latin-based ordinary Sunday mass to be excruciatingly boring and the only good things about the longer requiem mass on a school day were that it got me out of school for an hour or so and was not interrupted by a sermon from Fat Pat. Instead the red-faced old priest just got on with the job of saying mass while the shiny wooden coffin, with ornate silver handles, and topped off by a large spray of flowers, stood in pride of place at the front centre of the church with a tall brass candlestick burning at each corner. Fat Pat wore black vestments and all the accoutrements of the mass and the eucharist were black or fringed with black.

It fascinated me how the communicants, many of them weeping, had to file around the coffin to reach and leave the communion rail. I had to keep reminding myself that the big shiny wooden box contained a real dead person.

The mass proper changed at the end when Fat Pat came down from the altar into the body of the church — something he never did on Sundays — and walked around and around the coffin, which until then he had studiously ignored given that he faced the altar during the entire mass and so had his back turned to the coffin and the congregation. As he walked around the coffin he mumbled long and boring prayers in Latin, sprinkled holy water all over it with a brass knob, and waved a lidded incense burner hanging from chains and puffing smelly incense smoke, all over it.

Despite the tedium I couldn't help noticing the extreme misery of the dead person's family — young and old and everyone in between, some of them known personally to me or Mum and Dad — who sat at the front on the other side of the church. We stared at them openly, being fascinated by the sight of so many crying grown-ups, and were never discouraged from doing so. Perhaps it was part of the lesson to see such misery brought out into the open. But how they, the grieving family, felt about being stared at by so many unrelated, ungrieving and uncaring kids I don't know.

I liked it at the end, when the funeral itself was over, when six men came forward to carry the coffin by its handles in a procession down the centre aisle of the church, to the hearse outside, and to the other cars waiting to carry Fat Pat and the dead person's family to Waikumete cemetery. The little procession was led by a solemn altar boy holding a long pole with a shiny brass crucifix on top, complete with a dead Jesus, followed by a sad-looking Fat Pat holding to his fat stomach the prayer book he would use at the grave, and then by all the sad people dressed in black, bent over with grief, held and helped by supporting arms.

Road traffic was light in those days and it was the custom for motorised funeral processions — the hearse followed by the cars of those going to the cemetery — to drive slowly with their headlights on. And it was common, almost usual, for other cars going in both directions to slow down or stop until the funeral procession had passed, and for pedestrians to stop, and for men, who all wore hats at that time, to remove their hats, hold them at their chests, and bow their heads. Respect for even the unknown dead came naturally to people not far removed from war.

But we kids saw none of this, nor the burial at the cemetery. Once the church was empty we were required to file out of our pews and return to class. And then, while the details of the funeral and the obvious misery of the family members were fresh in our memories, Sister Ursula told us again about the burial service, how the coffin would be lowered deep into the wet earth and covered over with mud, and what Fat Pat would say. And she would remind us of how death must come to us all, sooner or later, and how the misery of the living, which we had seen again today, would be nothing compared with the awful and eternal pain in the fires of hell that awaited those — including kids — who died with the stain of unconfessed Mortal Sins on their soul. And then, turning to the blackboard, and picking up the duster which rested on the blackboard shelf, she wiped the blackboard clean and started the next lesson.

The inevitability of death, grief, heaven and hell, meant nothing to me. The requiem mass was simply tedious and being forced to attend hardly compensated for the hour or more it provided away from Sister Ursula and her lessons. But some kids I knew had a much more personal experience of death. Two Saint Michael's mothers died during my Marian year leaving kids in my class bereft. I didn't know the mothers personally and knew nothing of the circumstances of their illness and deaths; nor was I a friend and so had no idea of how much they must have suffered to have lost their mother so tragically. But I understood a bit when, at each funeral, I saw the kids involved sitting not with us, on the left side of the church with the school, where they would usually sit, bored, fidgeting and restless, but with their father whose hunched shoulders shook with tears and grief throughout mass, and who, whether boy or girl, tried hard to be brave for the sake of their father but couldn't hide their red eyes, and couldn't stop the tears flowing, when they left their pews and turned, so the whole curious school could see them, to walk with their broken father behind the coffin, out of the church and thence to the cemetery where they would personally witness what most kids never saw: the mysterious rites of a Catholic burial.

It must have been hard for them to return to school after only a few days, motherless at the age of ten. But they did return and only later, as a grown-up, did I understand how brave they must have been. But although they must never have forgotten their mother, and their awful experience, perhaps it affected them for life, other kids soon forgot. What sympathy there was — and I admit I then felt none in particular for their unimaginable misfortunes — soon evaporated to be replaced with curiosity about their family life. Who cooked their tea and made their lunch and washed their clothes? Indeed solo parenthood was so rare, and divorce so utterly unthinkable and unspeakable, that I couldn't imagine a family without both a mother and a father.

And then one day late in March another but different tragedy struck closer to home and helped me see just how awful death can be, up close, and how much people can and must suffer.

Was there ever a time when kids didn't leave their classrooms at the end of the school day without running, shouting and squealing with joy, swinging their schoolbags in the air over their heads? So it was for me that dreadful March afternoon. Despite the importance of my friends, and the games we had played together before school and at play time and lunch time, when the bell went at three o'clock nothing was more important than simply getting away from school. And so as soon as I had passed through the school gates, onto the normal streets which led through the shopping centre to home, I felt as though an awful burden had been lifted from my shoulders and that I had returned at last to the real world. Once out of sight of school I slowed down, idling along with groups of other kids, boys and girls, chatting with them about nothing in particular, who peeled away from the group as they reached their own street, or their home on the main road. Tessa was a little ahead of me, with her own set of friends, but when she turned into Winstone Street she waited for me and we walked home together. And all the time, without knowing it, a tragedy was unfolding not far away.

Mum was delighted to see us home. It was the same every day. She arranged her housework schedule so that the heavy, dirty and unpleasant work was done in the morning. By the time Tessa and I got home she was freshened up, wearing a clean house coat, her fair, wavy and lovely hair, of which she was so proud, freshly brushed and shiny, her young face and blue eyes bright and lively, with no remaining evidence — the grime, perspiration, aching back, sore knees and chafed hands — of the physically hard and repetitive work she had performed during the morning.

Now, at a quarter past three, as we ran merrily up the path and in the back door, throwing our bags into the corner of the breakfast room, she was there and ready with a pot of tea for herself and a big glass of cold milk each for us, with a buttery sandwich of fresh bread spread with Vegemite, and a piece of her own cake. Normally she'd sit down with us — she with her cup of tea and we with our milk — and talk to us about our day at school. But on this particular fine, warm and sunny afternoon early in autumn, as we sat down together in the breakfast room, there was a sudden scream; a scream so loud and piercing and horrible that Mum looked up suddenly, directly at us, frightened, and then in the direction of the back door. There was another scream, a woman's scream, even more horrible than the first, from perhaps three or four doors away. Mum's face went white — perhaps she recognised the woman's voice — and she stood up, crossing herself silently.

'Wait here,' she said firmly, leaving us at the table with our milk, leaving the house. 'Don't move.'

But she was gone a long time and we were ourselves frightened. We went to the front of the house, to Mum's bedroom. We kneeled on the window seat, let up the brown Holland blind, got inside the thick lace curtains, rested our elbows on the window sill, and looked out. There on the street was a small band of women, housewives and mothers, our own mother included, and a few young thumb-sucking kids pressing close to their mothers' thighs. The women weren't talking but looking, their arms folded, their hands to their mouths in fright and trepidation. Tessa looked to me for guidance but I didn't know what to do or what to think. So we waited anxiously where we were, watching, for perhaps half an hour.

We went back to the kitchen when we saw Mum coming home. She came in, white-faced and tearful, and told us briefly what had happened. It was an awful story for any grown-up to tell any kids but she had no choice. We had heard the screams as she had, and had seen the people on the street, and not least the fear on her own face and the tears in her own eyes. And so she told us bluntly.

'Phillip Swainson has drowned,' she said. 'Mr Thomsette had to tell his mother and that was what the screaming was.

'That poor woman,' she added, crossing herself again and then again.

Phillip Swainson was younger than I, older than Tessa, and without doubt the naughtiest boy in Winstone Street. He was what grown-ups called a scallywag; a mischievous rascal, handsome, blond, freckle-faced and charming, full of impish tricks that made grown-ups smile more than scowl. And now — I couldn't believe it — he was dead. Drowned.

Evidently he had not gone directly home after school, as he was supposed to, but to the estuary, where he was forbidden to go alone, and had taken a dinghy which had been stood against a bank, under a pohutukawa, and the oars which were hidden under it, and launched it into the water in the last and most foolhardy adventure of his short life. The sheltered water was calm but he was found floating face down beside the dinghy. One of the oars was missing.

I attended the funeral as usual, with my class and all the Saint Michael's kids, and it was the saddest and most meaningful funeral I had ever seen. And the Saint Michael's kids, boys and girls, usually not especially unhappy to be in church for a funeral instead of being in class for lessons, were especially quiet, shocked even, and a pall of sadness hung over the school for a week or more.

I had to walk past Phillip Swainson's house two or three times a day and could hardly bear to look in case I saw Mrs Swainson. Nor could I forget the funeral, nor the look of heartache that turned the poor boy's poor mother into a slumped and miserable wretch who never, as long as I knew, recovered from the death of her only son. Soon she and her husband moved away, never to be seen or heard from again. I believed the rumours that she had gone mad.

Mum cuddled me and Tessa more frequently after that awful day, and was even kinder to us and more tolerant of our childish ways than before, if that were possible. I knew — it wasn't hard to see — that like every mother in the neighbourhood she was grateful and relieved that it was Phillip Swainson and not her son who had been taken, and that it was Mrs Swainson and not she whose life had been ruined by a silly and boyish prank gone somehow and mysteriously wrong.

At the end of March I was unexpectedly in hospital. Doctor Richards had long believed that my tonsils and adenoids were diseased and that I would never be completely well until they were removed. Then, he said, my health and vitality would improve considerably and permanently. But of course I would have to wait a long time for an operation at Auckland Hospital because there was a long waiting list. Until then the only treatment he could suggest and Mum could provide for my winter earaches was a muffled hot water bottle for a pillow and one or two APC tablets. APC tablets contained a potent blend of aspirin, phenacetin and codeine, long since abandoned or even banned by the medical profession, which succeeded in relieving the earache pain by rendering me unconscious for most of the night.

Mum bought the APC tablets from Mr Olsen the chemist who frequently provided her with free medical advice and was therefore an important source of front line health support. Mr Olsen was tall and thin, with white hair, a white pencil-line moustache, and a pure white coat, and seemed to me to be older than the other shopkeepers. I knew nothing of chemists nor what they did and Mr Olsen's shop contained little to interest me. It was just a bright, white place that looked and smelled extremely clean. And I was intrigued by the huge jars and tulip-shaped bottles, with matching lids, full of mysterious and darkly-colour liquids that stood on a wide shelf high above the dispensing room. And I remember the APC tablets and his other pills less for their efficacy than for the cleverly made cardboard tube-like boxes in which they were sold. These wonderful dark-maroon pill boxes were always round, in a variety of diameters and sizes, some quite tiny. Each part, the body and the lid, was closed at the end by being crimped over a flat circular piece of cardboard of matching colour. The fit, of lid over body, was so neat and snug that quite some pressure was required to press out the trapped air. They were clever, simple and small packaging pieces, probably worth no more than part of a penny each, but when empty they had myriad uses as playthings for a kid with even a limited imagination.

Many of the other medicines Mum got from Mr Olsen were not prescriptions or mass-produced tablets and pills but liquids, creams, ointments and unguents made up in advance to his own recipes and formulas. His cough mixture was loaded with breathtaking alcohol and his dark, glue-sticky tonics, sold cheaply in his own labelled bottles and jars, were overwhelmingly sweet.

Mum told me that Mr Olsen's APC tablets were not a cure for my earache and that one day I would have to go to hospital for an operation to take out my tonsils and adenoids. I didn't know what that would involve — actually I didn't know what tonsils and adenoids were, nor what they were for — so I happily agreed to put the whole matter out of my mind. But suddenly, one school morning at the end of the month, without warning, and sooner than I had expected, Grandad and Gramma Little arrived in the big Chevrolet, Mum bundled me into the back seat with her, and off we went to hospital. But we didn't go to the big Auckland Hospital by the domain in Park Road but to Huia Hospital, a small private hospital on the corner of nearby Grafton Road. Mum and Dad wouldn't have been able to pay for an operation in a private hospital so it was probably paid for by Grandad Little.

The operation was horrible. I hated when I had to breathe in the ether and count backwards from ten. My hospital stay was short and it's true I was able to eat only ice cream at first — as promised by Doctor Richards, Mum and every other grown-up who knew about tonsil operations — but that was no compensation for the pain in my tender throat. It didn't last. I soon recovered and was out of hospital just three days after the operation.

April

ONCE I GOT HOME FROM HOSPITAL MUM MADE ME STAY
in bed for only a few days. The operation was a complete success and
my quick and total recovery was confirmed by Doctor Richards when
he called to see me on the third day and told Mum I could go back to
school. And so I resumed my life where I had left it feeling no different
from how I'd felt before. Mum was delighted with the result and told
everyone. She said I looked better, that everyone agreed, and that
Doctor Richards was a good doctor. She must have been right because
I was never again troubled by colds, tonsillitis, sore throats or the
debilitating earaches which had reduced me (and Mum) to tears two or
three times a year. And I never again had to take Mr Olsen's APC
tablets.

Easter, the most important feast on the Catholic calendar, was on
the way and Mum wanted me to look my best that long and important
weekend. So I had to have a haircut. A boy's haircut usually cost
ninepence at the barber shop except on Friday — the barber's busiest
day — when schoolboys had to pay the full half-crown price. But as
Good Friday was a holiday Thursday became the full-price day so I
had to get my haircut on the Wednesday after school.

At a time when men would openly scorn others for caring too
much about their personal appearance and grooming — condemning
them as vain and effeminate — and were themselves seriously and
justifiably afraid of being judged effeminate by their mates, it was
acceptable, desirable, even essential, for a man to care especially about
the short length and unaffected style of the hair on his head. A man's
hair had to be always neatly parted — a centre parting was very
fashionable — and combed, kept shiningly in place with an oil or
cream, while no stray wisps were allowed to show at the base of the
neck. And to have long hair — and hair that was allowed to touch the
top of the ears and fall slightly over the collar was considered long and
unruly — was to be categorised as someone scruffy and undesirable
deserving only contempt and creating in others only fear and loathing.
Dad and others called such men beatniks.

Long-haired men were therefore rare and bearded men even rarer
although a short and pencil-thin moustache, in imitation of those worn
by film stars like Clark Gable and Errol Flynn was thought to be

dashing. But the overwhelming majority of men conformed to the strict rules of male grooming which were unwritten and unspoken but were applied by all men to themselves so rigidly that a fortnightly visit to the barber was essential. That meant the barber shop was always busy, the owner of a barber shop was a wealthy man, that barbers who worked for him had secure employment for life, and that becoming apprenticed to a barber was considered a fine achievement for a young man leaving school, a ticket to a secure future.

The rules of men's hair grooming applied equally to boys and so every two weeks or so Mum met me after school for another visit to the barber. The barber shop was a purely masculine environment. It was painted outside with stripes of red, white and blue and had a vertical rotating pole at the door painted in red, white and blue spirals. As well as the strong visual signals on the outside there was a wafting of strong smells from the inside that easily reached the street. They were always the same quite pleasant but very masculine smells, instantly recognisable but impossible to describe, of sweet and damp unsmoked tobacco, the acrid smoke of burning cigarettes and cigars, the sweet scent of burning pipe tobacco, the heavy aroma of stale beer reminiscent of a public bar, and some male perspiration, all mixed with the strong and alcoholic aroma of bay rum, the only cosmetic of any kind accepted by men, which the barber sprayed liberally over the finished haircut. The look and smell of the barbershop combined to suggest that it was a strictly men-only place. Women, including Mum, rarely crossed the threshold.

I stepped alone into the barber's saloon with some trepidation fascinated by an atmosphere refreshingly devoid of feminine influence or power. The saloon was dominated by four large and elaborately decorated and engineered barber chairs facing a long and mirrored wall. 'Four chairs, no waiting' said the footpath sign but I always had to wait, and there were always men waiting, because all barbers were always busy. Four barbers were at work from Monday to Friday from early morning — so men could get a haircut before work — until five-thirty in the evening, Monday to Thursday, and until nine o'clock Friday nights. Each barber stood at his assigned chair dressed in a coat of purest white buttoned to the neck in a way that made him look like a dentist. The owner and obvious boss stood at his chair which was closest to the front from which position he could more easily supervise and consult the chain-smoking, hair-dyed, heavily made-up woman, perhaps his wife, who called everyone 'dear', 'love' 'sweetheart' or 'darl' and who sat all day in the tiny, cluttered and smoke-filled cubicle to dispense smoking and reading materials and collect the two-and-six payment from the customers as they left.

This miniature shop, a shop within a shop, always did good business for the barber. It had a counter open to the street as well as one next to the door and took up no more space than that needed for the serving lady to stand and turn and reach down, up or across to retrieve the customer's personal needs and take his money. It must have been especially profitable in relation to the space it occupied because its stock comprised only tiny items, easy to store and display: cigarettes in packets, cigarette tobacco and pipe tobacco, a range of pipes, cigarette holders for women, and other smoking accessories and requisites such as matches, lighters, lighter fluid, flints and wicks, cigarette papers, pipe cleaners, cigarette cases and tobacco pouches, and other small non-smoking items needed by men such as nail clippers, cheap pens and pencils, razor blades and hair oil and hair cream — after-shave was not then known — as well as newspapers, racing form guides, men's magazines, tickets for the national lottery called the art union, and Tattersalls sweepstake tickets from Australia. They were all available from the lady at the counter to be bought and paid for with the cost of the fortnightly haircut.

There were specialist stand-alone tobacconists too, invariably tiny shops, sometimes no more than a stall, with a range somewhat wider than that found at the barber's especially in the range of cigars, pipes, cigarette holders and special imported tobaccos that could be blended to the customer's particular needs. And they, like the barber shops, opened somewhat earlier than most shops — even earlier than dairies — to serve the desperate smoker who needed to replenish his smoking supplies before heading off to work.

The barber shop owner — everyone, staff and customers, called him Harry — positioned himself close to his lucrative little cubicle and was in charge of the small mantel radio of varnished wood that glowed at his end of the shelf which itself ran the full length of the mirrored wall. Each of the chairs swivelled on its own base which was so heavy — solid iron or perhaps filled with concrete or lead — that it might have been permanently fixed to the floor, and had a lever at the side which meant the barber could adjust the height of the chair to his own comfort and turn it at will so as to minimise his own movement around the customer's head. The body of the chairs was finished in white enamel while the armrests and footplate were cast in steel and ornately engraved in an *art nouveau* style. The seat of the chair and the armrests were of imitation leather called Rexene stuffed with a coarse material, perhaps horse hair.

The all-purpose shelf, at one end of which sat the radio, was laid with small white towels and littered with the tools of the hairdressing trade together with bulk jars of hair cream — the white formula known as lime, cream and glycerine was especially popular — small bottles of the green brilliantine, which some men preferred, and large bottles of bay rum fitted with an aerosol device powered by the squeezing of a rubber bulb at the end of a long rubber tube. The electric trimmers, essential for cutting the short back and sides style, the only known or acceptable style, hung from the ceiling on long electrical cords. They were in almost uninterrupted use creating, with the low-level volume of the radio, a constant hum and buzz meaning that the conversations between barber and customer and between the customers themselves, as well as with the waiting men sitting on the built-in and cushioned bench that ran along the wall of the saloon, behind the chairs and opposite the mirrored wall, who leaned forward to join the communal conversation, were necessarily loud.

Whatever they talked about during that half-hour or so every fortnight of those far away days, they always returned to the subjects of horses and horse racing. The racing pages of the *Herald, Star* and *Truth,* heavily marked in pencil with circles and underlines, lay about untidily on the bench having been discarded by earlier waiting customers. Small race books, about the size of a paperback novel but thinner and printed on newsprint — *Best Bets* and *Turf Digest* — were for sale at the counter and were bought, seriously studied and marked by the waiting customers. A piercing bugle call from the radio told everyone that a race was about to start and so Harry leaned across and turned up the radio volume. Hair-cutting and conversation were then suspended while each man present, whether standing, poised with comb, clipper or scissors, sitting in the chair with a cloth apron around his neck, or waiting patiently on the bench for his turn, inclined head and ear to the corner of the room and concentrated on the droning race commentary the expert delivery of which increased in speed, pitch and volume as the race came to its climax, and then wound itself down, reducing its speed pitch and volume like an old-fashioned wind-up gramophone player that had lost its clockwork power. Then Harry turned down the radio slightly and the talk resumed, somewhat tentatively, about the result although it was turned up to full volume again when the dividends were announced a few moments later. Only when the announcement of the dividends was over did the participants in this little drama — no doubt being performed by similar players at the same time and in exactly the same manner in barber shops throughout New Zealand — resume their conversation, and what they were doing, pleased or disappointed with the result of the race and its effect on their wallet.

I didn't know anything about horse racing. And, for reasons I came to know only later, Mum hated it, forbade all mention of it, and turned off the radio at home whenever there was a commentary. As a result it was only during my visits to the barber that I heard — but didn't understand — racing words and terms such as 'the first (or second) leg of the double', 'dividend', 'win and place', 'the off-course substitute', as well as the strange names that men thought up for race horses and the exotic names of far-away race courses which, unlike the familiar Alexandra Park, Ellerslie and Avondale which were close to home anyway, sounded so strange — like Trentham, Te Rapa, Rangiora, Riccarton, Waverly, Wingatui — that they might have been on the moon.

What else did they talk about in the barber shop that day? The weather, and politics and sport — the subjects which still fascinate most men everywhere — and certainly rugby which was then more than now the most important sport in New Zealand.

I didn't know then if the men limited their subject matter or modified their language when I and other boys were there. I knew only that when I was there, waiting or in the chair, the barbers and the customers, those in the chairs and those waiting, talked constantly to each other, although not to me, and to the room in general, and that they swore only mildly and occasionally. Men left the conversation when their haircut was finished while others joined it as they arrived which meant that conversation flowed in an endless stream that didn't stop until the last customers was gone and the shop was shut.

Once the customer's hair had been trimmed with the electric clippers to the required short back and sides the barber finished the work on top with fine blue-steel scissors, wielding them with unnecessary clicks and flourishes, before applying the customer's preferred dressing. And all men used some sort of oil or cream to both help keep their hair in place and add a fashionable glossy finish no doubt to please themselves as much as to please the opposite sex.

Although the barber's saloon was an exclusively male place there was plenty of evidence of women although not of the type that wives, girlfriends, mothers and daughters would have approved. Their sex was represented by many so-called pin-ups, pictures of film stars in swim suits, and models in what would later (but not then) be called sexy poses, that were pasted or taped to the walls and mirrors. They jostled for space with pictures of boxers and race horses, footballers and cricketers, and all sorts of sports headlines and photos, yellowing and curled, torn from the *Weekly News*, *Herald*, *Star* and *Truth*. Most of the sports pictures meant nothing to me but thanks to Dad I knew the difference between the Kiwis and the All Blacks, recognised the team photos from both codes, and recognised one fine glossy photo in particular, framed and hanging properly on the wall, of All Black Bob Scott caught in the action of kicking a goal.

The pin-up pictures were obviously torn from the old and used men-only and American movie magazines which were on sale at the front of the shop. There was one men's magazine called *Man*, and another called *Adam*, the content of which would now be considered as little more than slightly saucy but was then thought distinctly rude if not downright indecent. And while none of the men seemed to mind if I looked at the magazines I did so only briefly and with not a little embarrassment, wondering if looking was a sin. There were also plenty of old well-thumbed copies of the large, cheap, trashy but popular Australian magazines — *Pix*, *People* and *Australasian Post* — as well as the local and highly popular *Truth*, which, crumpled and dog-eared, lay about at random where they had been dropped on the waiting bench or even on the floor. They were cheap and trashy but they must have satisfied a general hunger for light entertainment and humour before it was served by television and the internet. And they fascinated me because Mum would never have had them near the house. But here, waiting my turn in the bowels of the barber shop, where Mum would never come, even to see how long I would be, I was free to page-turn my way through them at leisure, at least until it was my turn to go to the chair.

Oddly I felt more guilty about hearing all the talk of racing and betting. While I guessed that Mum would have disapproved of the rude and trashy magazines I knew for sure she would have condemned gambling outright as being a Mortal Sin. And yet it puzzled me that so many men — the whole country in fact — gambled so openly, apparently legally, and without guilt.

'C'mon, mate,' said the first free barber — his name was Reg — flicking his last customer's cut hair from the large fabric bib, and knowing somehow that it was now my turn.

I liked it that barbers, like butchers, treated me as their equal. But clearly I wasn't entirely equal. Evidently even the hugely complicated lifting hydraulics of the barber's chair wouldn't extend to a sufficient height to lift me within easy reach of Reg's hands and tools and it was embarrassing when he reached under the shelf for the varnished wooden bench, made for the purpose and polished smooth by thousands of juvenile bottoms, which he placed across the chair, resting on the arms, to raise me another twenty or so centimetres. It was even more embarrassing if he tried to help me up as I climbed awkwardly from the floor to the footplate of the chair and then onto the bolster seat.

Once he started work on my hair Reg hardly spoke to me but picked up the communal conversation where he had left it only a few moments before. I was happy to listen to the men talk, to let my mind wander, as it always did when I was having a haircut, and to study the pictures — framed and otherwise — pin-ups and newspaper cuttings on the walls and mirrors, at closer range.

'You want bay rum, young fellah?' asked Reg.

He had finished the job by massaging hair cream through my short crop, making a sharp parting on the left and deftly combing my whole head of greasy, glossy hair into a neat presentation. Now he was standing behind me with the bay rum bottle in one hand and the rubber squeeze bulb in the other.

'Yes, please,' I said even though I knew Mum despised the smell. 'Plenty, eh.'

And so I closed my eyes while Reg squeezed a fine mist of bay rum over my head. When he was finished I was worried that he might want to help me down from my elevated position. But knowing boys, and knowing his place, he stood back and waited while I climbed down to the floor again and waited while he used a coarse brush to flick away any stray hairs.

'There ya go, mate,' he said. 'She'll love it.'

'Who?'

'Your girlfriend.' He said with a wink.

I blushed. I couldn't help it. And I was still blushing when I went outside. Mum was waiting for me on the street. She had seen me coming and had already paid the required ninepence to Harry's wife, the lady in the cubicle. She didn't seem to notice my blush. But she noticed my smell.

'Johnny Boy, you stink,' she said.

'I know,' I said. 'Can't help it. He did it without asking me.'

'He should've asked. They ask your father.'

'He just did it, eh.'

'It's horrible,' she said.

Easter weekend, in the middle of April, was the first break from school that year. I was glad to get away from school, if only for a few days, because things were not going well for me. For some reason Sister Ursula had taken a dislike to me and was picking on me mercilessly. She was without doubt the most cruel and vindictive old woman I had ever met until then or since. She was thoroughly unpleasant and certainly old, being deeply wrinkled, and so stooped as to require a walking stick. Perhaps she was too old, ill or disillusioned to teach kids, or perhaps it was a vocation to which she had never been suited. Whatever the cause she was thoroughly crabbed, inclined for no apparent reason to take a dislike to this child or that, and proceed to ridicule him in front of the class, and slap him cruelly with her open hand about the head and face, and altogether make his life miserable for an entire year.

Unfortunately, in nineteen fifty-four, she chose me as her target and her unkind and bullying treatment reached its climax just before Easter. That's why I was more happy than usual when we were let out of school early on Thursday afternoon and I managed to suppress all my worries about Sister Ursula and her bullying for the entire long Easter weekend.

Mum knew nothing of my unhappiness at school. Like all devout Catholics she was preoccupied with lent, the hype of Holy Week — the full week leading to Easter — and the anticipation of Easter itself, the climax of the entire church year being even more important than Christmas. Holy Week began with Palm Sunday, the Sunday before Easter, when Saint Michael's was decked out ostentatiously and somewhat amateurishly with the so-called palm leaves. These coarse, smelly and somewhat sticky macrocarpa branches were draped over and across the statues of Our Lady and Saint Joseph at the front of the church, across the fourteen carved stations of the cross which were fixed in order around the walls of the church, over every other statue, picture, shelf and window sill as well as over the top of the organ, around the altar and over the communion rails. There was so many of them that their pungent, gummy smell made the little church smell like Andersons' paddocks.

It was all done to commemorate the day Jesus came into Jerusalem on a donkey, in the week before he was crucified, to be greeted by people waving real palm fronds. Many of the Saint Michael's parishioners attending mass on Palm Sunday collected a piece of the greenery, keeping it in their missal as a book mark although it usually went brown and brittle and eventually disintegrated. Mum kept her bit on the little table in the breakfast room with her rosary beads and beside the statue of Our Lady before which we were supposed to say the rosary every night.

Gloomy Good Friday; that it was a holiday from school was its only redeeming feature, otherwise it was a day of unrelieved boredom. All but essential work was forbidden on Good Friday, not only by the church but by the government and by convention. All shops and picture theatres were closed and no sport or entertainment of any kind was permitted. I had to go to mass on Good Friday, another holy day of obligation, which was bad enough, and the gloom and despondency of the miserable day — why, I wondered, was it ever called 'good' Friday? — was broken only by the eating of delicious cinnamon buns, called hot cross buns for the pastry cross on top, which were served hot, or cut in half and toasted, and spread with butter that soon melted and soaked its fatty, salty taste into the sweet dough. Gramma Little baked her own hot cross buns, many women did, but Mum bought ours from the baker who made them especially for his Catholic customers.

Easter Monday was also a public holiday and the Tuesday was a holiday from school. Easter Saturday was normal — the misery of Good Friday forgotten — and that was followed by Easter Sunday and all its special pleasures. They began after mass with chocolate Easter eggs, many of them eaten before and in preference to breakfast. There were eggs big and small. Some were simply hollow shells of chocolate but I much preferred those which, whatever their size, were only vaguely egg shaped and were in fact two chocolate-covered pieces of sticky white marshmallow, some with a dull yellow centre to represent a yolk, each roughly the shape of half an egg, stuck together so that there was a double layer of chocolate through the middle of the egg's length. Such eggs were available individually loose — their rippled chocolate covering unprotected — or in bags of six, twelve or more. The bigger and more expensive eggs were covered in brightly coloured or patterned tinfoil or for those with very expensive tastes, although all Easter eggs tasted the same regardless of their size or cost, there were very large eggs in elaborate printed boxes.

But there wasn't much time for Easter egg eating on Easter Sunday morning. As soon as we got home from mass and had something to eat — a quick and simple breakfast on this occasion — we were off again to the main road to catch the tram to Gramma and Grandad Little's in Sandringham for Easter lunch. Getting to Sandringham meant going not across town — the trams didn't run that way and the cross-town Green Line buses didn't run on the weekends — but into town on one tram and out on the Dominion Road line on another. Tessa and I were accustomed to taking tram journeys with Mum but the Easter Sunday trip to Sandringham, and then, after lunch, farther along Dominion Road, almost all the way to Mount Albert Road, to Gramma Fahey's stop, was all the more exciting because it was one of the few times we rode on the tram with Dad.

'It's the Crystals,' said Dad as the tram came into view.

'Of course,' said Mum. 'Fancy working on Easter Sunday.'

'Someone has to do it,' said Dad. 'And they get double for their trouble.'

Mr and Mrs Crystal were one of the many husband and wife motorman/conductress teams that worked on the trams. They were notable locally because they actually volunteered to work on Sundays. They did it because they didn't have children and didn't care about Easter or Christmas because according to Mum they were atheists.

'What are atheists?' I asked Mum once.

'They're worse than Mormans and the Watchtowers put together,' she said.

'What are they?'

'What are what?'

'Mormans and those other things.'

'Well they're worse than ordinary protestants, Johnny Boy. But at least they believe in god.'

'But what are atheists?'

'Atheists don't believe in anything.'

'Not anything?'

'Nothing.'

Now the big red black-topped tram was grinding to a halt at our stop and I could see Mr Crystal the atheist at the front in the motorman's cabin. He waved to us but I didn't wave back.

'Come on, you kids. Off we go.' Dad lifted Tessa onto the first step and Mrs Crystal the atheist was at the top to help. Then she slid open the door to let us into the passenger cabin. I thought Mr and Mrs Crystal the atheists were nice.

I liked the big, loud, dark-red Auckland Transport Board trams with their black tops and an elaborate arrangement of springs and other tackle below, with large iron wheels that ran noisily on steel rails from power that was delivered down a black pole from wires strung over the road. I liked the whine of the wheels on the tracks, the screeching noise they made on corners and points, the zinging electric noise of the pole sparking on the wire — which I often heard distantly at night as I was going to sleep — and the distinctive clanging of the foot-operated warning bell which trams used instead of a horn. I admired the brightly varnished and yellowed wooden interior and furnishings of the trams too. Their contoured seats were made of similarly varnished and shiny wood slats. The handles and hand rails were made of brass made shiny by a million hands, and the small electric light bulbs were housed in round upside-down glass domes. I enjoyed the way the tram moved forward, slowed and stopped so smoothly — unlike a bus or a car — and yet rocked sideways, sometimes quite rhythmically, something buses and cars never did.

Mr Crystal, locked in his forward cabin, a replica of which stood empty at the back, stood for most of the journey resting his bottom on a high stool. He turned a big lever to move the tram, and slow it down, but he didn't have to steer. And when it was necessary he pumped his foot to ring the clanging bell that served as a traffic and pedestrian warning.

Mrs Crystal was in charge of the passengers. She stood, legs wide apart, swaying this way and that and checking herself, only sometimes, against a brass post, watching the doors and pulling the central bell cord twice when the stairwells and doors — which were permanently open — were clear of people getting on and off. I watched, amazed, as she managed to issue tickets, clip them and make change from the leather pouch which was slung around her waist, without ever losing her balance.

The seat backs of the tram could be flipped to change the direction they faced. When we travelled together Dad arranged two of the double seats to face each other. Tessa and I were facing forward, facing Mum and Dad who were going backwards.

Mrs Crystal tore off orange tickets for Mum and Dad, grey tickets for me and Tessa, arranged them together with her left hand and clipped them with a special clipper which swung off the little finger of her right hand. I took the coloured paper tickets from her and hid them behind my back.

'Guess,' I said.

Mum and Dad knew the game.

'Hearts,' said Dad.

'Mum?'

Mum pretended to think hard.

'Show me, show me,' said Tessa grabbing at my hands behind my back.

'Quit it, Tess,' I said. 'Mum?'

'I don't know,' said Mum. 'I think it might be a star. Yes. A star.'

I had a look.

'Wrong. They're clubs,' I announced, spreading out the little tickets to reveal the playing cards motif Mrs Crystal had punched through the tickets with her clipper. There were, I knew, many clipping designs, including the familiar hearts, diamonds, clubs and spades of playing cards.

'Let me see,' said Tessa. I gave her the tickets and she held them for the duration of the journey although I knew we'd get another set when we changed trams in town.

During the long two-part journey I kneeled on the seat, despite the fact that it was hard and hurt my bare knees, so I could look down into the cabins of the motorcars, and at the people inside, passing to the inside of the tram on the left or going in the opposite direction on the right. The tram was nearly empty by the time we got near Gramma and Grandad Little's stop which meant I could freely move from one side of the tram to the other. And then, when our stop was in view, near the lingerie factory, Mum nodded to say yes I could stand on the seat and press the brass button in the middle of the round brown bakelite housing that activated the electric bell. 'Only once,' she said, holding up one finger. It was well known that motormen got annoyed by multiple bell rings.

Compared to the rowdy Easter Sunday afternoon to come at Gramma Fahey's, playing with my cousins, our lunch at Gramma and Grandad Little's was quiet, dignified and civilised. Dad had only one brother, my Uncle Cliff, and he and Aunty May had only one child, Sandra, who was only a little younger than I. This only cousin on Dad's side of the family was somewhat spoiled and indulged and, compared with tomboyish Tessa, as prim and proper as you might expect from a spoiled girl without brothers or sisters. Sandra was learning dancing and so she walked about Gramma and Grandad's house with her thin, pale arms held down, stiff and tight to her side, her long and dainty hands held out at right angles, dragging her limp and unnaturally splayed feet behind her in the manner of a ballerina. When we were settled in the lounge, waiting for the luxurious Easter eggs which I knew Gramma and Grandad Little had for us, we had to wait while Sandra showed off her newly-learned ballet steps, and her prize-winning accomplishments at Scottish country dancing and the Irish jig, while her parents and grandparents looked on with pride. I thought Mum and Dad — who seemed hardly to know where to look — must have been ashamed of their own scruffians, me and Tessa, and our apparent lack of artistic accomplishment, but I realised later that they were more embarrassed *for* their niece and by a performance that was evidence of parental skiting more than childish precocity. Poor Sandra. It wasn't her fault. Yet when she was dancing I found her, bold and self-confident, almost beyond contempt. I didn't like her frilly blouses, tartan pleated skirts, white ankle socks and expensive-looking patent-leather strapped shoes. And I definitely didn't like her silly dancing. Tessa, more used to romping with me and the kids in Winstone Street, and with more rough and tumble boy and girl Fahey cousins, found this pale, thin and delicate creature, to whom she knew she was somehow related, to be so strange and alien that she didn't know how to treat her or what to say and so, as much as possible, she simply ignored her.

But Sandra's turn at dancing and jigging didn't last long and her innocent conceit was less her fault than the fault of over-indulgent parents and proud grandparents. Once her turn was over she joined me and Tessa on the floor and became quite normal again. Then I found her interesting and approachable; we became good friends.

Gramma and Grandad Little loved to see their grandchildren — they often complained aloud that they didn't see enough of us — and so had plenty of Easter eggs waiting as well as some other special treats and novelties such as big chocolate Easter bunnies which I knew were very expensive. They gave me a small plastic yellow hen standing on orange legs which when pressed to the floor released and would leave behind a tiny white plastic egg. It was a silly and cheap toy but it and its internal mechanism amused me and I treasured it for years.

Many of the more expensive Easter treats were packed in darkly coloured cellophane — hardly seen these days — and I enjoyed holding up a sheet of this strangely transparent and crackling material to my face to see how magically my view of the world changed when everything in it was tinted red, blue, yellow, orange or green. It was, I thought, like entering another world and although I was equally fascinated by all the colours, walking around Gramma and Grandad's house and garden holding a sheet of coloured cellophane in place with my hands on each side of my head, turning this way and that to see everything I could, I always preferred the warm golden glow of the world when seen through a yellow sheet.

For their daughters-in-law Gramma and Grandad had a special Easter present: a new pressure cooker from Farmers'. Mum thanked them of course but later I heard her say to Dad: 'Fraser, here we are without a brass farthing and your father buys me a new pressure cooker. I don't even like cooking in a pressure cooker.'

She and Aunty May also received an expensive collection of imported chocolates in a luxurious satin-lined box. 'So extravagant I'm sure,' said Mum who, having felt beholden to her well-to-do and generous in-laws for many reasons for many years, disliked being even slightly obliged to them for yet another favour, even the smallest. She was embarrassed by their generosity, found it hard to thank them adequately and impossible to openly display any affection for them.

For some reason she had never even found a suitable name for them. 'Say thank you, Gramma,' she said to me and Tessa while she herself managed nothing more than a plain and somewhat awkward 'thank you'. On the other hand Dad had no trouble calling his own mother-in-law Mum and wouldn't hesitate to give her a kiss on the cheek or an affectionate hug. But as I became more aware of the topsy-turvy nature of grown-up relationships I saw that Mum cared for her father- and mother-in-law more than she could possibly show while Dad cared considerably less for his mother-in-law than he so glibly demonstrated.

We had lunch together at Gramma and Grandad Little's and although it was only a simple and cold ham salad Tessa, Sandra and I were too full of chocolate and marshmallow to enjoy a proper lunch. As usual the visit and the meal were spoiled by an awkwardness of which I was acutely aware but over which I had no influence. I knew the cause of the discomfit: Gramma and Grandad Little were only nominally Catholic — they were called lapsed Catholics by those who were steadfast — and although they had raised Dad and Uncle Cliff as Catholics, sending them mostly to Catholic schools, I doubt they were ever devout. Nor were Uncle Cliff and Aunty May. But *they* were all aware of Mum's piety — recently reinforced this Marian year — and usually indulged her unspoken wish to say grace. But on this important occasion — Easter lunch — they forgot, and Mum's silent prayer, and silent sign of the cross before and after it, caused more embarrassment than if she had asked if we could all say grace or if she had said it to herself without the sign of the cross. She was also somewhat duplicitous in her Easter lunch grace-saying as we, at home, usually said grace only before tea and even then sometimes only perfunctorily.

'Easter and Christmas are special days, Johnny Boy,' she said when I asked her about it. 'You should know that.'

'Don't question your mother, boy,' said Dad sternly.

I thought that was strange. Dad always looked and sounded embarrassed when it was his turn to say grace at home. He even blushed a little as he hurried through the few words in a mumble. Tessa tried to say grace nicely but only Mum said the short prayer with any feeling, bowing her head and closing her eyes, beginning and ending with the sign of the cross. If it were my turn I rattled it off in a fast and continuous stream of words, running them together without taking a breath, without modulation. I said the words but hardly knew what I was saying, nor what they meant, and I couldn't have cared less.

In the name of the father and of the son and of the holy ghost amen bless us oh lord and these thy gifts which of thy bounty we are about to receive through Christ our lord amen.

I said it fast. I didn't know what '…of thy bounty…' meant and I didn't know anyone who did. But that was grace at forty-three; a standard recitation as it was at all Catholic tables. I was amused at the way people in America, in the pictures, and on the rare occasion when I would be present at a protestant table, protestants, seemed to talk directly to god, rambling away in a one-sided conversation, thanking 'The Lord' for this and that, apparently making it up as they went along. It also puzzled and disturbed me that for one thing they didn't start properly, as I thought they should, with the sign of the cross, and for another that because they didn't say the only grace I knew, the Catholic grace, there was no way of knowing in advance how long their grace would take nor, without the sign of the cross at the end, quite when it was finished. In fact I believed that the Catholic grace was the only proper grace even if it were rushed, as it almost always was, and meaningless to kids.

After Easter Sunday lunch, and much sooner than Gramma and Grandad Little liked, we left Sandringham for the short tram journey up Dominion Road to Gramma Fahey's street. That my grandparents' homes — the family homes of Mum and Dad — were so close explains how they so easily met as teenagers in the nineteen-thirties. But that they met so easily, and were evidently attracted to each other, doesn't mean they were perfectly suited. They were probably just as different and incompatible as teens in the mid nineteen-thirties as they were as a young married couple in the mid nineteen-fifties.

Our family photo album contained many photos of Dad as a boy and youth and, later, as a young man at war. Oddly, there were none of Mum as a girl or teenager. Mum treasured this album and kept it up to date not only with blurred little snaps of me and Tessa but with all sorts of certificates and mementoes from church and school. It had hard covers wrapped with a brown brocade patterned with gold thread and so naturally had an expensive and important look and feel. Additions were not permanently glued to the matt-black pages but were held in place in each corner by small, stiff, triangular, black corners which, after a generous lick of the tongue on the back, were glued in position on the page. The pages themselves were held between the covers with black ribbons fringed at the ends.

The early snaps of Dad were small, deckle-edged, brown and somewhat faded, but he was easily recognisable as simply a boyish version of the man I knew. Those of him in uniform during the war, and in civvies immediately after, were sharp and not faded and showed him to be a strikingly handsome, slender and dark, with wavy hair, black and brilliantined. There was always a cigarette sticking, not drooping, from one corner of his ever-smiling mouth, and his eyes were wrinkled at their corners from years of laughing in the tropical sun of the Pacific Islands where he spent the war and which he loved so much; indeed, his Ngapuhi heritage meant his already brown skin tanned to almost black under the tropical sun.

Like many good-looking men Dad seemed to have a natural ability to charm everyone, old and young. With a quick wit, a ready joke, a love of sports and a preference for beer and Scotch whisky, he was always the life of the party. Men enjoyed his company while young women found him dangerously attractive and older women (except his own cynical mother-in-law) immensely appealing. Even kids, my friends and cousins, all of whom he called 'boy' or 'girl' regardless of their names, liked and admired him because he was entertaining and funny. He had a happy way of treating kids as grown-ups, using language and conversation carefully judged to be sufficiently risqué to impress them with its frankness and naughtiness but not enough to offend their parents. But he rarely entertained us, Tessa and me, in this way and so I was always torn between resentment (born of jealousy that he tried hard to amuse other kids), pleasure (bathing in the reflected glory of his popularity), and bewilderment (knowing that he wanted desperately to be liked, even by inconsequential kids, but not understanding why).

Before the war, as a young man growing up in Sandringham during The Slump, Dad suffered none of the money worries of his friends thanks to his father. Grandad Little had returned from his own war, the first world war, to a wife and two babies, and under the pressure of poverty and an earlier depression had earned his living as a bookmaker, on the fringes of polite society, and his sons, young Fraser and Cliff, had helped. Evidently when the horse races were on the boys were used as window look-outs, sitting on a window seat each, in different rooms at the front of the Sandringham house, one watching up the street, the other down, and missing school in the process, while Grandad Little went about his bookmaking affairs. And they were used as fixers of the gambling machines Grandad Little imported and installed in the back-rooms of barber shops throughout the North Island, so arranging their internal workings to fix the odds.

As a young man therefore Dad had a car, money and freedom when most other young men had none. And so he was able to easily charm and romance the girls of his neighbourhood. Somehow though he set his eyes on Eileen Mary Fahey, a pretty young woman from a family that was poor, modest, honest and devoutly Catholic. It seems an unlikely match as Dad's family were neither poor nor modest, not quite entirely honest, and only notionally Catholic. But somehow it developed into romance and this unlikely pair got married during the second year of the war when they were both twenty-one. And then Dad went to war and Mum went back to live with her mother in the family home in Mount Roskill.

By the time I was born, thanks to a generous leave pass granted to Dad nine months earlier — or rather, according to Aunty Maureen, to Dad purloining an American Jeep from Papakura camp and going A.W.O.L. for a night — my handsome and dashing father was fighting with the Americans in the Pacific war. Too young at the beginning of the war to be sent to the theatres of Europe and North Africa, where so many young New Zealand men had distinguished themselves, and so many more had died anonymous and bloody deaths, he was called up when New Zealand's attention was turned to the Pacific and the dangers of a Japanese invasion and so was attached, with others of his generation, to the American armed forces.

From the stories he told me later I knew that Dad enjoyed not the war but where it took him and what it allowed him to do. He loved his life in the Pacific Islands, and the people there, mentioning Fiji, New Guinea, New Caledonia, the Solomons, Guadalcanal and Guam in his narratives. In Fiji he had learned to play the ukulele and the guitar, tolerably well, and could sing many Fijian songs in the Fijian language. He also became acquainted with malaria, a companion who followed him home, not to be dismissed, and who seized him regularly for years afterwards with sweats and violent shivers. He told me about the malaria, about the people, the songs and the food of the Pacific, the quality of the American rations, the shabby way Americans treated their black soldiers, but like many returned soldiers he would talk about anything in the war except the war itself. Despite pleadings he never — not once — described fighting or battles, or facing the enemy, or shooting or killing anyone. He was away for years, I know he had seen action — he despised the Japanese for the rest of his life — but he said nothing, choosing to keep whatever he saw, whatever he did, completely to himself.

Meanwhile Mum, always shy, naïve and prudish, was, by the end of the war, careworn, nervous and fearful of life. She became more devout in her Catholic faith and more devoted than ever to her own widowed mother with whom she had lived and upon whom she had depended during the war. She therefore brought to her delayed marriage and motherhood a simple and unchallenged intellect, demanding little from life but love and security for herself and her son — little me — for whom her own love was absolute, unlimited and unconditional. But to Dad — experienced, Americanized, tanned and handsome, muscled and hardened by war — his new life of routine factory work on low wages, supporting an unfamiliar and somewhat changed wife and her new baby, seemed monotonous and unrewarding. And so despite his profound and sincere peacetime desire to conform and please, to be a good husband, father, citizen and Catholic, he could not escape his past. A misspent youth followed by years of soldierly freedom meant he was poorly equipped for family responsibilities in a place that was as small, quiet, conservative, conformist, prim and provincial as New Zealand in the nineteen-forties and –fifties. Husbandry, fatherhood and religion never did come easily or naturally to my father.

These then were the grown-ups who inevitably governed my world from the moment I entered it: an ill-matched young man and woman born into the British Empire in the reign of King George the fifth, being at the end of the second world war not quite twenty-six years old and who, due to circumstances beyond their control, including The Slump and the war, looked older than their years. They were both, in their own ways, somewhat bruised, damaged and changed by life. Indeed, so much had happened to them and to the world that by the time I arrived in nineteen-forty-four they were no longer the same confident, carefree and happy young people they had been when they met, somehow, somewhere between Dad's home in Sandringham and Mum's home in Mount Roskill to which, on this Easter Sunday afternoon in nineteen fifty-four, we were now heading.

We got off the tram at Jimmy Ivory's farm. It was hardly a farm any more being reduced to an ill-kempt and empty half-acre corner paddock bordered on the two road sides by a scoria wall of the type common in Mount Roskill and other places. But it was once a large working farm.

'We used to get milk and eggs from Jimmy Ivory during The Slump,' said Mum. 'When I was young,' she added somewhat wistfully. And while 'when I was young' was a time passed beyond my imagination it must have seemed to her, at that melancholy moment, like only yesterday.

While Mum and Dad waited, patiently I suppose, I clambered up Jimmy Ivory's stone wall and looked across the unkempt field, through the tall stands of dead dock and some green thistle, to the leaning and rusting corrugated iron shed under the ancient and broken macrocarpa which provided shade in the far corner, nearest Jimmy's old brown villa. I was searching for the big Clydesdale Robbie who was always there.

As soon as Robbie saw me on the wall he came clomping heavily across the field, dragging his huge and heavy hooves through the long grass and rank weeds, his big black head bobbing up and down, his shiny black and bloodshot eyes staring at me, hoping for a handful of fresh grass. And so as Mum fed Robbie with one hand, with handfuls of grass torn by Dad from the base of the wall, she held me loosely with the other, by the back of my shirt. I was entranced. I locked my feet into gaps in the dry wall and stroked Robbie's lovely deep neck; it was warm and smooth and richly brown, with prominent blood veins, as thick as rope, that I could press in. And as I watched him delicately pick the grass from Mum's hand with soft, fat lips, and manipulate it into his mouth, I listened to the crunchy-munchy sound of his chewing molars on the fresh, moist grass. Robbie didn't mind if I ran my fingers through his thick, stringy and sticky mane or felt his silky, soft and floppy mouth parts and coarse whiskers. I was quietly astonished that such a big and powerful creature should have such kind-looking eyes and should always be so gentle and placid. I loved him dearly and wanted so much to wrap my arms around his neck. But even if Mum had allowed it my little arms would never had reached around that thickness. Poor Tessa, meanwhile, so small and timid, stood looking up enviously at her brave big brother.

At last it was time to leave Robbie and set off on the last stage of our Easter pilgrimage to Gramma Fahey's house.

'Goodbye, Robbie,' I called, looking back at the big horse for as long as I could while being tugged by the hand up Gramma Fahey's street. Robbie stood still, looking back at me, and I thought he looked sad.

Gramma Fahey's house was a small, non-descript three-bedroom wooden bungalow, with a corrugated iron roof, two bay windows at the front, and a separate garage at the side, typical of the street and the times. Gramma Fahey had lived there since she and her family had arrived in New Zealand in nineteen-twenty-four. Grandad Fahey had died there ten years later, a young man still, her children had grown-up there, and it was there she remained to rule over her family of six daughters and an increasingly numerous clan of grandchildren all of whom she unknowingly and unintentionally intimidated, none as much as me. How or why she was so intimidating I don't know. She was only small — tiny even — and bent and wrinkled, with swollen knuckles, bent fingers, and hands deformed by arthritis; her white hair was thin and wispy and she wore it tied in a bun at the nape of her neck. She spoke through loose dentures in a Glaswegian accent that was so strong she could be understood by few outside her own family. She was in fact a very ordinary old lady. But she bewildered, intimidated and sometimes even frightened me, and all her grandchildren to some extent. She seemed to have some invisible and unexplainable influence over us and while I didn't have the language to explain it I accepted it as a manifestation of the power all grown-ups always have over all children. I accepted that, but I didn't understand how or why she had the same power over grown-ups.

She was, I knew even then, only a small and harmless old woman; in fact she may not have been especially old. But she *seemed* old to me, evidently much older than Gramma Little who was tall and thin and erect and who was always cheerful and quick with the praise that children love. But Gramma Little had the advantage of having been born in New Zealand and having grown up, healthy and strong and well adjusted, on a farm in the shadow of Mount Pirongia, while Gramma Fahey had had a tough start in life in the damp and dirty streets of a nineteenth century Scottish slum. As a tenement child she had known poverty, hunger and paternal drunkenness, and had many times felt her father's leather belt across her face. As a result she knew how too much drink and not enough money can destroy a man and wreck a family. She had survived her childhood to marry, emigrate to New Zealand and have children, but a better climate and abundant fresh food didn't help her carry good health into old age and she suffered dreadfully from asthma and advancing arthritis. In New

Zealand she saw the demoralising effect of depression on her husband and young family and at just forty years old she was left a destitute widow to bring up six children in The Slump, with war looming and no hope of ever being able to return to faraway Scotland.

I never knew Grandad Fahey; he died many years before I was born although a large hand-coloured photographic portrait of him hung in Gramma's lounge. His early death meant that he was virtually canonised by his widow and children, despite the fact that he left them destitute in the middle of The Slump, so that, to me and my cousins, his opinions, words, character and personality were always out of reach, shrouded in a halo of soft light, protected by his widow and children's unreasonable and irrational worship of his sacred memory. He had left behind a household of women, run for and by women, in which men — including boyfriends and, later, husbands and grandsons — had no chance of being heard or respected. As a result the girls of the family — Mum and her sisters — grew to womanhood with little understanding of men or, later, of their own boy children.

But I knew or understood none of that then. My cruel and pompous judgement of Gramma Fahey was based only on what I saw and experienced in my own little world; at that time, and at that age, I had nothing else to go on. However, despite what I might have thought of her, Gramma Fahey was worshipped by her grown-up daughters — although Dad and my uncles were less than utterly adoring — and apparently had plenty of friends, mostly Scottish immigrants like her, who visited her often. But she was impatient with children and I simply didn't like her. I didn't like the way she longed for what she called home and her generally cross humour especially, I thought, towards me and her other boy grandchildren. I didn't like her thick accent and her apparent unwillingness to modify it to suit the New Zealand ear; her use of Scottish idiom especially annoyed me. Indeed, the many strange words she used were, as far as I knew, used by nobody else but her and her own daughters. Babies were called bairns — 'och, look at the bonny wee bairn' grated terribly on my sense of being a Kiwi — while girls and boys were 'wee laddies and lassies', and tired, unhappy, impatient and hungry grandkids who complained aloud, doing what infants do, were admonished for their 'greetin and girning'. A naughty granddaughter, especially if she were being insolent or disobedient, was referred to as 'the wee besom', and it wasn't meant kindly. I don't know why such words and phrases irritated me but they did.

She was also full of peasant-like contradictions: a blind and equal belief in Catholic dogma and old-wives' tales mixed with a propensity for superstition and an apparent talent for reading tea-cups. That my grandmother could read the future in the random assembly of wet and swollen tea leaves clinging to the bottom of a china tea cup was to me, even as a child, unscientific and silly and I knew that Dad silently agreed. But when she peered up mysteriously, theatrically, from reading a tea cup, her wrinkled face framed with wispy strands of pure white hair, she sometimes looked like a witch or a gypsy fortune teller. She held the tea cup in one hand, at a slight angle, and made her prognostications in her strong accent, shaking her head slowly, mysteriously, without explanation.

'Is this your wee cup, Eileen?' she asked Mum.

Mum nodded, straining forward with the others to listen.

'I see,' she said. Then, mysteriously, she asked Mum, 'How's Mr Little?'

'He's fine,' said Mum. 'We had lunch there today. Remember?'

'Och, aye,' said Gramma Fahey, peering into the white depths of the Royal Albert cup and nodding slowly.

'What is it?'

Gramma Fahey looked up and put the cup back on its saucer.

'Och, it isnae guid what I see, Eileen, but I cannae see it all so it's better to see nothing and say nothing.'

Mum looked worried and frightened, and so did my aunts, and Gramma Fahey saw their looks and so picked up the cup again, tipped it gently, rolled it a little to redistribute the tea leaves, peered into the bottom of the cup and looked up again, smiling.

'But I *can* see money,' she said cunningly. 'Pounds and pounds of it.'

And she laughed. And Mum and all my aunts laughed too, with relief, but their laughter was somewhat sour and their sideways glances at each other contained a hint of doubt. I think they secretly feared if not truly believed that Gramma Fahey had some uncanny and inexplicable gift of prophecy. And, as it turned out, perhaps she did.

Mum and her sisters shared many other petty and inconsequential superstitions inherited from Gramma Fahey including beliefs such as: spilling salt would bring bad luck which could be averted only by tossing a pinch of the spilled salt over the left shoulder with the right hand; a cracked or broken mirror would bring seven years bad luck; walking under a ladder would bring bad luck as would opening an umbrella indoors or cutting your fingernails indoors; hanging a horseshoe over a door would bring good luck although it had to be hung with the two ends pointing upwards otherwise gravity would cause all the good luck to drip out the ends; the number thirteen was unlucky and any Friday dated the thirteenth was especially unlucky; the first day of the month was lucky but only if you said 'white rabbits' three times to the first person you met that morning; finding money was lucky (which seemed rather obvious to me); seeing a shooting star was lucky and a silent wish made immediately would undoubtedly come true. One could also expect a wish to come true if it were made while blowing out the candles on a birthday cake but only if all the candles were extinguished with one breath.

There were many other commonplace actions which Mum did her best to avoid in the course of her day and many other accidental, random or unpredictable events which when they occurred she involuntarily interpreted as omens or warnings. Some of these demanded a ritual antidote which she performed routinely, with an assumed nonchalance, nevertheless obeying some irresistible urge and so mocking her own religious beliefs. So many were these silly, harmless and unfounded beliefs and superstitions that with Dad's silent but smiling approval I made a conscious effort to ignore them all.

Although I didn't care for Gramma Fahey I didn't have to spend much time with her on Easter Sunday. Having said hello to her and all my aunts and uncles, and later, having seen and heard her read Mum's tea cup, we — all the cousins — were largely ignored by the grown-ups and were free to go outside and play away the day with 'chasie' and 'hidey' and 'go home stay home' and many other such games until it was dark and we were utterly puffed out. Meanwhile the grown-ups spent the afternoon and evening of Easter Sunday inside, eating and drinking, talking and laughing and leaving us entirely to our own childish devices.

At last — although quite late because the next day, Easter Monday, was not a work day or a school day — it was time to go home. A taxi must have been an extravagance, hardly affordable to Dad, but no doubt he and Mum couldn't face a long double tram ride home so late at night with two tired children. It had been a day as wonderful for us

— Tessa and I and our beloved cousins — as Christmas, although it grew dark earlier and so ended sooner, but with one particular difference: with so many Easter eggs available, and grown-ups who, for reasons of their own, were happy to abandon the usual meal routines and regimes, we indulged ourselves in the unregulated consumption of chocolate and marshmallow, surely committing together the sin of mass and wholesale gluttony. None went home with a face and clothes unstained by chocolate and many, the younger ones especially, inexperienced in such sinful behaviour and unfamiliar with nature's own signals and defences, suffered an hour or so of misery at day's end, with unsympathetic parents, losing everything they had consumed that day before they fell asleep that night.

I fell asleep in the taxi, my head in Mum's lap. But not before I heard her say to Dad: 'Such a lovely day but I wish your father and mother wouldn't spend so much on us at Easter.' But I didn't mind how much Gramma and Grandad Little spent on me at Easter. Or at any time.

After the excitement of the holiday I returned to school on the Wednesday after Easter with some trepidation. I knew I would have to face Sister Ursula's bullying again and I didn't know what to do about it. I guessed that my propensity to show off my reading skills annoyed her, especially when combined with my complete lack of ability in arithmetic, but the fact was I had absolutely no aptitude for numbers.

May

BEING GOOD AT NUMBERS WAS BOTH MORE important and more difficult then than now. More important because without electronic calculators, computers or cash registers ordinary people like Mum and Dad, shopkeepers and tradesmen, anyone working with money or the measurement of anything, had to make routine calculations in their head, many times every day, aided only by paper and pencil or sometimes their fingers; more difficult because everything important in life, including especially the management of time and money, was based not on the number ten — the oh-so-simple decimal system — but on the number twelve. Twelve was a magical number used for so many important calculations, for hundreds of years, because unlike the number ten it could so easily be divided by two, three, four and six. Provided, of course, that you knew your times tables up to twelve.

Mum and Dad both knew all their times tables. They had learned them at school in just the same way as I was now learning mine: by rote. We spent many hours of every school week at the daily repetitive chanting of the times tables. A visitor to Saint Michael's then, at any time on any school day, would have heard the high voices of classrooms of kids — thirty or more per classroom — monotonously sing-songing their way through their current multiplication table. That each class would be chanting a different times table, starting earlier or later than another, and at a slightly different tempo and pitch, meant that for the visitor it must have been like listening to three or four marching bands playing different tunes in different keys to different beats at different volumes.

Short of restaging the daily performance, using real children in real classrooms, there is now no way to describe the unique sound of thirty or more young voices in a closed room chanting the times tables in unison. In Sister Ursula's standard four class we did it over and over and over again until each one of us, without exception, could first recite the entire given table on his own and then, later, could automatically and immediately, without hesitation, provide the answer to any line of multiplication from the table in question.

'You,' said Sister Ursula, pointing directly at me with a wooden ruler and locking my eyes with hers. My heart sank. Would I know the answer?

'Seven nines?' she asked.

I had to shoot back an instant answer. Luckily, thank god, and much to her surprise, I knew it.

'Sixty-three,' I said with hardly a pause.

I was lucky that day. If I hadn't answered correctly and immediately, without hesitation — and I rarely could — my hesitation would have brought a groan from the rest of the class knowing that my failure meant they would all have to chant their seven times table a few more times until I and everyone could provide every answer immediately and correctly without failure.

The rhythmic and repetitive chanting, sing-song fashion, following the beat established by Sister by whacking her walking stick on her desk or sometimes, after pushing up the deep sleeve of her habit to reveal a white and unweathered arm, waving her hand vigorously like the conductor of an orchestra, served to etch the times tables deeply into our soft young minds where they remained, permanently embedded in the subconscious, to be recalled faultlessly on demand for as long as the mind was alive and well.

The times table chanting began in standard one with the two times table — *'two ones are two, two twos are four, two threes are six, two fours are eight, two fives are ten, two sixes are twelve, two sevens are fourteen, two eights are sixteen, two nines are eighteen, two tens are twenty, two elevens are twenty-two and two twelves are twenty-four'* went the monotonous chant — and ended in standard four with the twelve times table. I found the twos and tens the easiest and even the eleven times was easy up to nine — what could be easier than eleven nines are ninety-nine? — but eleven tens, eleven elevens and eleven twelves were stumbling blocks. But the twelve times was the hardest by far especially by the time I got to *'...twelve nines are a hundred and eight, twelve tens are a hundred and twenty, twelve elevens are a hundred and thirty-two and twelve twelves are a hundred and forty-four.'* I did eventually learn them all — what child or parrot is not capable of learning anything by rote? — so by the time the process was complete we all knew our times tables up to twelve by heart without ever making a mistake. Evidently it was a system that worked.

Just as essential, but impossible to learn by heart, was adding or subtracting simple sums. (Doing any form of arithmetic was then called 'doing your sums'.) These little calculations were cleverly arranged in the early lessons to avoid the need to 'borrow' or 'carry' until the concept of 'borrowing and carrying' a number from or to the neighbouring column, which took me a long time to grasp, was introduced. Then came fractions which were a complete mystery to me. However, the idea of simple fractions was not laboured but gently introduced as a concept yet to be discovered and explored in full. But having been touched upon gently, perhaps to quietly test our intellect for the sake of report writing, fractions were left for another year, another school, another teacher. But I was troubled even to discover that such complex mathematical concepts existed and that they would have to be addressed in the unknown future by an intellect grossly lacking in arithmetical aptitude. I wasn't wrong and perhaps as a result Sister Ursula's bullying increased, reaching it zenith just before the May holidays.

Children have a natural sense of what is fair and while they may be impotent, if angry, in the face of grown-up power they always recognise an injustice and they never forget it or forgive it. 'It's not fair,' they say in frustration and they're usually right. It wasn't fair that Sister Ursula dragged me by one ear to the front of the classroom where she humiliated me by asking me questions of arithmetic that she knew I couldn't answer. It wasn't fair that she slapped me hard across the back of the head — 'You stupid boy,' she said contemptuously — to show her scorn for my ignorance and that she then laughed humourlessly at my show of pain. Her derision caused me to blush with embarrassment and shame and it then wasn't fair that she taunted me for my blushes which made my face redden more and made the rest of the class laugh aloud.

Her bullying was merciless. If my arithmetic book was untidy, with mistakes and rubbing out, she would, without hesitation or warning, bring down the edge of a wooden ruler sharply on the back of my fingers. Then she would open the offending book and hold it up to show the rest of the class what *not* to do. Then she would throw it on the floor at her feet and make me pick it up. I was never favoured with the benefit of the doubt, a good mark, an encouraging comment or a spoken compliment even for my spelling, reading and comprehension which was the best in the class. So much humiliation, more than the physical pain of punishment, brought stinging water to my eyes, making me blink, but I didn't cry. Perhaps I should have. Meanwhile, unaware — or unconcerned — that she was making an innocent child miserable the old woman carried her bullying, tormenting and belittling out to the playground or wherever and whenever she encountered me around the school.

And then one day, just before the May holidays, it stopped.

'Fraser,' I heard Mum say to Dad that night, after tea. 'I couldn't believe it. She's just a real old meany. A horrible old woman just like they said.'

It was late and cold. I should have been in bed but I was sitting in my pyjamas on the floor in the hall, outside the closed door of the breakfast room where Mum and Dad were sitting at the fire. I sat there often at night and learned a lot to my advantage.

'Well what's the old bitch doing teaching kids?'

'Fraser!'

I knew whom they were talking about.

Evidently Mum had deduced enough from my reluctance to go to school after Easter, inferred even more from what I was saying, and then learned for the first time, from other more experienced mothers in the Legion of Mary, of Sister Ursula's reputation for bullying, to pluck up the courage to confront the unpleasant old woman about her unkind behaviour. It couldn't have been easy for her, a devout Catholic drilled from childhood to respect and revere any religious sister as a *de facto* virgin Mary, but she did it and I was glad.

'Well, she sounds like an old bitch to me. Why's she still teaching?'

'I don't know. She seems so old.'

'How old?'

'Dunno. She looks about, well, eighty I suppose.'

'Eighty!' Dad sounded astonished.

'Oh, I don't know. You can't tell with her veil and everything. Maybe seventy.'

'Well, seventy even, she shouldn't be teaching little kids.'

'I know. Molly McArthur said that Sister Olivia is always receiving complaints about her.

'I didn't like her at all,' she added.

I don't know what Mum had said but Sister Ursula's attitude to me changed immediately and from the next day she treated me not kindly but with a complete disregard, as though I now didn't exist. It was wonderful. And then suddenly it was the May holidays and nothing else mattered.

The May school holidays were the first of two poorly timed winter breaks. They arrived, two weeks in the middle of May, at the very beginning of winter while the second, two weeks in August, came during the very coldest and wettest part of the year. There were other holidays, such as Easter just passed and all the other public holidays of the year including Anzac Day in April, the Queen's Birthday in June, and Labour Day in October, but my best school holiday highlight came in the first week of the May holidays: it was my birthday.

I got a wrist watch for my birthday. My tenth birthday and my first watch. It was a sturdy but probably inexpensive little job in a man's style but smaller, with a brown leather strap, a sweep second hand and big numbers that glowed eerily in the dark.

'Don't forget to wind it every night before bed,' said Dad, 'but not too much.'

He explained that over-winding a watch, winding it hard until the winder wouldn't turn any more, could cause the clockwork to jam; a problem that could fixed only by an expensive visit to the watchmaker.

'And don't wear it in the bath,' he added. 'It's not waterproof.'

My little watch kept perfect time providing I remembered to wind it every night. It was an every day ritual, literally, which has disappeared from modern life. Clocks too had to be wound and most if not all people had an alarm clock on their bedside table. Dad's was a cheap tin model with a real jangly bell on the top that was hit repeatedly and rapidly with a tiny steel hammer every morning except Saturday at half past six. You don't hear the sound of alarm clock bells any more nor the constant ticking of clocks which was then ubiquitous. Most grown-ups fell asleep to the loud tick-tock-tick-tock of a cheap alarm clock while the same sound from a similar tin clock was ever present in the kitchen. The ticking of a clock was a strange sound to me; a sound that disappeared not necessarily when there were louder sounds in the room but when I was busy doing something, and yet the moment I stopped whatever I was doing the ticking clock seemed to start up again and grow even louder.

Getting my own watch was a milestone. I thought I was really growing up when, like Dad and all men, I had to take off my watch each night and wind it gently ten or more turns before laying it on my bedside table. But it rarely stayed there long. I was fascinated by the ghostly green and pulsing glow of the luminous numbers and frequently retrieved the watch to closely inspect in the dark what I now know was radioactivity at work. And when sleepiness meant I could no longer keep my eyes open, staring into the frantic shimmering of bright green luminosity, I tucked my little watch under my pillow and fell asleep to its rapid and somehow reassuring ticker-ticker-ticker-ticker sound.

I had a similar night–time fascination with torchlight, taking my lighted torch — another treasured birthday gift — under the blankets and staring into the centre of the lens where the light of the tiny bulb was reflected back into my eyes, in myriad patterns, by the mirror-like surface of the reflector. This fascination was increased tenfold when Gramma Little gave me a large torch with a sliding control that changed the normal white light to red or green for signalling. I never used it for signalling — I hardly needed a torch at all and I didn't know anything about signalling — but I exhausted many batteries with the light experiments I conducted in my dark bedroom, throwing light, coloured and otherwise, onto the walls and ceiling, and inspecting close up the process of changing the colours under the blankets for maximum effect.

But May was the beginning of winter and for much of the holiday time we — Tessa and I — were stuck inside with Mum, she doing her daily chores while we amused ourselves as best we could. If it were cold and wet Mum made sure the fire was burning in the breakfast room and made it my job to keep the scuttle full of coal. We spent a lot of time there, in front of the fire, reading or colouring-in or doing jig-saw puzzles or playing simple games together. I always won the board games — like draughts, ludo and Chinese checkers — I played with Tessa. My ability to outwit her at these simple parlour games was the result of nothing more than my slightly greater age but it frustrated her terribly.

'Why don't you let Tessa win sometimes?' Mum asked quietly and conspiratorially. 'It wouldn't do any harm.'

But I thought letting Tessa win was only another form of cheating which Mum would otherwise have condemned. Little Tessa, so young and small and inordinately pretty, had a tough, stubborn and quite unfeminine streak to her nature — and a well-known propensity to fly into what Mum called a paddy — and although frequently reduced to tears, tempers and tantrums by her inability to beat me at games she refused to stop trying and would have been insulted to learn that Mum wanted me to 'let' her win sometimes.

Tessa liked to play card games designed for kids. *Old Maid* was a favourite, although there were others, but I thought they were silly and refused to play any of them. I much preferred to play real card games with real cards and play them with Mum — *Strip Jack Naked* was a favourite although she also taught me *gin rummy* which I especially liked and, of course, *patience,* the stand-by pastime of bored and lonely people everywhere. She tried to teach me *five hundred* — which she and Dad often played on Saturday nights with friends or relations, graduating later to the much more complicated *canasta* and then *samba* — but *five hundred* didn't work well with only two, or three if a reluctant Tessa were included, so she gave up on that but at least I learned about trumps and bowers and the hierarchy of suits.

'Who wants to go to town?' asked Mum.

The highlight of the second week of the May holidays was an all-day trip to town.

'We're going on Wednesday.'

'Are we going to the Farmers'?' I asked hopefully.

'Yes. Meeting everyone at the Farmers.'

'Are we going to the flicks, too?'

'Yes, Johnny Boy, we're going to the pictures too.'

Mum had made all the arrangements with her married sisters. We were all — except Aunty Irene — to meet on the roof of the Farmers' where we would have lunch and then go to the pictures. Aunty Irene couldn't come because she worked all day serving ice creams in the Nibble Nook at the Regent in Queen Street. And although we were going to the pictures we weren't going there and so wouldn't even see her on this occasion.

But my other aunties and cousins were all there, Aunty Doreen and her kids Robert and Peter, Aunty Maureen and Kevin and Margaret, Aunty Colleen with Tony and Leah, Aunty Kathleen with Richard, and Mum with me and Tessa, fourteen of us for lunch and the pictures. It must have cost a small fortune and none of my aunts was any better off than Mum. But they managed it somehow, a treat for themselves as much as for us.

The big cinema companies always arranged special school holiday shows in some of their Queen Street cinemas. With three screenings during the day — at eleven in the morning, two o'clock and five o'clock in the afternoon — as well as the eight o'clock evening session, there was a huge range of theatres and programmes to choose from. We were going to the twos which gave us time to meet everyone, have an early lunch in the Farmers' roof-top tea rooms and then spend some time on the adjacent playground.

Mum and her mother and sisters, and everyone they knew, loved to shop at the Farmers'. They liked its vast range of products, its keen prices aimed directly at working-class families, and its easy and friendly hire purchase terms. The Farmers' Trading Company — to give it its full name — was New Zealand's biggest retail business with branches throughout Auckland and the country as well as a huge mail-order business serving farmers and the folk of country towns. Its flagship store was the huge multi-storied building in Hobson Street, the biggest department store in the country by far. Although it was located off Queen Street it was easy enough to reach as many trams stopped directly at the main door while the company provided a free electric trolley bus service from Queen Street up Wyndham Street to the store and back to Queen Street via Victoria Street, as well as a free tram service to and from Pitt Street and Karangahape Road.

And so, on the assigned Wednesday morning, as soon as Dad had gone to work and Mum had made the beds and we had helped her do the dishes and tidy up the kitchen, the very minimum amount of housework, we set off to the tram stop for town. Although I knew Mum loved shopping — or at least window shopping — in all the big Queen Street department stores like Smith and Caughey's, John Court and Milne and Choyce, she didn't linger this day but headed straight for the Farmers' free bus stop at the bottom of Wyndham Street. The free bus — in fact there must have been two or three of them, so constant was the service and so short the wait — was the only electric trolley bus service in the country. It left every five minutes or so, or sooner if it were full and it often was, so there was no delay. I marvelled at the way the pale green bus on soft rubber wheels effortlessly hauled so many passengers up steep Wyndham Street without making any more noise than a soft hum. Other petrol or diesel buses — like the squat Green Line buses which we sometimes took to Mount Roskill, which had their engines in the front, more like a car, and whose rounded shape behind combined to remind me of a teapot, short and stout — sent out a variety of loud mechanical noises from their gears, brakes and engine, and always smelled of hot oil. And the iron wheels of the trams riding on steel tracks were especially noisy to people in the street as much as to the passengers they were carrying. But the Farmers' free trolley bus was quick, smooth, silent and odour free.

Once we had been carried so easily and quietly up Wyndham Street, to be delivered across the road from the store's main door, the greatest attraction at the Farmers', for Mum and her sisters and thousands of women like them, was the wonderful and romantic tea rooms on the top floor. It was there we went, after some token window shopping, carried up on one of the lifts as smoothly and silently as we had been carried on the trolley bus. The lifts — there were many of them — were operated by a man or a woman in a smart brown uniform who stood at the front to one side, started and stopped the lift by turning a brass knob on a big brass wheel in one direction or the other for up and down, who announced between floors the number of the next floor on the journey, and the name of the departments which called it home, in a dreary monotonous drone of a voice which was perhaps the result of boredom brought about by frequent repetition. And then, when the lift had stopped with a slight and soft bounce, the operator leaned across the front to open first the inner doors, using a long and levered handle, worn smooth and shiny from frequent use, and then the noisy outer safety grill which could be opened only from the inside. And there, what joy, waiting for us on the top floor, were my aunts and cousins. Everyone was so excited. And Mum and her sisters found enough money between them for a cup of tea, a sandwich and perhaps a cake.

The Farmers' tea rooms were a model of design and styling right down to the multi-levelled silver-plate dish holders, the English china, real silverware, and the silver tea services which were standard. Every possible fitting was made of a dull stainless steel curved this way or that combining an elegant form with unmistakable function. There were large bevelled mirrors, cut to geometric shapes, stylishly engraved and sand-blasted, filling every possible vacant wall space; leadlight glass was used wherever a division was required, and the lead-light and angular wall lights were complemented by elaborate chandeliers. The waitresses — there seemed to be no men employed in the Farmers' tea rooms — wore black uniforms and white caps and aprons trimmed with lace, and were all old, surly and unhelpful. Unbelievably, the entire vast area was plushly carpeted from wall to wall although there was one area, at one end of this vast and noisy room, where a parquet floor, bordered with large potted palms, was set aside for tea dances.

A huge fish tank stood on a tall plinth at the height of my chin, populated by a seemingly random collection of large, lazy and bored-looking goldfish — black, white and multi-coloured and patterned as well as simply gold — that shimmered like expensive un-named jewels under the tank's artificial light. It was to the fish tank that we cousins went first. I stood in front of it, entranced, looking up, moving my head this way and that to counteract the reflective glare from the glass, fascinated by the beautiful gulping and sometimes bulging-eyed creatures that seemed to nibble at something on the tank's pebbly floor, or at the swaying green and slimy weeds that waved gently in the current created by a stream of air bubbles, or wobbled idly through and around the decorative artificial rocks, shells, china shipwrecks, mermaids and deep-sea divers which littered the floor of this mini-ocean.

While we were standing at the fish tank we could hear the awful and irritating squawking of Hector the parrot coming from the playground. Hector — a yellow-crested cockatoo housed in a tall wire cage — was resident on the playground that day because it was the school holidays. Otherwise his time was divided between the toy department and the pet department, both of which were attractive to kids which I suppose was the point. Hector was reputed to be very old and although no age was mentioned it was generally believed that he was at least a hundred years old, probably more. He was a sort of mascot for the Farmers' and Hector's Birthday Sale was an annual fixture. But despite his fame Hector was a very ordinary looking bird, somewhat scruffy and not at all special, clever or even friendly. Nevertheless we wandered out to the playground to pay our respects to the irritable old bird.

The wonderful Farmers' rooftop playground: its attraction to children can hardly be overstated. A bench ran around three sides, the fourth side being open to the tea rooms, together with some iron tables and chairs, where mothers, aunts and grandmothers sat with infant charges watching the older children at play. Behind them was a high glass wall through which visitors could see the whole of the Waitemata harbour, busy with ships large and small, and green-and-white steam ferries, blowing black clouds of smoke into the wintry sky, moving constantly between the ferry building and the jetties of Birkenhead, Northcote, Bayswater and Devonport on the North Shore beyond. It was all laid out like a harbour-side toy town; a spectacular view of

Auckland, the best available. Later came the tall buildings of Queen Street to rival the Farmers' playground for its view but even then only the Farmers' roof, with its own elevated observation tower, was open to the public.

The playground was big enough to accommodate, for the holidays at least, a merry go round and a little train — three pence a ride on each of them — and still leave plenty of room for all the pedal cars which were free to any kid who wanted to use one. There was no queue, nothing to pay, and no time limit. A boy who was alert, patient and fast could claim any pedal car as soon it became available and ride it anywhere in the playground until the sad but inevitable moment when he was called away by his mother. True, the pedal cars were somewhat dented and battered, and lacked the embellishments and trims they must have boasted when new, but they were well maintained by somebody, greased and oiled so carefully and regularly that the pedals and steering always worked to take me and my cousins, and thousands of others like us, on a wonderful journey, high above Hobson Street, to imaginary places grown-ups could never go. I always longed to have my own pedal car but I knew, without being told, that I would have to be satisfied with the occasional visit to the wonderful Farmers' rooftop playground.

Much as I loved our occasional visits to the big Farmers' store in Hobson Street the weekly reality for Mum was a visit to the local branch store. It was a long and narrow shop, painted a dull cream, and dimly lighted, and so nothing at all like the big parent store. It had only a token range of furniture, bedding and other household linen, perhaps some tools, a lawnmower, and a few kitchen appliances, displayed on each side of a straight and central aisle. It was down this aisle every week that Mum marched resolutely, her hire purchase payment book and money in her hand, avoiding the temptation of looking either left or right, directly to that part of the shop which was in fact the point of the local store's existence: the cashier's cage set into the back wall. It was at this barred window, and others like it around the country, that the furnishings, clothing, bedding, tools, hardware, toys, and all manner of farm and household essentials and luxuries, selected with such breathless excitement and anticipation at the main store, or from one of its regular mail-order catalogues or advertisements, had finally to be paid in regular weekly instalments. The payments must have seemed small when the contract was signed but they grew in significance every week as the novelty of the new purchases wore off. Then the small amount, perhaps only a couple of shillings, being taken from an almost empty purse, at the end of the week, represented not that which was now owned and in use but that which was needed but could not yet be afforded. Such were and are the perils of credit. But then, as now, credit was the last resort of the hard-up; a willing but dangerous friend whom Mum came to know well.

But all that was forgotten on our day out. It was a day of escape. A time for Mum to forget her worries and enjoy a modest lunch at the Farmers', and a trip to the pictures, enjoying the company of her beloved sisters, her two children and her nieces and nephews. She must have enjoyed herself because whenever I glimpsed her across the Farmers' playground, sitting at an outside table with my aunts, enjoying a cup of tea and a cigarette, she was smiling, or tossing her head with laughter, and she looked truly happy and beautiful.

After lunch, and after just a short hour or so on the playground while Mum and her sisters sat together chatting at the periphery, it was off to the two o'clocks. We, my cousins and I, were reluctant to give up our pedal cars too quickly or easily knowing that as soon as we got out they would be claimed by another set of sharp-eyed boys loitering at the edge of the playground, ready to pounce on the first available car. But once we saw that we were definitely leaving for good we surrendered our little cars willingly knowing that we were off to the flicks.

We took the free bus again, all together this time, down Victoria Street to Queen Street. The bus dropped us almost directly outside the Century where we all went in to see Walt Disney's *Snow White and the Seven Dwarfs*.

Birthdays and outings, school holidays or not, Mum had to keep up her routine household duties of cleaning, washing and ironing, shopping and cooking. And although I found going shopping with her to be tiresome and tiring Tessa and I couldn't be left alone at home. So, braving the wind, rain and hail of May, we trudged to, from and around the shops with Mum, learning how hard and boring her daily routine really was.

Mum walked everywhere. She didn't have a car of course but nor did any woman. And if any family did have a car it was driven and used only by the man of the house. Women didn't drive because it was believed that driving required an understanding of things mechanical which their minds were incapable of gaining. Nor for that matter did women seem to want to drive; Mum and my aunts had no such desire. And so, if they were not out with their husbands, and they were not taking the tram to town, or a bus across town, then women walked, whatever the weather, to do their shopping.

Because there were no supermarkets, and limits to what she could carry, and limits to what she could safely store without a refrigerator, Mum had to do the shopping almost every day, calling at one little specialist shop after the other in a manner that now seems archaic, almost medieval, until she had bought all she needed and could carry home. In the process she frequently met other women on their own shopping rounds meaning that going to the shops doubled as a social event. Women must have achieved a remarkable level of fitness from so much enforced exercise. But fitness is not the same as strength and none of the housewives then, certainly including Mum, would have been strong enough to carry home all the meat, fruit, vegetables and groceries so frequently and necessarily acquired. And so a free delivery service was routinely provided by grocers, fruiterers and some butchers, even chemists. Some would even take phone orders in the morning which would be delivered by a schoolboy after school in the afternoon. But the grocer's delivery services were used only for what housewives called the big order; more than they could manage to get home on their own.

Grocers had one or two bicycles especially made for such deliveries. They were heavy and clumsy machines — always black, and old even then — lacking the gears which would have made them easier to push up hills. A large box-like frame, made of the same heavy tubular steel of the bicycle's main frame, was welded to the frame over a disproportionately small front wheel. The frame was designed to carry cardboard boxes of the orders which had been phoned in by the customers and packed by the grocer during the day in readiness for the big boy's arrival. After a day at school the poor delivery boy had to pedal this old bicycle around the neighbourhood to deliver two or even three orders at a time. Sometimes it was loaded so high in the front with boxed orders that he could hardly see where he was going.

Roger Machynlleth was a grocer's delivery boy for Marriot's and I often saw him straining up Winstone Street after school, standing on the pedals of the old bike and zig-zagging across the road to reduce the climb (but increase the distance). It must have annoyed him to have to ride such an antique bike as his own was a new Phillips with Sturmey-Archer gears.

One day I found him sitting in the gutter on the corner of Studio Street, by the red post box, looking dazed. His school shorts were ripped at the pocket, he had a bad graze on his knee, and the old Marriot's bike was lying on the road beside him with one of the orders scattered all about. There were broken eggs, broken tomato sauce bottles and a split bag of flour.

'I'll be in for it now,' he said.

'What happened?'

'Stupid front wheel. Caught in that bit of wood,' he said. 'I absolutely *hate* that bike,' he added, lashing out with his good leg to give the old bike a kick.

Evidently he was delivering an order to Mrs McCutcheon, an old woman famous for her irritability and intolerance of children. Mrs McCutcheon herself rode a bicycle everywhere and had got her husband to set a small ramp of wood against the stone curb to make it easy for her to leave the road on her bicycle. It worked fine for her bicycle's full size front wheel but not for the small wheel of Roger's delivery bike. When he tried to use the ramp for its purpose the small front wheel of his heavy bike stopped dead, threw him off and tipped the orders he was carrying onto the road. The bike's little front wheel was bent and so the bike was crippled.

I helped him pick up the spilled groceries but there was nothing we could do about the broken and damaged stuff. He didn't go into Mrs McCutcheon's with her incomplete order — not then at least — but set off to walk his wobbly bike back to Marriot's.

The next time I saw him at work he was on his own flash Phillips bike. He had a canvas bag slung across his shoulder.

'Working for Mr Olsen now,' he said. He pulled out a tiny weightless parcel from his canvas bag. 'Just have to deliver this medicine. On my own bike. It's so easy.'

For their daily routine shopping most housewives used their own shopping trundler, a deep upright container on two-wheels with an upright handle set at a convenient height and a peg at the back to ensure it stood upright and stable, which they could fill with their purchases, sometimes to overflowing, and pull along behind themselves to home. Trundlers came in all shapes and sizes, some factory-made and stylish with a lightweight steel frame covered in tartan canvas and a fitted lid, some home-made by a husband who was handy and thrifty but lacking design skills. But whatever their design they were all used regularly, often daily, sometimes to carry impossibly heavy loads, and it was a dreadful day in any housewife's difficult life when her trundler broke or a wheel fell off or for some reason her little cart was out of action until her husband could fix it.

Mum's trundler seemed well designed and sturdy. Its body was made of unpainted cane basket-ware sensibly shaped to flare gently outwards from its solid wood base; its rubber-tyred wheels were narrow and cream and, except for the loosening of the cane that was wound around the wooden frame of the handle, it lasted Mum for as long as she needed it despite being used almost every day.

We had a choice of three grocers within walking distance, not counting the dairies. The Marriot's shop was closest but did not find favour with her. Another was the Self Help store, not a supermarket, as the name suggests, but one of a nation-wide chain of self help cooperative stores, but that didn't find favour with her either. Instead she was loyal to the local Four Square store — one of another cooperative still extant in country towns — owned and operated by the East brothers.

Whoever they were, whichever their shop, all grocers then were always smartly dressed in a white shirt and tie over which they wore a pure white apron which fell almost to the floor. They stood behind their counter while the customer opposite read through her list, her 'order'. The grocer then fetched what the customer wanted, one item at a time, from the long and high shelves behind him and around the shop, using a rolling ladder if necessary, frequently covering the same ground again and again in a remarkable display of personal, patient but inefficient service. Gradually a small hill of groceries was assembled on the counter, the grocer jotting down the price of each item as it was collected using a pencil stored behind his ear. Factory-packed goods were being introduced to grocery shopping but most dry goods were weighed by the grocer as required and packed in tall, upright and square-shaped paper bags. Even biscuits were mostly weighed out as required, the grocer drawing them from special biscuit tins — perfectly cube-shaped, each dimension being about thirty centimetres, with a hinged lid — which had been packed at the factory. These tins, made of a bright and especially thin material with dangerously sharp edges, were highly sought after when empty as useful and versatile containers. There was one brand whose tins were always printed on the front with the picture of a boy, much like me I thought, laughing with joy, running towards the observer, a neck scarf flying out behind him, carrying a biscuit tin under his arm. The fascination lay in the biscuit tin being carried: it was in fact a biscuit tin of the same brand printed with the same picture of the same boy with an identical tin under his arm with the same boy carrying the same tin and so on deep into the picture for as far as I could see, each biscuit tin diminishing in size until the last was no more than an imaginary dot.

At Easts' there were always two or three biscuit tins on a forward-sloping low shelf at the front of the counter labelled 'mixed broken biscuits', priced especially cheaply. Despite my pleading Mum always refused to buy biscuits from the broken biscuits tins. 'We're poor but we're not *that* poor,' she whispered while one of the Mr Easts was away fetching something. Mum enjoyed a biscuit with her cup of tea but her tastes were simple and she usually chose from the a limited range most of which I thought were boring: tennis biscuits, round wine, vanilla wine and Nice were her favourites as well as a round and salty cracker called Snax on which she liked to put a slice of tomato. I always envied boys whose mother bought broken biscuits because it meant there was so much variety, including colourful animal crackers, pink wafers and delicious chockie bickies of all sorts, mixed up in every bag. We rarely had chocolate biscuits.

Grocers didn't stock fruits and vegetables. They were the preserve of specialist greengrocers — more often referred to as simply the fruit shop — which were as great in number as grocery shops. For some reason fruit shops were almost always owned and operated by Chinese families and such shops were the only places European New Zealanders would encounter people so foreign, different and exotic. As at the grocer's there was no concept of self service. Mum would ask for what was required — measured by the pound — and Mr Wong would make his own selection from the display, put them into an appropriately-sized brown paper bag, cleverly mixing the under-ripe with the just ripe and over-ripe, the big with the small, weigh the bag on hanging scales, make a mental price adjustment for weight that was a little over or under exactly what was required, jot down the price on a flat brown paper bag using a short blunt pencil, and add it up quickly and mentally when the shopping needs had been filled.

I watched these processes with awe, fascinated by the quick way Mr Wong delicately picked out the produce, selected a brown paper bag of just the right size, deftly flicked it open with one hand, filled it carefully, weighed it, and then, once weighed, held the bag at each corner of the top and spun it quickly over itself a couple of times to close it without spilling the contents. I admired the way he and his family members could so quickly and accurately guess how much of the selected produce would be required to make a pound or two of weight, and then make the mental calculations necessary for the cost of each item and the total. It was remarkable that they did it so quickly and accurately when the weight was based on pounds and ounces (sixteen ounces to the pound) and the price was based on the complicated pounds, shillings and pence system.

Mr Wong and all the members of his extended family who helped in the shop were naturally and invariably small and delicate. Some of the women, especially the old women, were as tiny and frail as small and sickly children, no doubt from under-nourishment in their homeland, and yet they all helped out in the shop, even those with deformed feet, crooked fingers and bent backs, compelled by habit and culture to contribute to the family's welfare no doubt having brought memories of poverty and famine with them from China. Most of them — the older ones especially — could hardly speak or pronounce English but they knew the names of all the produce and had a complete mastery of the mental arithmetic necessary to calculate the costs. And if they couldn't clearly say the words they simply showed Mum the calculations and total they had pencilled on the empty brown paper bag. Money and numbers speak a universal silent language.

These encounters with such foreign people were difficult for a shy, unworldly and not necessarily liberal grown-up like my mother. She didn't like to complain to them, although she must have sometimes had cause about the quality of the fruit and vegetables she was given, and would suffer in resentful silence. And she felt awkward about other odd things concerning their foreignness and their race. For example the fruit which years later came to be called Kiwifruit was then known as the Chinese gooseberry and Mum found it difficult and embarrassing to say the words '…and a pound of Chinese gooseberries please' to whomever was serving her in Mr Wong's shop. She wasn't alone in her awkwardness; once I heard her saying to her sisters that she couldn't bring herself to ask the Chinaman, as Chinese men were then called, for Chinese gooseberries and would prefer to not buy them at all. And my aunts agreed saying they did the same. How many pounds of Chinese gooseberries went unsold in Chinese fruit shops for such a curious reason will never be known.

The Wong family had their own garden at the back of their house, which was at the back of their shop, to supplement the supplies they bought from the market. It wasn't a small garden — Dad said it must have been an acre or more, the equivalent of about half a hectare — and it was surrounded by a tall wooden fence. Often, before and after school and even on the weekends, I peered into the back of the garden through the gaps in the palings of the tall rough-sawn fence which marked the garden's back boundary. I was always impressed by the tidy unbroken rows of vegetables, reaching from one boundary fence to the other, and by the earthen paths between the rows worn smooth and hard. But it was a strange and exotic place. The shrivelled old men and women working there wore Chinese-style baggy trousers and smocks, and round pointed hats in the summer. Never — not even once — did I see the garden empty of people. It seems that those members of the family not working in the shop spent their long days digging and hoeing, watering and weeding; even the kids had to help.

'You should thank your lucky stars you're not born a chow, Johnny Boy,' said Dad. 'You'd have to work your arse off before and after school and all through the holidays. Just like a slave.'

One day after school, as I was standing at the fence, peering through a gap to watch the old Chinese people hard at work, I sensed someone beside me. It was Raymond Adams, a big boy from the states.

'Have they done it yet?' he asked.

'Done what?' I had no idea what he was talking about.

'The chows.'

'What do they do?'

'They shit in the garden,' he said.

'What?'

'They shit in the garden,' he said again.

'They do not.'

'Do so.'

'What for?'

'To make it grow. Have you seen one do it yet?'

'No.'

'Just wait. One'll do it. You'll see.'

'Quit it,' I said. 'They do not.'

'Do so,' he insisted. 'I seen it hundreds of times.'

I didn't believe him although I knew that Dad, who was a reasonable gardener, and quite knowledgeable, always wondered why he had to struggle to get a decent crop of anything from the same neighbourhood soil as that in the Wongs' garden. Of course his gardening was entirely part time and he put the Wongs' success down to time and effort.

'They work bloody hard those chows,' he said. 'That's what it is. The whole family working hard all day's what does it.'

I wanted to tell him what Raymond Adams had said but decided against it. After all, I didn't believe it any more than I believed another Raymond Adams story: that Chinese people in town cooked and served cats and dogs in their restaurants.

'How'd you like to pretend to be a chow kid, Johnny Boy. Help me in the garden all weekend? You can turn it over for some spuds. No playing. No pictures. Just bloody work.'

I knew he didn't really want me to help him in the garden but I could see his point. Even I could recognise hard work when I saw it and I could easily see that the Wong family worked really hard, all day, seven days a week.

I wasn't alone in being fascinated by the Chinese garden. Some kids, meaning to insult the old people, would adopt a high, sing-song and nasalised voice and call out silly and meaningless rhymes that all began 'ching chong Chinaman…'. There were many versions, all nonsense. But the people we could see through the fence, working patiently with a hoe or a fork, preoccupied with their work, took no notice. Perhaps they knew they were being insulted but it's doubtful they understood the English words nor cared about the chanting nonsense of local children.

There were many other Chinese gardens in the suburbs of Auckland including some on the poor land of a hill near Western Springs then known widely and colloquially as Chow's Hill (or more politely as Chinaman's Hill). Whenever I saw them I recognised the small and slight people with funny hats, bent over at work up and down the long tidy rows of the Chinaman's Hill gardens, as coming from the same hard-working culture as the Wongs who, with patience and hard work, had turned hard clay into fertile and productive soil on land that was later taken from them for a new motorway.

There was one local fruiterer who was a true Kiwi. A big, burly man called Mr Townsend. Mr Townsend's shop seemed small, dirty and untidy and lacked the variety and freshness of stock taken for granted at the Wongs' shop. Perhaps that's why it never thrived. But it didn't seem to matter. It was Mr Townsend's wife who worked in the fruit shop while Mr Townsend ran a lucrative winter business that would have been entirely beyond the powers of the small and frail Mr Wong. And so, when I heard Mum say 'Ah, there's Mr Townsend,' I ran to the street to watch him in open-mouthed amazement as he went about his work.

Mr Townsend was the wood and coal merchant and he called to forty-three three or four times in the winter to deliver coal. He was tall, broad and hairy-backed and wore a black singlet and a special leather hooded cape across his shoulders to protect his bald head and hairy neck. Nevertheless his head, face, neck, shoulders and arms were blackened with coal dust which made his teeth look especially white and his eyes especially big. He winked one of them at me as he got out of his small truck.

'G'day, Johnny Boy,' he said in his deep, gruff voice. He seemed to know everybody's name.

'G'day,' I said, trying to lower my voice.

He laughed at my attempted imitation. I watched as he put on his cape and went around to the back of the truck. There he stood with his back to the tray, reached his thick, heavily muscled and hairy arms over his head to grab a full coal sack by the corners, leaned forward and at the same time heaved the unimaginably heavy, hard and lumpy bag onto his back, and walked steadily and straightly down the side of our house giving me, running along beside him feeling small, feeble and clean, a smile and another wink as he walked. And then, at the coal box at the back of the house, he unlaced the coal sack and tipped it sideways off his back in such a skilled and practised fashion that the black shiny coal rushed out in a clatter into the coal box followed by a vast cloud of its own black dust.

Mum seemed to take for granted such a demonstration of might. She simply stood on the back step to pay Mr Townsend, apparently unimpressed, counting the money carefully from her purse while he, caped like a medieval peasant, with runnels of sweat showing though the coal dust covering his hairy body, despite the cold weather, waited patiently below, holding a limp, empty and dirty coal sack in one hand. I, meanwhile, stood to the side openly staring up at this giant of a man.

Meat was a daily essential. There were a number of family-owned butcher shops within walking distance and Mum patronised the nearest which was owned and run by the three Pellow brothers. They worked hard together, Monday to Friday, from well before dawn — when the dead and skinless beasts were delivered — until the middle of the afternoon when their stock was exhausted. In the meantime they butchered their raw carcases of whole lambs and sheep, pigs and oxen, and carefully prepared their stock of chops and steaks and roasts for the window and counter displays as well as the offal which was always popular. Somehow they found time to make their own mince and sausage meat, luncheon sausage and black puddings, prepare their own pickled pork and corned beef, and cure their own bacon and hams which they sliced to order. Their shop was therefore as much a factory as a shop, a place where everything on sale had been prepared by the same self-employed men who served the results of their efforts to their genteel lady customers with hands still bloody from their macabre work.

Service was provided over a high glass-fronted counter where stood the cash register and the scales. On a forward sloping shelf behind the glass, set off by fresh fronds of ponga, were displayed the offal products: grey-looking, lumpy and veined brains; small and creamy-looking sweetbreads; shiny slabs of smooth liver; kidneys like large, black and wet river pebbles; whole hearts, dark and shiny, large and small, cut from sheep and oxen, which animals also contributed their cut-out tongues, black and rough on top with their own maroon-coloured and fibrous looking muscle below; a whole pig's head with hairy ears, blinded white eyes and a drooling tongue; ox tails full of fat, bone and rich flavour; creamy sheets of honeycombed tripe that looked like a wet and cold blanket; the butchers' own fatty mince meat and sausage meat, and pound bricks of white dripping moulded into waxed paper bags. Then there were their own manufactured, smoked and cured products, already referred to, including horseshoe-shaped black puddings made with dried blood and barley, brawn, luncheon sausage, bacon, ham, pickled pork and corned beef. Long loops of linked sausages were hung like heavy chains from hooks on the back wall.

In the holidays I enjoyed going with Mum to the butcher's. Entry was through a heavy steel and glass door. Inside, the grey-painted concrete floor was spread with a thick layer of coarse sawdust, there to absorb blood and catch scraps of meat. The sawdust must have been freshly laid and raked each morning but was soon worn into tracks to, from and across the front of the counter, and traipsed out the door and in reducing trails along the footpath in both directions. The interior walls of the shop were lined with glazed white ceramic tiles although the very back wall was untiled but covered with a romanticised farmyard mural featuring fat and cheerful-looking cows, sheep and pigs, living examples of the red and dead carcasses which hung from their hoofless feet on vicious S-shaped hooks from a steel rail that ran high against the wall behind the counter. There was a cool-store at the back of the shop, secured by a heavy door, from which the brothers would retrieve the meat, limbs and organs that for some reason were stored there and not in the shop.

Adjacent to the cool-store door was the butcher's block: a section cut through the trunk of what must have once been a massive tree — about two-metres in diameter — upon and around which more than one man could slice and cut and chop and saw the trunk and limbs of the dead animals, their organs and bi-products, into the size, shape and weight required. The block must have lasted many years — I never saw it replaced — over which time it lost its level surface and acquired a series of shapely curves and contours unique to itself. Behind the block, against the wall, was a large square wooden box into which the working butchers threw the fat, gristle, skin, bone and fleshy inedible off-cuts of their work which were later sorted and used for Pellows' own sausages and puddings, or rendered into the lard and dripping they sold by the pound for cooking. In fact the pure animal fat bought from them was the only cooking fat used at forty-three. Cooking with oil was not known at that time.

The Pellows each wore a long bib apron of dark blue with narrow white vertical stripes, a protective garment that was usually wet, bloody and sticky and must have been replaced every day. Around their waist they wore a leather-and-chain belt affair from which freely dangled on one side a long stiletto-like sharpening steel and on the other a leather-covered wooden holster or pouch which held the three or four razor-sharp knives, long and short, straight and curved, which were their essential and personal tools of trade. Saws, like large hack-saws, and cleavers, which were used less often, and were too cumbersome to hang from the waist, were for communal use and so were hung somewhere within easy reach of the chopping block.

Sometimes, but only on Fridays, I visited the butcher alone on instructions from Mum. Friday was the butchers' busiest day. Without refrigerators and with no shops open on the weekends housewives needed to carefully plan their shopping for the weekend. To get the best meat — especially the traditional Sunday joint — before the butcher was sold out meant getting in as early as possible. Sometimes, if she were in the shop on a Wednesday or Thursday and had already planned her weekend menu, Mum would place an advance order and I would be sent off early on Friday morning, before school, to fetch it. If she had not placed an order then I would be sent off even sooner, at half-past-seven or earlier, with money and a hand-printed note which included an option in case her first choice was already sold out.

But on my own, stretching up to hand over Mum's note and money, I was especially vulnerable to the jibes and jokes for which butchers were notorious. Perhaps one of the Mr Pellows would pretend he couldn't reach my up-stretched hand implying to his brothers and everyone in the shop — or so I felt — that I was too small.

'Better tell mum to give you an extra sausage,' he said. 'Or ask Dad if you can stand in his manure,' he might say with a wink before, at last, taking the note and money easily. And when handing over the brown paper parcel of meat, tied with string, and then the change, he might say something silly of the type that men often said to kids. 'Don't spend it all in one shop,' or 'I'm going to ring up mum and tell her how much change I gave you'. Or most embarrassingly of all he might refer to my non-existent girlfriend: 'There's enough there to take your girlfriend to the pictures on Saturday, mate.'

Of course no harm was meant but I found these Friday morning exchanges excruciating. And I was ashamed that I couldn't find the words to match the butcher's cheek. Sometimes though a lady shopper stuck up for me.

'Leave the boy alone, Wal,' she might say. 'You're embarrassing him.'

'It's only Leeny Little's boy Johnny, love,' the butcher replied. And then turning to me with another friendly wink he said, 'You don't mind, son, do you,' and it wasn't a question. I did mind but I shook my head shyly and wished I were anywhere but there. But I did like it that Mr Pellow then gave me the end of a luncheon sausage, with a red skin crimped with wire, which he knew they couldn't sell. I ate it on the way home and didn't tell Mum.

The Pellows treated their overwhelmingly-female customers quite differently from the way other shopkeepers did. They joked with them, teased them, flirted with them, even called them 'love' and 'darling' and 'sweetheart', and while wrapping the meat would — with a mischievous grin and a cheeky wink — refer to the satisfaction awaiting their husbands that night in a way that no other tradesmen did or would dare. It was harmless fun and the women customers seemed to enjoy it, even expect it from butchers, and happily gave a little of their own cheek in return.

Of the meat she bought from Pellows' Mum had a special knack with stews and casseroles. She had renounced her new pressure cooker on the grounds that it was both too quick and too dangerous and instead cooked the meat long and slow, in the traditional way, with all the vegetables, in the same old pots and casseroles which she had always used. Oxtail was cheap, full of a viscous yellow fat and lumpy bones, which she turned effortlessly into a delicious stew full of onions and other seasonal vegetables including whole potatoes cooked in with the meat so that they absorbed the gravy's flavour. Fillet steak, which must have been expensive, was Dad's favourite but Mum could usually afford only cheaper cuts which she cut up with kidneys and served with doughy yellow dumplings laced with mixed herbs, or made into a steak and kidney pudding topped with her own buttery pastry. She even managed to turn Pellows' cheap and fatty mince into a delicious meal, cooked slowly in the pot with onions, carrots, parsnip and Swede.

Steak cooked and served on its own was always fried, overcooked and dry, and I couldn't understand why Dad liked it so much. Lamb or mutton chops, with a thick edge of yellow fat, and pork chops with a crackling edge, were more moist and much preferred although I personally preferred Pellows' fried sausages over any other fried steak or chops. Mum usually bought the pork sausages which Dad preferred.

'I like beef sausages better,' I said.

The contents of the pork sausages seemed to be smooth and pasty while that of the beef variety were more coarse.

'They put more meat in the pork snarlers,' said Dad. 'And more breadcrumbs in the beef.'

In fact there was no way of knowing quite what meat or what else went into the butchers' sausage grinder but whatever the variety and contents Pellows' sausages were always delicious and always had a very meaty and peppery taste. I was only expressing a personal preference.

'Anyway,' said Dad, pointing his knife at me for emphasis. 'You just stop complaining...'

'But I wasn't complaining.'

'...stop complaining, eat up what your mother's cooked for you and thank your lucky stars.'

'I do.'

'And thank your lucky stars you're not going hungry tonight like millions of people all over the world.

'The snags are lovely, Leen,' he said to Mum. 'Cooked just beaut.'

I knew that cooking sausages was simple. Mum fried them gently in dripping, turning them frequently to avoid burning them, and pricking the skins where necessary to release the copious bubbling fat and so stop them from bursting open and losing their shape. They were served plain although Dad added plenty of Wattie's tomato sauce while Mum liked to cut them down the middle and add butter which of course melted through the already fatty, greasy meat. Sometimes though, especially in the winter, she braised the sausages which is to say she cooked them slowly in the oven, in a covered casserole, with onions and carrots and a thin gravy.

Offal and other meat by-products were consumed with more or less regularity, probably because they were cheap, but I didn't like them all. I didn't mind sheep's brains which Mum poached gently in milk. Tripe, the stomach of a cow, was a favourite. Sometimes I helped cut the tripe into large squares which Mum then boiled hard, draining and replacing the water four or five times to eliminate the grassy taste and greenish tinge, adding plenty of sliced onions to the final stage and then blending in a white sauce flavoured with salt and plenty of chopped parsley cut fresh from the garden. Roasted pigs' trotters were a cheap way of enjoying the taste of roast pork which was a rare treat; but they were very fatty. Mum never bought sweetbreads, nor did her mother or any of her sisters, not because they were expensive — they weren't — but because they believed them to be the testicles of an unspecified animal. Dad scoffed at this belief but it was a half-hearted scoff as he didn't know what sweetbreads were either. Mum and Dad both enjoyed liver although I never did objecting more to the smooth unmeaty texture than the taste; Mum called it lamb's fry although I wasn't sure it didn't come from a calf, cow or pig. Whatever it was she fried it gently in shallow fat and usually served it plain for tea. Sometimes though she cooked it as part of the Sunday breakfast with bacon, black pudding and fried bread, perhaps with a lamb chop and a fried egg. Kidneys though were used only to add flavour to a steak and kidney pudding; they were never eaten alone. Hearts were rarely eaten but tongue was and it was always popular, especially cold.

Some purchases were made at home from travelling door-to-door salesman of which there were many. Such itinerants always called to the back door. For some reason only proselytisers called to the front door, and at forty-three they were always treated with predictable contempt, but Mum was always happy to leave off her chores to see a bona fide salesman although she rarely bought anything.

Of all the salesmen none was more reliable, more welcome, and had more and better merchandise, than the Rawleigh's man. There were Rawleigh's men everywhere in New Zealand, and they must have varied in nature and quality, but only one ever called to forty-three. He had no name I ever heard, and he seemed old to me although he travelled about on a bicycle which must have required some residue of youthful strength and fitness. His bicycle had an elaborate-looking Rawleigh's tin sign painted in faded gold and red on both sides and fixed in the triangle of its frame, and a flat carrier with a spring-loaded gripper over the back wheel. It was upon and within the grip of this carrier that the man carried his brown leather suitcase which was, when he opened it, 'a wonder to behold'. Like many of her neighbours and friends, Mum would defer certain purchases from the grocer or chemist preferring to wait for the Rawleigh's man. His products — they were always and only Rawleigh's branded products — were considered, without exception, to be superior in quality and much cheaper than the more famous grocery and pharmacy brands. Samples of ointments and salves, toothpastes and tooth brushes, hair combs and hair curlers and much more were revealed, department by department, as the Rawleigh's man put one knee on the back step upon which he rested his case, and opened it backwards, towards himself, to reveal layer upon layer, compartment after compartment, of Rawleigh's products. Each sample sat in its own cubicle, some open, some lidded, which was just the right length, breadth and depth to accommodate its particular sample in what I thought was a wonder of design.

'This is new, Missus,' he would say, and Mum was then free to take as long as she liked to sample, rub, sniff or otherwise handle or feel or examine the new product or whichever of the standard products took her fancy. Sometimes though, having just run out of a Rawleigh's favourite, she knew exactly what she needed.

'Am I glad to see you,' she said.

'At your service, Missus,' he said. 'And how can we help you today?'

Perhaps if he hadn't turned up she would have been forced to buy a substitute from the grocer or chemist which would have cost her more and cost the Rawleigh's man a sale.

The arrival of the postman — the postie was always a man — was an every-morning highlight for Mum. The postie walked everywhere, and wore a smart black uniform edged in red, including a jacket and a cap with a shiny peak, a military look which reminded me of the uniforms worn by the tram motormen, conductors and inspectors. He carried his burden of letters and parcels in a large brown leather bag with myriad pockets, compartments and flaps. A silver whistle hung on a chain around his neck and his progress up and down the street was marked by a sharp and regular whistle blasts given not so much to denote a delivery — most houses got a good fistful of mail every day — but to signal his arrival and progress along the street to the busy housewives indoors.

'Oh, good, there's the postie,' Mum would say to me during the holidays, sending me to the letter box to await his arrival and so collect what was almost always a good bundle of letters.

The postie knew me, as he knew almost every mother and child in the street, and happily handed me our post. And while he rarely met the working men of the neighbourhood he was thoroughly familiar with their names and the names of each member of every family on his route, and he used his knowledge to ensure the correct delivery of every letter even when the address provided was inadequate or wrong.

As sometimes the only means of communication between people even across town, let alone from around the country or the world, the arrival of the post was an event of daily importance, something to look forward to, and my hardworking mother used it as a chance to stop whatever she was doing. In fact it was an intimate and sometimes sentimental and emotional time which I wished I could share but never could or did; I was, during the school holidays, merely a mute observer.

'Make us a cuppa, Johnny boy,' she said, a familiar request from a weary mother. And then, putting aside a duster or a cloth, or dropping a scrubbing brush into a bucket of soapy water, she wiped her hands quickly on her housecoat, turned down the radio, took the bundle of letters from me, sat at the table and rifled through them, to 'separate the wheat from the chaff' she said, putting aside the bills — there were always plenty of them — for Dad to deal with later.

Meanwhile I made her a pot of tea. Tea was essential part of daily life and Mum would have a cuppa — meaning not just one cup of tea — at least half a dozen times a day including the tea that was taken during as well as after each meal. A large china teapot, covered by a woollen tea cosy especially hand-knitted for the purpose, with openings for the handle and spout, full to the brim with freshly brewed tea, was always on the table at meal times together with the teacups and milk jug and, in case of visitors, a sugar bowl although neither Mum nor Dad took sugar with tea.

As making a cuppa was such an important ritual I was taught at an early age how to make it properly so I could be called upon if Mum were busy so it would be brewed and ready for her as soon as she sat down. Tea was made to a standard and traditional recipe using dry black tea leaves, always from Ceylon. Tea bags had been heard of but were not freely available and most people thought their contents to be no more than the sweepings off the tea factory floor and so worth nothing but contempt. People were particular about their choice of tea: Mum preferred a brand known as Bell perhaps because each packet contained a tea coupon worth a penny which she collected although many other popular brands, including Amber Tips, Roma, Red Rose, Choysa, Lipton's and Bushell's, also provided a penny coupon.

Whichever the brand the tea-making process was always the same. First the teapot had to be thoroughly warmed by filling it with hot water from the tap while the kettle was coming to the boil. The tea itself was stored in an airtight tin — a tea caddy — with its own deep scoop which held something more than a teaspoon. Most households had more than one teapot varying from a tiny model suitable for one person to a large and quite monstrous thing which was so heavy when full that it could hardly be lifted for pouring. Most times though there was a medium-sized china pot suitable for two or three people. Whatever the teapot's size the same tea leaves rule applied: one spoon for each person and one for the pot.

Electric kettles were low and squat then, modelled on the traditional kettle used on a fire or gas ring and therefore less likely to tip over than the tall and narrow electric jugs of a later time. But the handle across the top, over the lid, not only made them awkward to fill but meant that the hand could be exposed to escaping hot steam. I was drilled by Mum in all such safety matters including the dangers of electricity, especially in the presence of water. I knew that before the kettle was moved it had to be switched off at the wall and the electric cord removed and that when holding and pouring it I had to be careful of escaping steam.

The water in the kettle had to be boiling and bubbling furiously before it was added to the teapot otherwise, I was told, the full flavour of the tea leaves would not be properly infused. In cold weather the tea cosy would be fitted at once and the teapot brought to the table where it would stand for an unspecified time, a duration that was sensed rather than measured. And then, before the brewed tea was poured, the teapot had to be rotated by the handle two or three times, clockwise and then anticlockwise, but never stirred.

Milk had to be put into the cup first — adding milk to hot tea was thought to scald it and was therefore forbidden — although the amount of milk varied according to individual taste and preference. Few people took their tea without milk; those who did were considered eccentric. Sugar, if taken, was added to the hot mixture and stirred with a teaspoon until it was dissolved. For some reason the adding of any sugar was considered 'common' at forty-three but most people added some sugar from as little as half a teaspoon to two or even three teaspoons full.

Immediately the tea was poured I had to return the teapot to the kitchen to be refilled from the kettle; a cup from this refilled pot was considered less than ideal but acceptable although if the tea stood too long in the pot it was considered to have stewed to bitterness in which case if more tea were needed — and it often was — a fresh pot would be made.

And so it was in the holidays that I made a small pot of tea for Mum and brought it to the breakfast table where she sat with the morning's post, turning over each letter in turn and inspecting it carefully and with much anticipation, checking the stamp, postmark and date. And then, having arranged the letters in some sort of personal order, she opened and read each one in turn. She was a slow reader as she was a slow but careful writer — she had an immature hand due, no doubt, to having left school when she was only twelve — but it didn't matter. She took her time and there was no one there to judge her for her slowness or occasional lack of comprehension. It was a personal and intimate time and she shared none of the news with me. I saw only her changing expressions — a smile, a frown, a puzzled look, a hand up to her mouth (signifying what, I didn't know), sometimes even a tear — until all the letters had been read, refolded slowly and neatly, and thoughtfully, replaced in their original envelopes, and set aside for Dad to read when he got home.

She looked across at me wistfully.

'Back to the here and now, Johnny Boy,' she said, draining her cup and replacing it carefully and slowly on the saucer.

She pushed back a stray wisp of wavy hair and, resting her chin in one hand, looked somewhat sadly out the window at nothing. The radio was playing softly in the background but she didn't hear it, and I could sense nothing in the room but sadness. But having no idea what news had come in the post I felt excluded and inadequate, as if Mum had forgotten I was there, and could only wait with uncharacteristic patience until the moment passed and she returned to normal.

I went back to school after the May holidays and never gave the postman another thought but I now know that whether I were there or not Mum must have put aside her chores every morning at the same time to enjoy a cuppa while she slowly and quietly read the day's post. Then, every day, she must have sat at the table for a few moments, staring out into the back yard, thinking her sad and secret thoughts about the letters she had just read.

I had looked forward to going back to school for the second term because I knew that with my new watch I would be able to see exactly how long I had to wait until each play time, lunch time or home time. But I soon learned that time passes slowly when you watch it and quickly when you're busy and so, with Sister Ursula now ignoring me altogether, I discovered that the harder I worked the faster time passed and more easily I learned. As May became June my school work improved, and so did my marks, and I found that I rarely even looked at my new luminous watch.

June

I NEEDED ALL MY NEW-FOUND ENTHUSIASM FOR school in the second term because for no apparent reason Sister began drilling us harder than ever in what was called revision. Revision meant going over again and again what we had already learned to check that we really had learned it. Evidently she had to be sure that we knew all our sums before moving on because just knowing our sums — the simple adding, subtracting, multiplying (using the dreaded times tables) and dividing of simple numbers — was now not enough. Now the lessons learned earlier with ordinary numbers had to be applied to the adding, subtracting, multiplying and dividing of money using the utterly illogical system which New Zealand had inherited from England.

I rarely handled large-value coins, or even saw large-value bank notes, but I became well schooled in the imperial money system. It, the system, although it hardly deserved to be called a system, was referred to as L.S.D. Even its name — the L.S.D. standing for pounds, shillings and pence — was illogical and therefore confusing. The stylised L sign, a script-like flourish of a capital L crossed with two short horizontal lines (£), still used in Britain, represented a Roman measure of weight because the English pound's value was once based on a pound weight of silver. (To add to the confusion, the pound weight was symbolised by the letters L and B together: *lb,* or *lbs* for the plural). The S in L.S.D. stood sensibly enough for the shilling while the D, always written and printed in the lower-case form, from the Latin word denarius, the name of the Roman penny, stood for pence.

I knew none of that historical stuff. All I knew was that money was important, that money sums were hard, that it didn't make sense for L.S.D. to stand for pounds, shillings and pence but they did, and whether I liked it or not, and despite its complexities and illogicalities, L.S.D. *was* our country's monetary system.

Dealing in pounds, shillings and pence was thought to be an immutable fact of life never likely to be changed or abandoned, and that meant we kids would have to understand it and use it for the rest of our lives and should therefore be taught it from as early an age as possible. But for me, who struggled with ordinary sums, it was really hard to understand how to add, subtract, multiply and divide pounds, shillings and pence. But I had no choice. It was especially hard to understand the importance of 'borrowing' and 'carrying' when values had to be changed in the process. A pound borrowed from the pounds column suddenly changed from being one pound to become twenty shillings while a single shilling borrowed from the shillings column suddenly became twelve pennies. With Mum's help at home I did eventually come to understand the mysteries of L.S.D. which I once considered insoluble, learning in the process that I was capable of learning anything, perhaps the most important lesson of all.

I knew that there were twelve pennies to a shilling and twenty shillings to a pound. But there were many coins in use between the penny and the pound note, each a different size and design. The penny was a big copper coin with a tui on the back; his little brother, the copper half penny, which everyone pronounced as hape-nee, featured a tiki; the tiny silver three penny piece, which everyone called a thripp-nee bit or thruppence, depicted a pair of crossed Maori mere; the slightly larger sixpence, which was usually called a six-pinny bit, but was sometimes referred to by men as a tanner, had a lovely but extinct huia on its back while the even larger shilling, which was worth twelve pennies and was called a shilling although more often, usually only by men, a bob, had a crouching Maori warrior on the back; the even bigger two-shilling piece, which was logically worth twenty-four pence and which everyone called either a two shillings, a two bob, or a two-bob-bit, but never a florin even though it was engraved with that name, had a Kiwi; and finally there was the large and heavy half-crown, with its elaborately engraved New Zealand coat of arms embellished by Maori carving designs, which was worth two shillings and sixpence — that is to say, as people did, two-and-six — and was variously referred to as a two-and-six, a half crown, or sometimes by men as a half dollar or half a dollar. And although the name of the half crown implied the existence of a crown there was in fact no such coin just as there was no such coin as a dollar.

Each coin bore a shallow relief sculpture of a royal head on the front, usually of King George the sixth who had reigned since nineteen-thirty-six, almost as long as New Zealand had had its own silver coinage and before the introduction of the New Zealand penny and half penny. There were many coins in circulation bearing his bearded father's portrait as well as many English coins still circulating, still legal, bearing his even earlier ancestors; I frequently handled a

Queen Victoria English penny. But by my Marian year new issues of New Zealand coins all bore the head of the new young queen, Elizabeth the second.

There were notes too of different colours, and in sizes that grew larger with their increasing value, and although I saw them at home I rarely handled them. They were issued in denominations of ten shillings — printed in brown, the note which was the most familiar to me — one pound, five pounds, ten pounds as well as the rare fifty pounds.

Working with money was never easy for me; in particular I found it impossible to mentally calculate change under pressure. But one day after school Mum taught me an easy way to do it. It was a quick and easy-to-learn method that was practical and foolproof. She tipped all the coins in her purse onto the plastic tablecloth that covered the breakfast table.

'Now, Johnny Boy,' she said, 'say you bought something from Drakes' for one and fourpence hape-nee and you gave Mr Drake a pound note.'

The Drakes owned our dairy.

Surveying all the coins spread across the table in front of us she used the first and second fingers of her right hand to draw a halfpenny across into the palm of her left hand.

'That's one and five pence,' she said.

Next she selected a big brown penny.

'One and six.'

A silver sixpence came next.

'That's two shillings now. Do you get it, Johnny?'

I nodded. It really did make sense.

'This shilling makes three shillings and this two shillings—' she picked up a florin '—makes five shillings, these two half crowns are worth five shillings so that makes ten shillings, and this ten shilling note—' she took a brown note from her purse '—makes up the pound. Easy, isn't it.'

And it was although it didn't help me at school where I was expected to be able to do sums, at least on paper, representing the adding, subtracting, multiplying and dividing of money that could reasonably be expected of me in my grown-up years. It wasn't easy when adding something like £1/12/7 and £2/9/8. While seven pence plus eight pence might have equalled fifteen pence it had to be converted to shillings and pence; with twelve pence to the shilling the answer was 1/3 (one and three, or one shilling and three pence). The three had to be 'put down' and the twelve pennies converted to a single shilling and 'carried' to the next column where it was added to the twelve shillings and nine shillings which were waiting there making a total of twenty-two shillings; that twenty-two shillings then had then to be converted to pounds and shillings.

With twenty shillings to the pound the answer was one £1/2 (one pound two, meaning one pound and two shillings). The two had then to be 'put down' and the single pound 'carried' to the next column where it was added to the one pound and two pounds waiting there to make a total of four pounds.

The whole answer therefore — adding £1/12/7 to £2/9/8 — was £4/2/3 (spoken as four pounds, two and three, meaning four pounds, two shillings and three pence) and the sum was printed:

$$£1.12.7$$
$$+\underline{£2.9.8}$$
$$£4.2.3$$

It bends my mind even now to look at such a strange sum. And, when it came to money sums, it was even more difficult to subtract, multiply and divide.

Incidentally, there was another amount of money called the guinea which was a complete mystery to me when I first heard it mentioned. I was at Gramma Fahey's place. Aunty Irene had bought Gramma a fox fur stole; that is, the fur of a skinned fox, complete with legs and head, that a woman draped around her shoulders ostensibly for warmth but more for fashion. Gramma was showing off her new stole to her admiring daughters, parading around the room and pausing, like a model, looking back over her brown-and-silver fox fur shoulder back with an assumed and silly coquettishness. Meanwhile the fox's four dangling legs, two at the front and two at the back, flopped about as she walked; they were complete with feet and the feet were complete with dull claws and leathery pads much the same as those of a dog. The furry head — with ears, an open mouth, white needle-like teeth, and glass eyes — hung down the middle of her back. I thought it was horrible, and that to wear such a thing was downright cruel, but evidently it was exceedingly fashionable and something Gramma Fahey had always longed for.

It was also very expensive but Aunty Irene had bought it for a bargain price in a sale at Stern's. She said it cost 'only so-and-so guineas'. I didn't hear or care what the 'so-and-so' was but my ears pricked up at the word guineas. All the ladies present gasped although I don't know whether that was because they thought the price was low or high.

'What's a guinea?' I asked Mum later.

Evidently there was no such thing as a guinea. It was in fact a complete fiction. It existed only in the minds of sellers and buyers where it was mentally agreed to be worth one pound and one shilling. It was used to price such things as fashionable and expensive furs and gowns, hats and coats, expensive items of jewellery and furniture, even motor cars, and was therefore used purely as an instrument of snobbery.

Prices in guineas were always given in round figures — no shillings or pence — and written for example as 100 gs or, in full, 100 guineas (that is, £100 plus 100 shillings = £105). In this way guineas might have served to partly disguise a higher price although it hard to imagine how anyone was fooled. More usually a price in guineas was used as a signal — in a way that has now passed into history — that the goods in question were somehow 'superior'.

Just as utterly illogical, and hard for kids to manage, was the so-called system of weights and measures. Like money it was a system that had been inherited from England and was then the standard being used throughout the British empire. We had to learn all the details — getting them off by heart — if we were to ever master their sums and, as far as the sisters were concerned, if we were ever to get and hold a job.

We had to know, for example, that there were sixteen ounces (abbreviated to *oz* or *ozs*) in a pound (abbreviated to *lb*), fourteen pounds in a stone — although the stone was used only in the weighing of people — two stones in a quarter, four quarters (or one hundred and twelve pounds) in a hundredweight (usually written as *cwt*) and twenty hundredweight, or two thousand two hundred and forty pounds, in a ton.

Small lengths were measured by the inch, which was usually divided into eighths or even sixteenths. Twelve inches made a foot with three feet to a yard. Longer distances were calculated by the mile in which there were one thousand seven hundred and sixty yards or five thousand two hundred and eighty feet. There were a few other standard measurements of distance — including the furlong and fathom, the rod, perch and pole — but their values were not material in everyday life and were therefore not taught with any vigour.

Liquid capacity was mostly measured by the pint (in which there were twenty fluid ounces), quarts (two pints) and gallons (four quarts or eight pints). Temperature was measured in the Fahrenheit system in which water froze at thirty-two degrees and boiled at two hundred and twelve degrees, a difference of one hundred and eighty degrees, so easily managed by a system based on twelve not ten.

Learning my sums earlier in the year — how to add, subtract, multiply and divide simple numbers — was now seen as easy compared with the onerous and unrewarding rote learning of all the various, illogical and unrelated details connected with doing sums in the standard weights and measures that were in everyday use at that time.

Of the other conventional lessons — in English, printing, spelling, comprehension, geography, social studies, nature studies, art as well as catechism — I especially remember lessons in English grammar, learning how to manage tense, past, present and future, and about nouns, pronouns, proper nouns, adjectives, verbs, adverbs and prepositions, subjects and objects, and especially subject-verb agreement, as well as the basics of punctuation including the use of the full stop, comma, semi-colon, colon, exclamation and question mark. There was an emphasis on the proper use of the apostrophe, to indicate missing letters and words and, by extension, possession, lessons we learned well and never forgot but the importance of which now seem to have passed into history. I learned to spell groups of cleverly-clustered words contained in a small spelling book with a limp blue cover and was often called up, apparently at random, to spell this word or that aloud in front of the class, something I could do with ease. I also had to write down words in my exercise book as they were called out by an unbearably demanding and exacting but no longer bullying Sister Ursula who checked and marked them later.

Connected I suppose to our English lessons was the regular fortnightly visit of an attractive but misfortunate young woman who taught elocution. Her name was Miss Staines. She dressed in fashionable street clothes, and was addressed as 'Miss' by the class, and was therefore a somewhat disconcerting figure as our teachers were always dressed in long brown habits and veils and were addressed only as Sister. In contrast to the old, drab and shapeless sisters, mean and spinsterish, Miss Staines was young, tall and slim, with a pretty face, perfect skin, and a head of short, wavy, auburn hair. She was also friendly, funny and fashionable. But to me — and surely for most of the kids, although, oddly, it was never mentioned — Miss Staines's most noticeable and memorable feature was her right leg: it was short and withered by polio.

Poliomyelitis was a feared disease in the nineteen-fifties. It was not uncommon and tended to flare up in unpredictable but short-lived epidemics. I knew all about it from Michael Sturgess whose left leg had been struck by polio. He was my age, handsome and cheerful, and he rather enjoyed the notoriety of his handicap and happily let me and other kids examine his purple, thin, limp and useless leg. But I knew that not every polio person was as nonchalant as he and guessed that the older Miss Staines suffered much embarrassment if nothing else from hers. But children can be overwhelmed by curiosity and I wanted terribly to see more of Miss Staines's leg. For one thing I wanted to know if it was the same funny colour as Michael's but it was covered by a thick stocking. Like the young Michael the older Miss Staines wore an elaborate and adjustable steel calliper, complete with hinges, clips and leather straps, which was fixed at the bottom into the built-up heel of a heavy and clumsy boot. She walked with a severe limp — no prosthesis could compensate this pretty young woman for her lifeless leg — and with every limping step, made by throwing her leg sideways and then ahead of her in a swinging action, the boot made a resounding clomp on the bare planks of our dusty classroom floor.

Who hired her and why I don't know; perhaps elocution was part of the official syllabus for which the sisters of Saint Michael's had no training. During her short lessons she tried to coach us in proper pronunciation and although the girls tried hard to please her we boys were not only distracted by her handicap but found the whole process of learning what we considered posh pronunciation to be a silly exercise in sissiness and something that was absolutely nothing to do with us. And surely we were right to be sceptical: the New Zealand accent was firmly established even then and any attempts to modify it by coaching children were going to be futile.

During the elocution lesson Sister Ursula retired to the back of the room as if to superintend the young teacher, overriding the lesson and applying Saint Michael's-style discipline from behind whenever she thought we were being unduly inattentive. Sister's presence, and her participation in the lesson, must have been disconcerting to the enthusiastic and qualified young teacher, an unspoken judgement on her ability to teach and control a class. As if she didn't have enough to deal with.

Near the end of June Sister Ursula's behaviour changed suddenly in the most peculiar and contradictory ways. On the one hand she became more exacting than usual in her demands for not only the correct answers to her questions — in particular her questions on English, spelling, arithmetic and geography — but also in her strict requirement that, when chosen apparently at random from a classroom of lively kids pumping their arms in the air for attention and approval, we should stand up straight and deliver our answers clearly and confidently. But on the other hand she seemed to become more kindly disposed than usual towards us, almost unctuous, in a way that was disconcerting and confusing but nevertheless a wonderful relief to me — and surely to many others — who usually lived in day-to-day fear of her bad humour and petty meanness. Sister Ursula's classroom, rarely a happy place, was suddenly full of happy, good humoured and well-behaved kids.

The reason for this happy change of classroom atmosphere, brought about entirely by a change in the mood of the only grown-up in the room, was soon revealed to be entirely for our benefit, at least according to Sister Ursula. At the end of the month — on a Wednesday — we were to be inspected. That is we were to be visited by an official inspector of the department of education, a very important person.

He was indeed, said Sister, a very important man and so it was essential that the whole class should behave properly during his visit although she didn't say what would happen if we didn't. And so Sister Ursula, surely one of the rudest people in the world, set about coaching us in courteous behaviour. She began by teaching us to say, loudly, clearly and respectfully, when the inspector entered the room and in response to his greeting of 'good morning, everybody', 'good morning, sir', rehearsing us by leaving the room, pausing outside, and re-entering it in the role of the fearful inspector. This coaching was necessary because just as Miss Staines was the only civilian woman we ever had to address as Miss so the inspector was the only civilian man whom we ever had to address as Sir. The only other man who regularly entered the classroom was Fat Pat. Whenever he entered the room, and he seemed to do it often, quickly and without warning, hoping perhaps to take Sister Ursula, us, or both, by surprise, we knew we had to quickly stand up and say 'Good morning, Father'. During Fat Pat's visits he grilled us on religious matters, drawn from our catechism, and was, in effect, a *de facto* inspector of our religious education.

But we now knew that the real inspector was to be feared much more than Fat Pat. And so, having coached us on how to properly greet the very important man, Sister then went over our revision, grilling us in English, spelling and mental arithmetic, encouraging us to hold up our arms decorously to signal that we knew the answer, and to refrain from the usual air pumping and calling out of 'Sir, Sir, Sir' to gain attention. And when choosing someone to give the answer she chose carefully to ensure, as the inspector surely would, that the shy would be chosen as often as the rambunctious, the dull as often as the clever, the poor as often as the rich, and that none would be made to feel foolish in front of the class.

On the day of his visit the inspector's importantness was confirmed by his tallness and stately bearing, his silver hair, and above all by his black uniform with silver buttons and the black cap with a shiny black peak that made him look rather like an American policeman. And yet we found that, contrary to Sister's warnings, and despite his uniform, great stature and obvious authority and importance, the inspector was softly spoken and kind towards us and not the slightest bit frightening or intimidating. Indeed, he so quickly and cleverly put us at ease that, in contrast, Sister Ursula seemed to be more nervous than all of us kids put together.

And for good reason. It was only later I understood that it wasn't we who were being inspected at all but Sister Ursula who, as soon as the inspector's visit was over, resumed her nasty and vindictive behaviour, perhaps relieved that the ordeal was over for her for another couple of years.

Winter had truly set in and while Auckland wasn't very cold in the winter, not as cold as more southern parts of the country, it was cold enough to be uncomfortable, and much rainier than anywhere else. Our house in Winstone Street, built of wood in the California bungalow style of the late nineteen-twenties, was rambling and spacious, cool in the summer but cold in the winter. Its rooms were large with high ceilings and casement windows. It had a steeply gabled corrugated iron roof, and so a vast and airy attic, and the ceilings were lined with patterned fibrous plaster resting on heavy wooden beams. The concept of insulation was unknown which meant that vast amounts of heat must have been lost through roof and walls. The internal walls were lined with flat, undressed kauri timbers to which was tacked what was called scrim, a coarsely woven hessian-type fabric to which the wallpaper was glued. The windows and doors were weather-tight but not airtight so draughtiness was considered normal. And in stormy weather the wind whistled under the closed doors and around the closed windows and reached under the house and up between the wall cavities to push the scrim and wallpaper out into the rooms with an eerie breathiness. Heavy rain or hail on the tin roof was deafening and made conversation or radio-listening impossible. The roof was pierced by three tall brick chimneys, one each from fireplaces in the breakfast room and lounge and from the copper in the wash house where every couple of weeks Dad had to manage the fire to boil the water Mum needed for the washing.

Nowadays the dreariness of an Auckland winter is hardly noticed indoors but in our large and airy wooden house without insulation, and with only an open fire for heating, fuelled by Mr Townsend's expensive wood and coal, winter evenings at forty-three were sometimes an ordeal especially when electricity was in short supply and there were frequent blackouts caused by power rationing or a systems failure.

'Oh, it's getting cold,' said Mum, rubbing her hands together vigorously, each afternoon after school. 'Time to light the fire, Johnny Boy.'

There was plenty of dry kindling stacked beside the fireplace, cut by Dad from old wooden boxes, and a few split manuka logs, so while Mum started things going with screwed up newspaper I went out into the cold, to the coal box, to fill the coal bucket. That fire in the breakfast room, set and lighted in the late afternoon to ensure that the coals were hot and glowing by tea time, was essential to our evening comfort but its warmth was confined to that room, and then not evenly to every corner, so we spent our winter nights together as close to the fireplace as we could comfortably manage.

Winter and summer, whether Dad was working overtime or not, Mum always had tea ready at five o'clock. But despite this early hour there was no time after tea in winter — or rather no daylight — for playing outside even if it were fine. And so, whether Dad were there or not, we settled into an after-tea winter routine in the breakfast room.

I don't know why that room was called the breakfast room as we ate all our meals there. These days it might be called the dining room but even that wouldn't properly describe a room which was in fact the centre of family life including the eating of all meals, all indoor leisure activities, the winter fire, and of course the home of Mum's little shrine to Our Lady in front of which we were supposed to say the rosary every night.

There was another large room, the lounge room, which another family might have used for relaxation but which Mum kept neat, tidy and clean by simply not using it. 'It's for important visitors and special occasions,' she said, but as important visitors and special occasions were both rare at forty-three the room was rarely used at all. Because its door was always closed its space and contents were unfamiliar to me. When I was allowed in I felt as though I were in another house. It seemed quieter in that room and I felt intimidated by its formal order and discomforted by the dimness caused by the weight and thickness of the cream lace curtains which seemed to hang heavily, ominously, without moving, and the low position of the brown and waxy Holland blinds. And because the lounge was the only room with windows on that side of the house, the east side, even the view through the thickly patterned curtains, across the side path to the high boundary hedge and the wall of the neighbouring house beyond, was disconcertingly unfamiliar. As a result I much preferred the brightness of the breakfast room, its carpet, threadbare in places, its worn but comfortable furniture and its familiar, cosy and cluttered informality. And so it was in the breakfast room — with the fire burning and the doors closed — that we spent our winter evenings.

It was a large room, the largest in the house, and easily big enough to accommodate the big and bulky extendable wooden table which stood against the windows, where the light was best, and its six matching chairs. There were four softly upholstered armchairs, with wooden arms made shiny by use, two of which were permanently drawn up to the fireplace while the other two were set against the south wall, one each side of a china cabinet. It was in this cabinet, dark and unfashionable, with curved side doors glazed with leadlight panels, that Mum kept her few pieces of special china and silver, mostly wedding presents. The whole room was papered in a light non-descript colour which set off the dark wood of the deep skirting boards, wide architraves, panelled doors (with hollow tin door handles too high for me and Tessa to reach) and the thick ceiling beams framing the white and lightly rippled plaster ceiling. The floor was covered in a worn maroon-coloured carpet of indeterminate pattern, which was not fitted to the floor but so positioned to leave a wide margin of dark varnished wood showing around the room's edges. The deep and generously proportioned casement windows were set into the west wall with doors to the kitchen and hall in the opposite wall, a single door to the back porch and the wash house in the south wall.

The deep brick fireplace was built into the middle of the north internal wall — the unused lounge boasted a much more elaborate iron fireplace flanked by brightly-coloured tiles — and was surrounded by varnished wooden panels and topped by a deep mantelpiece in the centre of which stood a modern streamlined-looking chiming clock. A large oval mirror on a tarnished chain was hung above the clock and at an angle down into the room. Of the cavities created by the forward-jutting fireplace the one to the left, adjacent to the table, was filled by a floor-to-ceiling storage cupboard — Mum called it the press — and the one to the right by a tall wooden radio turned at an angle into the room.

On cold winter nights in front of the fire Mum and Dad listened to their favourite serials and quiz shows on the big radio. They also read a lot at night, in front of the fire and later in bed, getting through three or four books each between fortnightly visits to the library.

The Auckland City Council took special pride in its wonderful libraries, then as now, and at that time our library was one of the biggest buildings in the shopping centre. It was open some evenings and it was always fun to visit it with Mum, sometimes but rarely with Dad, every two weeks or so, after tea, winter and summer.

On the library porch I got the same reminder from Mum, although Dad seemed to care less.

'Remember, Johnny Boy, it's always very quiet in a library,' she said. 'Don't bang the furniture or drop your books. And don't talk loud.'

And as the heavy doors swung closed behind us the sounds of the street were suddenly blocked and we found ourselves in a large open and high-ceilinged space surrounded by thousands of books. The atmosphere was warm and vaguely musty. And utter silence ruled. Even the occasional cough seemed to echo rudely around the building.

'You choose your own books, Johnny Boy,' whispered Mum. 'Then wait for me at one of the tables.'

There was a vast range of reading available in the children's section. I made my choice quickly, putting aside three or four books to take home, and then chose others to read at the low children's table while I waited for Mum. She chose three or four books for herself and another three or four for Dad.

Books being returned were left at the counter on arrival. When all the new books were chosen Mum handed them over to the librarian who opened each in turn, quietly, removed the index card and stamped the return date — two weeks forward — on a special piece of white paper that was tip-glued into the front. I always finished my selection in plenty of time, especially in the winter when we spent our evenings indoors in front of the fire.

The importance of the library — that so much knowledge and entertainment were available without charge — cannot be overstated and I shall never forget the luxuriously pleasant warm hours Tessa and I spent early on winter evenings, lying on the floor in front of the fire while Mum and Dad sat in their armchairs, all reading from books that were free from a source of infinite supply and variety.

Later, perhaps by seven or half-past, Tessa and I were sent to our chilly rooms to get into our pyjamas, slippers and dressing gowns after which we joined Mum and Dad for a while before having to go to bed. Perhaps then, instead of reading, I worked on a colouring book, or did a jig-saw puzzle, although sometimes I simply sat on the floor and looked deeply into the fire's leaping flames, fascinated by their ever-changing shape and colours.

Although the breakfast room was warm and cosy it was the only room in the house that was. I quickly became chilled and shivering during the pre-bed ritual: a trip to the toilet, not in the bathroom but in the big, dark, unlined and wooden-floored wash house.

The wash house — what would now be called the laundry — was a special room at the back but still part of the house with its own door off the back porch opposite the kitchen door. In houses older than ours the wash house was a separate small building in the back yard but even when it was part of the main house, as it was at forty-three, it was still called the wash house as if it were a separate building. Our wash house was a large, dark, gloomy, cold and spider-webbed room, unlined and unceilinged, in which Mum had to spend so many hours of every day.

In the extreme corner, farthest from the door, was a large and permanent brick and concrete construction known as the copper but in fact a freestanding fireplace in the shape of a cube. This cube, much more than a metre tall, wide and deep, stood on its own concrete foundations hidden beneath the floor but buried deep in the earth. It had a brick chimney reaching up through the roof while the fire chamber below was lined with firebricks and accessed by a small cast iron door set just above the concrete hearth which was itself set just above the wooden floor. Set into the top of this construction, where its bottom and sides would be licked by the fire, was the eponymous copper bowl with a loosely fitting wooden lid.

The copper — meaning the whole affair not just the copper bowl — was a major and important construction in the house, carefully built for safety, and taking a lot of space in the wash house. But starting it, keeping its fire roaring, and moving heavy, wet and scalding hot washing from it to the wooden wash tubs for rinsing, was more than Mum could manage alone and so it was used only every fortnight or so, usually on a Saturday morning or another time on the weekend when Dad was available.

It was at the washing tubs that Mum worked every day. These deep wooden tubs, in fact one large tub divided in two in which the back and sides stood vertically while the front sloped upward and outward at a gentle angle, were fixed against one wall, under the wash house window for light. A set of hot and cold brass taps was fitted over each tub while their dull and tarnished copper pipes, snaking up from beneath the floor, were fixed with copper brackets to the framing of the unlined wall. A hand-turned mangle was clamped to the central wooden divider which separated the tubs. The mangle — a sturdy steel and alloy thing, painted a dull green, with cream rubber rollers, partly perished, which were turned by a crank handle — had a wide knob on the top which was used to adjust the spacing and pressure of the rollers, and was so designed that whichever way it was turned the water being wrung out by the rollers was directed via a rocking tray back to the source tub.

I knew Mum's washing routine well. One of the tubs was half-filled with water as hot as her hands could stand to which she added a soluble washing powder: Rinso was a famous brand but Mum also used a brand called Persil as well as Lux Flakes which was more expensive and so reserved for 'delicates'. Whichever was used — many full tubs might be required in the course of one washing session as the water would have to be replaced when it got too dirty — it was complemented with a cake of hard, yellow Sunlight soap which was rubbed into stains or marks which were especially stubborn. A coarse wooden-handled scrubbing brush was also at hand and was frequently required.

First Mum added the washing powder to the hot water tub and swirled her hands through the water to speed up the dissolving process and create the suds which were assumed to be essential to the process. Meanwhile the other tub was filled, and refilled as necessary, with cold water. It was icy cold water in the winter. One day I found her leaning against the wash house wall, crying real tears. Her shoulders were hunched, her arms were crossed, and she had her hands pressed into her underarms.

'Mum.' I was genuinely alarmed. 'What's the matter?'

She looked down at me pitifully. 'Oh, Johnny, my hands are aching so much.'

'But why?'

She nodded towards the tub of water.

'The water's like ice,' she said. 'I don't know if I can stand it any more.'

I tried it. I dipped my own hands in the water for only a few seconds. She was right. It was almost freezing. How could she stand it? But she had to. More than once every day.

Hand washing in the hot and soapy washing water must have been a relative pleasure. She stood in front of the hot tub and vigorously rubbed the soiled items against the corrugated wooden washboard. This board, standard equipment in every wash house, was made of a piece of two-sided horizontally-corrugated wood, perhaps thirty centimetres square, held between two legs each about a metre long. It stood in the water, half submerged, resting on the front of the tub where Mum stood. The garment being washed was rubbed on the board and then turned and rubbed again and again, not unlike the way some people of the world still rub their clothes on a stone beside a river. The really stubborn dirt or stains were rubbed over with the Sunlight soap and attacked again by holding the item against the washboard and scrubbing the offending part with the brush.

Each item was then swished through the hot water and rubbed and turned and swished again and again until Mum considered it to be clean. Then she passed it through the wringer into the cold water of the adjacent tub where it sat while the next item was attended to. When the cold rinsing tub was full its contents were swirled by hand through the water which then lost much of its clarity and coldness. Another wringing out was required into the adjacent tub in which the warm, dirty and soapy water had been replaced by clear, fresh cold water for the second rinse. More swirling by hand completed the process and the now clean items were put through the mangle for the last time. This time they were collected by hand, as they emerged from the rollers, and dropped into the large, oval wicker basket which was another item of essential and standard equipment in the wash house.

There was one other step, not always taken, in which the clean whites — underwear, shirts, pillow cases, (sheets were not washed by hand but saved for the copper) — were steeped in cold water to which a faint blue dye had been added. Mum used the little white cotton bags of a powdered dye called Reckitt's Blue — a colour in concentration as bright and blue as the radiant blue ink from Dad's fountain pen — which were tied at the top like an old-fashioned money bag and left hanging by their string-tie to dissolve in the cold water. Evidently a trace of blue dye in newly-washed whites masked the natural yellowing which occurred when white cotton and linen were washed by hand.

Some housewives also starched their whites, especially their husband's white shirts, and the frills and laces of their own petticoats, but my factory-working father rarely wore a white shirt while pretty petticoats were not part of Mum's wardrobe, so the occasional starching was not part of her washing routine.

And so, progressively, after so much scrubbing and rubbing, filling and refilling of tubs, rinsing and blueing and wringing, a batch of washing was done. If the weather were clement Mum carried the heavy basket of damp washing out to the back yard where a galvanised wire-rope washing line was strung between two poles from one of which hung a bag of wooden pegs. Mum put the basket of washing on the sometimes damp or even muddy lawn, and moved it along the length of the line as she progressed with the pegging out. Sometimes she carried the peg bag with her, hanging it around her neck, while at other times she took as many pegs as she needed, slipping them into the front pocket of her apron or housecoat, and drawing them, one at a time, from this supply. Some women preferred the new spring-loaded pegs but they were more expensive than the plain wooden pegs which Mum used, the design of which had been unchanged for hundreds of years.

Once all the washing had been pegged on the line — after two, three or more trips to and from the wash house — Mum used a long pole, known as the prop, a long stick of more-or-less straight manuka, chosen for the way it ended with a branched Y to hold the wire, to raise the heavy line high in the air to maximise the washing's exposure to sun and wind.

Regardless of how thorough the housewife might be — and my mother was especially conscientious about cleanliness and hygiene — hand washing in a tub was not considered good enough for many items and at least only provisionally good enough for others. And so once a fortnight, or whenever it was otherwise practicable, the copper was filled with cold water, the fire beneath it started with kindling and fuelled with split logs — but not coal which burned too hot for copper — and a process begun which could be neither stopped nor interrupted until it was over. The fired roared. The water boiled and rolled. Soap powder was added. And into the boiling copper went our white bed linen, cotton singlets and underpants, shirts and handkerchiefs, to be thoroughly boiled to sterility.

Some women managed the copper on their own but it was hot and heavy work, more suited to a well-muscled fireman on a steam train or ship than to a frail young woman. And so Mum needed Dad's help and waited until a suitable Saturday morning when he was home and willing and when the weather looked set to be fine. Apart from the labour required to light and feed the fire, the washing and rinsing process itself required manly strength. It was the boiling of the water combined with the soap powder which did the cleaning and bleaching of the linen but its heavy bulkiness, twisted and tangled in the rolling water, needed to be stirred frequently. Dad occasionally lifted the lid of the copper and energetically stirred the contents using a large wooden paddle, bleached and feathered with use, shaped for the purpose. Meanwhile the fire, roaring noisily up the chimney, sometimes needed feeding and I watched in awe as Dad, using the toe of his shoe, lifted the gravity latch on the iron door which let it swing open to reveal the fiery furnace inside — it made me think of Sister Ursula's stories of hell — into which he, now stripped to his singlet, his brown skin glistening with a fine sweat, managed to push in another split log of wood while ensuring that no burning embers fell anywhere but on the small concrete hearth. I was impressed by his methodical approach to the work, his confidence in his ability to control the fire, and the utterly effortless way he did work that was beyond anything Mum or any young woman could manage on her own.

And so when at last the boiling process was over Dad lifted out the copper's contents — heavy with hot and soapy water — using the wooden paddle, and moved them drippingly to one of the tubs pre-filled with cold water. There he used his superior strength to vigorously stir the washing through the cold water by hand, untangling it as best he could, and then helped Mum guide the heavy and ungainly items, especially the sheets, through the wringer. Once it had all been thoroughly rinsed a couple of times, and wrung out as dry as possible, Mum could manage to hang out most of the large items on her own but she needed Dad's help with the sheets, to carry them out to the yard and lift them over the line where they would be pegged in place. Finally it took a man's strength on the prop to lift the heavily-laden line high in the air where the now pure white linen would be free to move gently in the breeze, or flap and crack sharply in a gusty wind, soaking in the light and warmth of the sun, to dry slowly and naturally in the manner humans have dried their washing for thousands of years.

In fine weather the washing would be dry in a few hours and would stay in the sun for the rest of the day until Mum found time to bring it in. But her washerwoman's life was more difficult in the winter months when it sometimes rained for days at a time; and even when it didn't rain the air was cold and damp. At such times the washing might hang limp on the line for days ending up wetter than it started and acquiring an unpleasant damp smell instead of the natural light freshness that warm sun and moving air added to cotton and linen. Despite the hardships of winter Mum preferred to dry her washing in the air believing that the fresh air, and the sun in particular, was good for the clothes. Unpegging sun- and air-dried clothes from the line she would hold them up to her face and smell them with obvious satisfaction and pleasure before dropping them lightly into the wicker basket. For such sensory rewards most housewives would hang out the washing, even in showery weather, being prepared to rush out, at the first sign of rain, to bring it in again until the sun returned. Neighbours called out to each other to warn of a coming shower or, in the event that a neighbour was out, brought in a the dry washing knowing that she would one day receive the same favour in return.

But sometimes, in the depths of winter, when it rained continuously for days or weeks, or when the air was heavy with moisture even if it weren't raining, Mum would despair. At these times she used a clothes horse over which she draped the damp washing. It was a complicated wooden affair that unfolded from its neat and compact size to become a large standing, frail and somewhat unsteady frame with many wooden dowels. Loaded with damp washing it stood in front of the breakfast room fire, day and night, until the washing it carried was dry albeit with a smoky smell. In the very worst weather even the clothes horse couldn't accommodate all the damp washing which would have to be draped over the backs of chairs, in front of the fire or an electric heater, or hung on a rope line in the cold wash house.

Although I knew then that Mum worked hard I realise now that her life was in fact nothing *but* hard work. Indeed, wives and mothers worked constantly at nothing but keeping house for their husbands and children. Housekeeping was far from easy for anyone but for young mothers like mine, with small children to manage, it took all day and into the evening with no respite. It involved work that was often heavy, physically demanding, and always drudgery.

But to Mum 'cleanliness is next to godliness' was not an empty phrase but a motto to live by. And given that godliness was so important to her putting cleanliness next to it was to put it very high indeed on her list of standards. It went beyond personal hygiene, the washing of clothes, and the cleaning of kitchen, bathroom and toilet, to getting down on her hands and knees to scrub wooden and linoleum floors as well as vigorously scrubbing the back- and front door steps and scrubbing and disinfecting the outside drains and gulley traps. Dirty and unpleasant work for anyone at any time.

And so it wasn't until Tessa and I were in bed in the evening that Mum found a quiet hour or so to spend with Dad, to discuss the events of the day — hers and his — and apprise him of our activities and progress at school. By then she was too tired to do anything but read, perhaps listen to a serial or a quiz on the radio, before going to bed exhausted hoping to be sufficiently refreshed in the morning to face another day of plain hard work.

'I work like a navvie sometimes,' she said, often, comparing herself to the so-called navigators, the burly men who once worked so hard building and repairing railways, roads and drains. It was, I think, a fair comparison.

The toilet was also in the wash house. It had originally been installed in a little building in the back yard, where the coal box now stood, but had later been moved into the wash house in a little room built for the purpose. It was a small, light, warm, fully-lined and modern bright spot in one corner of the gloomy wash house. It had its own chrome-handled door, of a more modern style than the house's other doors, and a ventilation window with fixed louvres far too high to look through but letting in plenty of air and natural light. It was a proper inside toilet, lined with Pinex inside and out, painted primrose yellow with bright white joinery. The big white and shiny china bowl was new and uncrazed, unlike many old toilet pans, and the brown varnished wooden seat was shiny and unbroken. I was particularly proud of the modern cistern, set low in a wooden box with a chrome lever. In contrast, most cisterns, even those in other houses with an inside toilet, were no better than a rusty cast iron water tank fixed high on the wall above the toilet pan and operated not by a modern chrome lever but by an iron handle, shaped to take the four fingers of a hand, on the end of a long and rusty chain. The chain at the top was attached to a curved iron lever which protruded from the cistern and which, when pulled from below, clumsily opened the valve which allowed gravity to take charge of the cistern's watery contents to send it rushing down the long curved pipe and into the toilet pan to wash out its contents and discharge them I knew not where.

'Remember to pull the chain?' was a reminder that most children needed even at forty-three where there was no actual chain to pull, a reminder almost as important as 'remember to wash your hands'. But it often required a considerable effort to pull one of those old-fashioned chains.

Having been pulled and flushed the high iron toilet cisterns then made strange plumbing groans and water hisses during the interminable process of refilling. The noises didn't matter if the toilet were outside but they were the source of considerable embarrassment to Mum, if she were visiting where the toilet was inside, as its noise announced to everyone that someone had just 'been'. To be that someone made her cringe with embarrassment.

The smallest room in the house was in fact the biggest source of embarrassment to Mum as it was for many grown-ups who passed on their awkwardness to the next generation as unconsciously as they received it from the previous. As a result I learned that there were some things which simply could not — *must not* — be said about the toilet; words and phrases which were simply too rude to be heard although the details of what could and could not be said contained subtleties and nuances impossible to convey now as precisely as they were then understood.

Our toilet was so called but never called the lavatory, lav or lavvie, and never the dunny. The word loo was not then part of the toilet lexicon which was a pity because it has since proven to be utterly inoffensive and useful. Using the toilet for an unspecified purpose was called simply going to the toilet. To be more specific, as was sometimes if unfortunately necessary, it was acceptable when referring to urination to speak of doing or going wee wees but not going or doing wees, nor weeing and certainly not piddling, widdling or peeing. And a child speaking of piss or pissing would certainly be boxed around the ears as they said. Indeed weeing and peeing, widdling, piddling and pissing were things the residents of forty-three never did, not even Dad, at least as far as I ever knew or heard.

Passing a solid motion was referred to as doing a job although I knew some families who referred to jobbies in preference to plain job. 'Have you done jobs today?' was a question heard frequently at forty-three and it was a few years before I understood that it wasn't a real word for the function but was meant euphemistically, evidence that euphemisms for unpleasant words can themselves acquire all the unpleasantness of the original word if the original word itself is unknown or forgotten. In the meantime any conversational use of the word job in its proper sense — 'I see you've done a good job,' for example, or 'Have I got a job for you,' or 'He's found a good job' — brought at least a sly smirk to my face, and to that of my boy cousins or, depending on the circumstances, loud hoots and howls of laughter we sometimes found impossible to suppress.

But children soon learn to bypass grown-up niceties and so I, my cousins and friends, discovered alternative job words like poop, dung, shit and crap, and longer words like excrement and defecation. But we could use them only amongst ourselves which of course we did with delicious pleasure in being so rude.

Fart was a word I always knew although I don't know how, when, where or from whom I learned it. And I also automatically knew that it too was a forbidden word which only made it more interesting. Mum insisted that a fart should be referred to only as a rude noise although most people, even the most polite who renounced fart, found blowing off to be perfectly acceptable alternative. But of all the fascinating natural bodily functions only farts can and frequently do escape the body suddenly, surprisingly and in public. Even Mum farted aloud, in company sometimes, although not without blushing with shame.

The single, innocuous and all-embracing term rude noise was hardly adequate to describe an event with such a variety of characteristics and so much potential for natural and harmless humour. Farts could be loud or soft, short or long, pitched high or low, and came in an infinite variety of smells and stinks, depending on the farter's constitution and recent food consumption. Onions, cabbages and peas were known to produce farts of loud volume and strong odour, and then the intensity of each odour could itself be indelicately measured, compared and discussed.

Amongst ourselves we boy cousins never used the term rude noise. On the contrary we not only relished the use of the fart word but happily drew public attention to a pending fart, waited together in silent anticipation for its arrival and completion, and then reviewed its length, volume and odour with mock seriousness that lasted only until one of us burst out laughing. Farts could also be silent — we referred to such farts as being silent but deadly — or they could be both silent and odourless in which case only the farter would know of their existence, surely a waste of a good fart.

But despite the harmlessness of the fart — both the event and the word — and its frequent occurrence, Mum wished in her heart that farts didn't exist at all. But as they did, and as she could do nothing about their spontaneous eruption, she could only insist that, in her domain at least, a fart should be referred to only as a rude noise and that there should be no laughter following such an event nor any commentary on its volume, duration or strength of odour. But once during tea — and only once that I ever heard — Mum herself farted, and quite loudly. Dad, Tessa and I stopped eating at once, shocked. We all looked directly at her, immensely curious about what she would say or do. In the event that I accidentally made a rude noise I was expected to say 'Excuse me' or 'I beg your pardon' and on this remarkable occasion I expected the same from her. She looked at us, apparently as surprised by the event as we were.

'Oh,' she said, putting her hand to her mouth. 'I *do* beg your pardon.'

And then I noticed a faint smile which became a proper grin. And that grin relieved the tension and provided the permission we needed to laugh. And so we did. We all laughed out loud at both the fart and the farter while Mum, the farter, sat back apparently amused and not at all embarrassed by the whole affair.

Related to embarrassing toilet matters, impossible to avoid, were the few words used for intimate body parts. Bottom was the only allowed word for that particular part of both the male and female body while bosom or bust were the only words used for the female breasts; the female genitals were simply unnamed or called a fanny by those who were shameless.

Amongst my cousins and their own families a penis, in particular a boy's penis, was referred to only as a willy and it amused me later to learn that Mum and her sisters had inherited the name from their mother, Gramma Fahey, and that she must have adopted the diminutive of her only brother's name, Uncle William, who still lived in Glasgow. I could only assume that Uncle William's willy was the only one that Gramma Fahey had ever seen as a girl and that the name willy was adopted accordingly. But how Gramma Fahey, Mum and her sisters, all born without a willy, came to have naming rights over that uniquely masculine member, and at the same time why Dad and my uncles allowed them the privilege, remains a mystery. But somehow the women ruled and for many years my boy cousins and I had no other word to use but willy when discussing our, well, willies. I was soon aware that my willy, which finished with loose skin which Mum had taught me early in life to draw back and wash whenever I was in the bath, although she never asked me later whether I did, was quite different from Dad's skinless variety. But it was a difference about which I never asked, was never told, and never connected with the important feast of the circumcision. As usual, unprompted explanations were not provided.

Despite Mum's horror at all things intimate and rude I soon learned all the ancient and common words relating to willies such as cock, dork, dick, prick, knob, nuts and balls, ball-bag and scrotum, and all such variants, as well as bum, arse, arsehole and crack. I was given these secret and unbelievably wonderful words by the big boys who were their custodians. They held the end of a strong, long and unbroken thread of secret rude word knowledge that stretched back into history, and when they passed it to me and my friends they handed over not only their somewhat limited knowledge but the responsibility of preserving it, and then, in due course, passing it to the next generation of curious boys.

But our curiosity then was limited to our own organs and acts. What girls had and did was of no consequence to us and the only rude words we knew concerning the female body were tits and nipples. Indeed, the plain, short, four-letter Anglo-Saxon words for the vagina and the sexual act were not learned by boys until much later and even when the existence of such things was hinted at by big boys, who seemed or pretended to know about them, my friends, boy cousins and I refused to believe either that girls were like that or that our parents would do such things in bed at night.

But whatever we learned, discussed and believed, right or wrong, we were simply boys being boys and it was obviously beyond the power of prudish parents or any grown-up authority to control boyish behaviour and defy such a venerable and unbroken tradition. But Mum knew nothing about such male traditions and naively adopted and strictly applied Gramma Fahey's feminine rules about the discussion of intimate matters. Her rules were followed at home although I knew that Dad's language out of the house, and out of Mum's hearing, was often coarse and certainly more plain than that which he used at home.

Finally a survey of such matters at forty-three wouldn't be complete without mentioning the chamber pot. Despite a comfortable new toilet having been installed in the wash house, the wash house itself, at the very back of the house, was a long way from the bedrooms at the front of the house, especially on a cold night when it was only dimly lighted, cold and draughty. As a result Mum and Dad used a chamber pot — called variously the pot, the pottie or the po — at night. I knew that both Gramma Little and Gramma Fahey had and used a chamber pot but unlike their beautifully formed china pots, decorated with red roses, our cheap pot was made of white enamelled tin with a blue border, much like a big camping mug. It was stored under the big bed, on Dad's side, although Tessa and I were allowed to use it in the night if we had to. And although I never saw Mum or Dad in the act of using it it was nevertheless always full of a golden liquid, sometimes to the brim, in the morning, bringing life to Dad's saying that something was as full as the family po. Sometimes I saw that Dad, who smoked cigarettes in bed, had dropped two or three butts into the golden liquid where the paper disintegrated and the fine threads of remaining tobacco were left to float in the pot staining the already golden water with runs of tobacco brownness. In the morning, when she was doing the housework, it was Mum's duty to carefully carry the heavy and almost full pot to the wash house where she would empty its contents into the proper toilet and flush them away.

But to return to that cold, wintry evening in June. After my visit to the toilet, in the cold wash house, it was back to the warmth of the breakfast room and out again, this time down the hall to the bathroom where I stood, shivering, on a cold lino floor, to briskly, quickly, brush my teeth (with the Ipana brand tooth paste Mum favoured). Then back to the warm breakfast room to say goodnight to Mum and Dad then up the long, dark and cold hall to my carpeted but still cold bedroom where the wallpaper moved in and out as the whining wind moved under the house and up between the walls. If it were an especially cold night Mum would have earlier put a hot water bottle in my bed but even then the rest of the bed felt cold, especially deep between the sheets where I had to press my feet. I lay there, under woollen blankets and a feather eiderdown, embracing the hot water bottle to the extent that I could bear the heat, while I jiggled my cold feet between the even colder sheets to raise their temperature by friction, trying for a moment but failing to say my prayers, before going naturally and quickly to sleep unaware even of the transition to that blissful state. I simply slept, deeply and obliviously, for eleven or more hours, unacquainted with even the idea of insomnia. And Mum's question, posed to me at breakfast the next morning — 'Did you have a good sleep, Johnny Boy?'— seemed pointless. Like all children I wasn't aware of being refreshed by sleep or of my own health and wellness. That I might feel other than perfect every morning didn't even occur to me.

One day at the end of that wet and wintry June, as Tessa and I were arriving home from school, we saw a Hill and Stewart truck pulling away from the kerb outside forty-three and we knew that something big and important had been delivered. We ran around to the back door and inside, throwing our bags onto the porch floor, calling out 'Mum,

mum, what is it? What is it?'

We found her standing in the wash house. The front of her house coat was lifted and held by a tight fist to her shocked face. She was staring. And there were tears in her eyes. Real tears.

There in the gloom of the wash house, adjacent to the old wooden tubs where she had to work so hard, was a new electric washing machine; a Whiteway. It was only a simple contraption. Nothing more than a large, open-topped steel drum, enamelled white, with a flimsy tin lid, raised to waist height on long legs with castors on the end, together with an electric wringer that could be swung, on an upright axis set on the side of the drum, to any position over the bowl or tubs that was necessary or convenient for the wringing-out process. It stood, incongruously new and gleaming, in the dusty beam of light from the wash house window, waiting to be filled from the brass taps with the required amount of water, a mixture of hot and cold to achieve the desired temperature, using a special rubber hose hooked at the end to hold it in place over the edge of the bowl. It was waiting to be plugged in to the electricity that would set it working to help her every day — tirelessly, effortlessly, rhythmically — with one of the most important but onerous chores on her workday list. As she probably knew, as she stood there, crying, it would make the copper, the washboard, the scrubbing brush, the Sunlight soap, the little blue bags and the achingly cold water, redundant forever.

She looked away from it briefly, down at us, and smiled awkwardly through her watery eyes.

'Grandad Little sent it,' she said sniffingly, dropping her housecoat and dragging us awkwardly to her, one to each side, where we stood within her loose embrace and together looked at that simple, simple machine.

July

ONE DAY EARLY IN JULY TESSA AND I ARRIVED HOME
from school to find the house eerily quiet. Although it was after three
o'clock the breakfast dishes were still on the table and the kitchen was
a mess. There was no Mum, no fire, no cuppa, and no milk and biscuits
ready for us. We looked at each other, mystified and worried.

Dad had stayed in bed that morning, suffering a mild relapse of his
malaria, but everything else had seemed normal. Mum had been in a
happy mood. 'I'm going to do all the washing this morning,' she had
said cheerily. She was looking forward to using her new washing
machine.

What could have happened?

And then, from the front of the quiet house, I heard Mum call out
in a stage whisper.

'Is that you, Johnny Boy? Tess?'

Tessa and I ran up the hall. Mum and Dad were in the big bed. Dad
was asleep. Mum put her finger to her lips to shush us and then pointed
to Dad.

'Dad's still not well,' she said.

But she didn't look well either. Her bottom denture was out — I
could see it, broken in half, two shiny pink and white bits on the
bedside table — and she had a cut lip; and her mouth and jaw were
swollen and bruised. The black and blue looked shocking on her white
skin.

'What happened?'

She put her finger to her lips again.

'Shhhh,' she said, folding back the eiderdown to get out of bed.
'Pass me my dressing gown, Tess,' she whispered. 'And you go and
make a cuppa, Johnny Boy, and I'll get up and tell you about it.'

Evidently it was all the fault of the new washing machine which she
was still learning to use. At first she was fascinated — so was I — to
watch the new machine in action, its paddles working automatically
and effortlessly to do so quickly and easily what she had always found
so slow and hard. When the washing was judged to be finished — after
ten or fifteen minutes — it was time for the wringing. And so she
learned to disengaged the agitating paddles and swing the electric

wringer into place between the washing machine and a tub of cold water. Having started the electric wringer, and set the roller direction using a lever on the side of the rollers, she was able to use both hands to pass each item through the rollers, effortlessly extracting more of the by-now warm, sudsy and dirty water than she could ever have done using the old hand-turned mangle, into the waiting tub of cold water.

The electric wringer made wringing easy but it required constant attention and some new skills. If the roller pressure were not quite right, being too loose or too tight, or perhaps because of the nature or texture of the fabric, some item of washing would not exit the rollers properly. Instead of sliding smoothly down the exit chute into the cold water it would wind itself continuously around the upper roller. It wasn't a problem if the item were small, a handkerchief for example; it was easy to stop the wringer and extract the tangled item. But if it were a sheet — the washing machine could easily handle sheets — or something bulky like a pair of man's pyjamas, not noticed, the rollers would be forced unnaturally apart. This activated the safety mechanism so that the whole affair flew up and open, suddenly and without warning, to release the jam.

It was a dangerous result if at that moment the unwary and inexperienced user were leaning across the top of the wringer, as Mum was that morning, trying to make things right. The sudden impact of the steel wringer cover on her jaw broke her lower denture in her mouth, knocked her to the floor and left her momentarily unconscious. Dad, dozing in bed, weak and feverish, heard her involuntary cry of surprise and pain, and perhaps the noise of her slumping to the floor of the wash house, even from the bedroom at the other end of the house. He got up and found her beside the washing machine, unconscious, bleeding, and gagging on her broken denture.

It was only a mild and momentary concussion. He carefully took out the two parts of her broken denture, helped her stand, and together they made their way to the bedroom where she meant to rest and recover. But the effort of helping Mum was too much for Dad, weakened and sickly, and he fainted, falling against a door jamb, blacking his eye, and dragging Mum down with him. Unable to move any farther on her own she lay beside him in the hall until he recovered from his faint. Only then were they able to ring Doctor Richards and help each other to the bedroom.

'Oh, you two,' she said with a laugh, picking up her tea cup. We were sitting together at the table in the breakfast room. She looked strange without her bottom teeth and taking a mouthful of milky tea was awkward. 'He thought we'd had a ding dong row.'

She put down the cup and laughed again, thinking about what was to become a family joke: that the family doctor found them, husband and wife, both in bed, he with a black eye, she with a cut lip, a bruised jaw and a broken denture, all the signs and symptoms, not unfamiliar to a family doctor, of what was called a domestic.

Mum learned then that the electric wringer, like all machines, was powerful but mindless and that constant vigilance was required to avoid the consequences of a wringing tangle. She also had to learn to overcome her fascination with automation and leave the washing machine alone to do its work automatically and without supervision. Freed from standing at the wooden wash tubs she was able to return to the house and some other chores for each of the ten or fifteen minute periods that the machine was working, making its deep, rhythmical, swishing, thumping and somehow reassuring noises that echoed through the house. But it was a unfamiliar freedom, laced with guilt, which at first she hardly enjoyed. Unaccustomed to any form of mechanization she thought the new washing machine made things *too* easy, making her feel decadent and almost sinful. She thought that washing, being housework, was *meant* to be hard but now it was easy. All she had to do was load the dirty items into the hot water, add soap powder, engage the electric motor using an upright lever that emerged from under the washing drum, and that was it. When the washing was done, and the clean but still somewhat soapy clothes were standing in the tubs of cold water, she emptied the machine of the now grey, warm and used washing water — the washing machine had an electric pump and hose for the purpose — refilled the machine with fresh cold water, and repeated the agitating process to rinse the clothes free of sudsy residue more efficiently than she ever could have done by hand. And the electric wringer wrung them more dry than ever could have been achieved using the hand mangle.

Then, suddenly, awfully, her guilt at how easy the washing had become was surpassed by her shame. Shame because she saw, at the end of the wash, that the water in the washing machine was greyer and dirtier than she had ever seen washing water before. She realised that her new washing machine was easily extracting more accumulated dirt and grime from her washing than ever she had, despite her best and exhausting efforts of the past.

'No wonder it's called a Whiteway,' she said.

One evening, after tea and the rosary, we were sitting in front of the fire together. Dad was reading the *Star*. Suddenly he stopped reading and leaned over to Mum, the paper open, to show her something. An advertisement.

'Fifty-six quid,' he said.

Mum stopped her knitting, put it on her lap, looked at the paper. Comprehending, she put a hand to her mouth.

'Oh, Fraser,' she said. 'Fifty-six pounds. Imagine it.'

I knew they were talking about the cost of the new washing machine. And once again I saw that Mum wasn't comfortable about Grandad Little's generosity. But there was nothing she could do about it but be grateful.

Meanwhile neither the guilt nor the shame lingered when she happily acknowledged that doing the ordinary household washing was no longer a difficult daily chore and that boiling day was eliminated forever. Now all the washing could be saved up to be done only once or twice a week and without Dad's help. It might take a morning or more but the time it took, only once or twice a week, was nothing compared to how much easier doing the washing had become, how she could leave the machine to work while she did other chores, and how her hands didn't have to spend hours and hours a week going between boiling hot and freezing cold water. Above all the new washing machine left her family's clothes cleaner than ever she had achieved by hand. It was a machine-age lesson in the value of the many new labour-saving devices which were being made available to her, and to housewives all over the world, to reduce or even eliminate the tedium and the physical demands of housework.

If only they could be afforded.

Mum's high standards of cleanliness could be met only within the limits of economy and facility, and our standards of personal hygiene in particular were not nearly as high as those set and more easily attained by later generations. Showers, for example, were then hardly known in the home — a shower was considered somewhat contemptuously as an American affectation — and a bath was taken only once a week. Hot water was used sparingly, not to save water, which was free, but to save electricity which was not only expensive but was rationed for many years. A shallow bath was often used by one of us after the other, being topped up with hot water only to maintain a comfortable temperature.

Even Dad, whose work was hard and dirty, and who was meticulous about his grooming, bathed only once a week otherwise being satisfied with stripping to the waist after work and vigorously washing his upper body in hot soapy water over the bathroom basin. Toilet soap was used liberally. Mum bought Rexona brand, a green soap, although there were many other brands including Palmolive, Knight's Castile and Lifebuoy. She used a shampoo for her own hair but considered it an expensive luxury, not necessary for children, so our hair was washed with Sunlight soap, brought in from the wash house, which Mum thought to be 'softer'. Hair conditioner was not known. Mum did use a deodorant called 'Mum', and of course she used the face creams and hand creams which all women used then and for centuries before. She also applied scent, make-up and lipstick lightly when she went out. However, male cosmetics — deodorants and after shaves — were unknown and had they existed would almost certainly have been anathema to Dad and all men.

I knew nothing of Mum's personal habits but I did know that Dad changed his underpants and his winter singlet, and his pyjamas, once a week. As a working man he had few and simple clothing needs for the working day as his employer provided a full overall. To go to and from his work by bicycle, or by tram on very rainy days, he usually wore a pair of grey trousers — men called their trousers their strides — leather-soled shoes that were once his best but were now somewhat shabby, a plain shirt with the large pointed collar turned out over the collar of a tweed sports coat with leather buttons. He wore a grey felt hat — all men then wore a hat at all times — except when he was riding his bicycle. He had few casual clothes; comfortable casual clothes, such as jeans, cotton trousers, t-shirts and light-weight jackets, were unknown then and most men relaxed in sports trousers and sports coat, or even suits, that were considered casual only because they were no longer new. And when even those clothes became old and past it they were kept for wearing in the workshop, garage or garden.

In summer Dad wore shorts of a boxer style, with an elasticized waist and built-in underwear, properly meant for swimming; tailored dress shorts were rare. But for church on Sunday, and the occasional evening out, to the pictures or a party, he liked to dress as well as he could afford and always had at least one good suit and one good pinstriped shirt in his oak tallboy as well as a selection of mostly paisley ties, a pair of shiny brown shoes in good repair, a smart gabardine overcoat, a white or maroon fringed silk scarf — a look so fashionable at the time — and a brown fedora.

During her working day at home Mum wore an all-purpose apron-cum-housecoat. This cheap, loose and light cotton print wrap-around garment served as a protective all-purpose overall with generous and convenient pockets. But it was never worn out of the house and a change to her second-best dress and hat was required for a trip to even the local shops. Her best dress, shoes and hat were saved for church, a shopping trip to town or an outing to the pictures or a party. Despite her best efforts I thought Mum always looked somewhat drab compared with Dad — a peahen compared to a peacock — because like most wives and mothers she made sacrifices for her husband and children which he and they didn't notice or appreciate.

Like Mum's housecoat my school uniform served as a versatile *ensemble* suitable for almost every occasion which is why I wore it almost all the time. A school uniform, while an awful expense at the beginning of the year, was economical in the long run because it was well made, serviceable and versatile, and rendered unnecessary the purchase of many other clothes.

Whatever the garment, whether worn by grown-ups or kids, male or female, it was inevitably made of entirely natural materials — cotton, linen or wool — as were all the household items, including table cloths, bedding, towels, face cloths, tea towels, even cleaning rags — that needed washing more or less often. And while synthetic materials such as nylon must have existed they were not used commonly and, except for their use in women's stockings and lingerie, of which I knew nothing, were quite unfamiliar. While doing the washing was hard work for the housewife it was, together with drying and ironing, at least uncomplicated by the peculiar characteristics, delicate nature and special demands of the myriad synthetic materials of a later age. Cotton and linen made sturdy garments which could be washed, dried and ironed without fuss, coming back from crumpled dirtiness to always look clean and fresh and crisp, while the quite different demands of wool were easily learned and managed.

While the new washing machine made life easier for Mum it did nothing to ease the worry of getting the washing dry in the middle of winter. But once it was dried and aired ironing it all — a time-consuming but not unpleasant task which she did only once or twice a week — was almost a pleasure. She saved the ironing until after lunch on the chosen day when all the regular morning chores were behind her and she had been to the shops. And so the afternoon stretched ahead to be broken only by our homecoming, a cuppa and a biscuit. She brought armloads of stiff, dry clothes into the breakfast room where she dumped them onto an armchair. Then she returned to the wash house to get the folding ironing board and the yellow ceramic-encased iron, switched on the big radio which stood in the corner of the breakfast room, to listen to the afternoon women's session with Marina, and began working her way through the tall pile.

Marina was a minor radio celebrity in Auckland. Her rambling and apparently extemporized talks were always about her visits to the many and familiar department stores and fashion shops of Queen Street and Karangahape Road. Her voice was somewhat but not too cultured, as smooth as silk, and she used it in a lazy and relaxed fashion that was strangely soothing.

'Why, only this morning I popped into Milne's— ' she said, referring to Milne and Choyce, the Queen Street department store '— to see their new season's hats and the whole department looked wonderful all decked out with summer colours. I was talking to...'

Listening to someone who sounded so nice and kind and motherly talk interestingly, charmingly, about nothing at all seemed to lull Mum into a detached and dreamlike trance. And so she listened idly to Marina while she ironed, as if she were listening to a friend who had popped in for a brief visit, standing the iron on end while she turned, flattened and smoothed whatever she was working on, then working the hot and heavy iron backwards and forwards in smooth sweeps, or in short and repetitive strokes as she worked around a button or along a tight pleat. When something needed steam pressing she ironed it though a damp, almost wet, cotton cloth — toasted brown from repetitive use — and the hot iron sent steam into her face so that she had to draw her head away to better see what she was doing. Then, as each item was finished, she stood the iron on its end again while she put the finished item on its flat pile, or draped it on a hanger, and then drew the next piece from the pile that seemed to get smaller only very slowly.

Gradually, as the hours passed, the breakfast room was transformed. The air took on a warm, steamy and slightly burned but quite pleasant smell; very domestic. And every flat surface — of table, chair, sideboard — became covered with smoothly ironed and sharply creased clothes and underwear as well as handkerchiefs, sheets, pillow cases and tea towels. And every door handle, knob and chair back was hung with coat hangers of shirts and blouses and dresses.

Meanwhile the big radio in the corner droned on. It was the most important and reliable source of free entertainment and Mum always had it on when she was working. It was so large an affair that when I was young, not more than an infant, I thought — only fleetingly, until Mum laughed at me but not unkindly — that there must have been a man hiding in it or behind it to do the talking; it was certainly big enough to accommodate a small man. Of a style known as a console it was built of wood to look as much as possible like a piece of expensive furniture, and was treated as such by Mum who polished it regularly and ensured that there was always a small vase of flowers or an ornament on its top resting in the middle of one of Gramma Fahey's string doilies. It was a little taller than grown-up's waist, and about a metre wide and half a metre deep, and was stained or sprayed in a delicate vignette from dark at the edges to a light tan colour around the dial and controls. There was a distinctly soaring and vertical feel about its design, with elaborate fretwork decorations in the *art nouveau* style over a large fabric-covered speaker, and a highly-geared dial that spun quickly and smoothly with no more than a slight turn on the centrally-located station selector knob. There were only two other knobs, one to each side of the station selector: a volume control to the left and a tone adjustment — turned anti-clockwise for more bass, clockwise for more treble — to the right.

Although it was extravagant in design and size it was typical of its age, and its size was not merely for show: its body had to accommodate a metal chassis, fixed at the upper half, packed with valves, warm and glowing when the radio was on, and all the electrical components and wires which went together to somehow make a radio work. A large speaker —thirty centimetres or more in diameter for the sake of sound quality — was fitted low behind the fretted wooden front and tweedy fabric cover. It was no doubt an old fashioned wireless receiver even then — radio was usually referred to as the wireless especially by older people — but it served us well although I was always annoyed at having to wait a few seconds for the radio to warm up. Even then the sound came up to listening volume only slowly but that was a characteristic of all valve radios, apparently accepted by grown-ups, which I, of a new and impatient generation, found quite unsatisfactory.

Only four stations — all government owned — were available in Auckland although at forty-three only that station called 1ZB was considered worth listening to. It began broadcasting at six o'clock in the morning and closed down, like almost everything at that time, including street lighting, at midnight. 1ZB was a commercial station which catered for ordinary people — like our family and all the people we knew — with sponsored dramatic and comedic serials, quiz programmes, specialist programmes for gardeners and sports lovers, popular music and weather reports.

1ZB was always on on week-day mornings as Mum started her day in the kitchen and Dad, Tessa and I breakfasted together in the breakfast room. The breakfast announcer was a man called Phil Shone who was liked by Mum and Dad for his humorous patter and mildly seditious attitude to broadcasting, an approach that was refreshingly entertaining in a country as conservative as New Zealand especially when coming from the government's own bureaucratically managed New Zealand Broadcasting Service.

'By Jove, he's a beaut,' said Dad every morning as he got up to leave the table.

'What did he say today?' asked Mum and Dad would tell her the joke or the story before kissing her on the cheek and saying ta-ta to us.

Phil Shone was followed at nine o'clock by the raucous and irritating voice of Aunt Daisy, a famous radio celebrity who had a half-hour session on 1ZB every week-day morning. Mum listened to Aunt Daisy as she worked whenever she could, the radio's big speaker easily filling the house with a rich and undistorted sound. Aunt Daisy — she must have had a real name but I didn't know what it was and I suppose few people did — was famous for the fast, breathless, machine-gun style delivery of her commercials, endorsing this cleaning product or that tea in her own unique style which probably matched the frantic tidying, dishwashing, bed-making and dusting faced by her housewife listeners every morning.

Mum tried to have all these regular and routine chores finished by ten o'clock so she could sit down with a cuppa and a biscuit to listen to her favourite serial, *Doctor Paul*. This fifteen minute serial — 'a story of adult love' — marked the beginning of a full hour of sponsored soap opera serials. *Portia Faces Life* was another daily serial which for years I thought was about the life of a woman called Portia Face not knowing that life for grown-ups was something which had to be faced. But *Doctor Paul* was Mum's favourite and the only one she tried hard to catch every day. She especially liked the character of Virginia, the doctor's wife, but she left the radio on to hear the others playing in the background. And I would hear them too if I were home.

There was plenty to listen to on 1ZB in the evenings, after tea, including serials, plays, dramas and quiz shows, mostly from America, or from Australia with an American flavour. Mum and Dad did most of their evening radio listening when Tessa and I were in bed and they could relax and listen in peace to their favourite programmes, whatever they were.

Saturday radio on 1ZB was dominated by horse racing commentaries including the announcements of dividends and regular racing summaries. Mum hated — not too strong a word — anything to do with horse racing, and for good reason given Grandad Little's past, and so the bugle call which preceded racing broadcasts on 1ZB was the signal to switch off the radio for a few minutes until, it was hoped, the racing was over. And yet racing broadcasts of one kind or another — whether a race commentary, the announcement of the official results and dividends which followed, or one of the regular summaries of results from meetings around the country — were so frequent that on Saturdays the big radio at forty-three was more often off than on.

There were no news programmes on 1ZB, the reporting of news being left entirely to newspapers. The only news events of any consequence on the radio that I remember were the announcement, in June nineteen fifty-three, that a man called Edmund Hillary had reached the top of Mount Everest, the highest mountain in the world, and later, in May of my Marian Year, nineteen fifty-four, when it was announced that someone called Roger Bannister in England had broken the four-minute mile running record.

1YA was the serious station. It broadcast mostly British programmes from the BBC — comedies, dramas and documentaries — as well as the BBC news. The news was always serious and was always preceded by the serious announcement: 'This is the BBC in London,' and the painfully slow chimes of London's Big Ben. I heard the BBC news broadcasts occasionally — if Dad were listening — but I didn't understand what they were about and I thought the announcers sounded so impossibly plummy and posh.

'Why do they talk like that?' I asked Dad.

'Like what? All scratchy?' He was referring to the poor short-wave reception. Sometimes the quality of the broadcast from London was so full of static and echoes that it sounded as though it were coming from the moon which, in the days when shortwave radio was the only form of international communication, it might just as well have been.

'No. All posh.'

'Oh, that. Poms,' he said as if that explained everything.

Dad invariably called English immigrants — and there were plenty of them about — poms, pommies or even, providing Mum couldn't hear, pommie bastards. But that didn't make sense to me because none of the poms I knew spoke anything like the BBC announcers.

'But the Greenfields and the Newmans and them, they don't talk like that.'

'All poms talk funny one way or another, boy. Just thank your lucky stars you're a Kiwi.'

Like 1ZB, 1YA closed down at midnight. There were two other stations which broadcast for only a few hours of the day but Mum and Dad didn't listen to them.

On Sunday mornings, whenever we could, Tessa and I listened to the children's request session on 1ZB. It started at seven o'clock and continued until nine although going to mass meant I rarely heard the whole thing unless I were sick. The programme was mostly stories, short and long, dramatic and funny, produced in America. Kids wrote to the station to hear their name read out for their favourite story but I never wrote in because I thought I would miss hearing my name while I was at mass. And anyway the same stories were repeated in a different order each Sunday and I knew most of them by heart. An intimate knowledge of the plots and their outcomes did nothing to spoil the excitement and drama of the stories many of which could bring a lump to a small throat and wetness to a small pair of eyes, a wetness I hid, successfully I think, from Tessa. I especially liked *The Golden Palomino*, written so beautifully, narrated so sensitively and acted so well that I could easily see the handsome horse called Amigo and the brave boy Bobby who cared for him so much. *The Happy Prince, The Small One* and *Dianna And The Golden Apples* were other favourites. Tessa liked the story of *Flick*, the little fire engine who was too small and young to fight fires but who did it all the same, in defiance of his deep-voiced father and sweet-voiced mother, and in the end became a fire-fighting hero. In a similar vein — the triumph of the underdog, just the sort of story kids love — were *The Little Engine That Could* and *The Ugly Duckling*. There was much fun and humour too: the story of *Gerald McBoing-Boing*, the boy who speak only by making funny noises; *Sparky's Magic Piano, The Emperor's New Clothes* and *The Three Billy Goats Gruff* as well as many others. Some people requested songs like *How Much Is That Doggie In The Window?*, *All I want for Christmas is my two front teeth* and *Tell Me A Story (before I go to bed)*, but I thought songs took up precious story time and that the people who requested them were silly.

My only complaint about the Sunday morning request session for kids was about grown-ups. The announcers — whichever reluctant male announcer was rostered on for that time — didn't know or care about the stories or the characters they contained nor how important they were to their avid little listeners. To them it was just a tiresome job and I thought it was another example of how the grown-ups of my world not only didn't know what was important to kids but didn't care.

The children's request session on Sunday mornings was followed on 1ZB by Brass Band Parade, a programme of military marching music aimed, I suppose, at R.S.A. members, which Dad enjoyed but I definitely didn't, and various religious programmes of preaching, sermons and hymns, often featuring a children's choir of appallingly low standard called the Sankey Singers. The religious programmes were always protestant and were always switched off by Mum. The Sunday request session proper, for grown-ups, began at noon and ran until two o'clock and although, like the kids' programme in the morning, its content was merely a reordered version of the weeks before, it was always on in the background during our Sunday lunch.

And so the big radio provided plenty of free daily and evening entertainment and as she was doing the afternoon ironing, during the week, Mum hummed or sung along with the popular songs that were played before and after Marina's session. And then about three o'clock, or a few minutes later to coincide with the end of school, she turned the radio down and switched off the iron, temporarily at least, and moved to the kitchen to put on the kettle to make a cuppa and so stop to spend some time with the homecoming Tessa and me.

But much as Mum enjoyed her afternoon tea break with us it was no more than a short intermission in the progress of her long day as she worked her way through a seemingly endless and repetitive list of monotonous chores. After finishing the ironing, and putting everything away, she had to start making tea for us and her soon-to-be-home hungry husband.

If he were not working overtime Dad got home from work, tired and hungry, about five o'clock and he expected his tea, the evening meal, to be on the table within a few minutes of his arrival. It now seems an early hour to be eating but most working class people ate dinner about then, the exact time being determined by how long it took the father of the house to get home from the factory where work usually stopped at half-past four. On the nights Dad worked overtime Mum still had our hot tea on the table at five o'clock and kept Dad's warm on a plate in the oven, or over a pot of simmering water, until he got home, somewhat irritable as well as tired and hungry, about eight o'clock.

Dad was always hungry. I don't know what he had for lunch. Mum would happily have prepared a lunch of sandwiches, cakes and biscuits and fruit for him, as she did for me and Tessa, but I never knew him to require it. Perhaps like me he didn't care for Mum's sandwiches but I sensed instead that he considered taking a simple lunch from home to be unmanly, even sissy. Appearances were especially important to him and always appearing manly was of paramount importance. Did he eat at the factory cafeteria? I don't know. If he did it was an expense he probably couldn't afford. And if he didn't, if he preferred to miss lunch rather than appear unmanly to his workmates, as I suspect, then it was no wonder he came home from work so hungry and demanded his tea so early.

I knew Dad's work was dirty, smelly and tiring. I knew because sometimes, on a Saturday morning, he took me to his factory if he had to make a quick visit there. I knew the work was dirty because the huge ink rollers had to be cleaned by hand; it was smelly because the cleaning was done using rags soaked in strong chemical solvents; and it was tiring because the machine in question — a big Roland — was especially long and high and so required strength and stamina to climb its ladders, ramps and gantries all day. So Dad undoubtedly ended each day physically tired and very hungry. No doubt he had a good wash at work, standing in the staff washroom with his colleagues, swearing and joking with them at the end of the day, the top half of his dark blue overall, sticky with thick printer's ink, hanging from his waist. He used solvents to remove ink from his hands and forearms, and face if necessary, before vigorously rinsing all the exposed skin, including his hairy and sticky underarms and the back of his neck, and his hair, first with hot soapy water and then with plain cold water. After drying himself, again roughly and vigorously, he stepped out of his heavy overalls, changed into his street clothes which had been hanging all day on a hanger in his tall wooden locker, carefully combed back his black wavy hair, before setting off for home.

The evening paper, *The Auckland Star,* was delivered to forty-three every day except Sunday by big boys on bikes. The paper boy rolled the paper tightly on his knee as he pedalled from one house to the next and managed to slip it into the home-made tube, usually made from a drainpipe of tin or pottery attached to every home-made letter box, without stopping. Dad expected the *Star* to be waiting for him at the end of each day.

During July and August, and on any wintry day, Dad encouraged the idea that I should put on my raincoat and gumboots and wait at the gate to take the paper directly from the paper boy. It was the only way to be sure that his paper would be dry when he got home as the delivery boy was notorious for pushing the paper only partly into the letterbox tube. I took the dry paper in and lay it on the table beside his place, awaiting his arrival. Dad insisted that no one, not even Mum, should open the *Star* before he had. Once he got home he did no more than kiss Mum on the cheek, tousle our hair affectionately, go to the bathroom to wash his hands again before sitting down expectantly for tea. Depending on his mood, and on the importance of the world, national, local and sporting events of the day, he would either leave the unopened paper on the table beside him to be read at the end of the meal or open it to the page that interested him, fold it to a convenient size, and rest it against the teapot so he could read as he ate. We, however, were forbidden to read at the table. After tea, in the course of the evening, he read the *Star* from cover to cover, taking it to bed to finish the news and do the crossword puzzle.

The New Zealand Herald — known universally as the *Herald* — was the morning paper. It too was delivered by big boys on bikes in the very early hours of the morning, well before school. No doubt Dad saw the *Herald* at work during the course of his working day but he and most grown-ups in my world considered it to be a Tory paper — Dad called it Sid Holland's paper after the prime minister — loyal to, written for and supported by farmers and the wealthy and not to be read or trusted by working-class people like us.

As for Dad's tea, Mum was a good but not enthusiastic cooker of manly meals. She had an aptitude for cooking, and a fund of recipes, but perhaps because she was tired by the end of the day cooking tea was more of a duty than a pleasure. And yet it was the biggest and most important meal of the day, the one that required the most planning, shopping, expenditure and preparation.

Having grown up in a house of fussy, finicky girls, dominated by a fiercely independent mother, Mum seemed not to have properly appreciated that her young and hard-working husband, not long returned from war and now burdened with the responsibilities of a family, had a manly appetite to be satisfied at the end of every tiring day with good hot food, and plenty of it. It was a strange flaw in her wifely character which I didn't see in any of her sisters. They loved to make big, hearty, hot and meaty meals for their husbands and seemed to enjoy their end-of-day meal as much as their families did. But Mum said she couldn't enjoy a meal she had taken so long to prepare. And she believed that working-class men were so hungry at night, because they worked so physically hard during the day, only because she had been told it so often. She didn't understand it for herself, and had only a small personal appetite.

Despite this lack of understanding, and therefore acting on faith, with only a limited experience in preparing man-sized meals, and a limited budget, she managed to provide Dad, Tessa and me with a hot, hearty, nourishing and tasty meal every evening. True, she did it somewhat dutifully, but she had the best intentions, and she served it with generous helpings of love, perhaps the most important ingredient in any meal. Dad always thanked her, and complimented her often.

Weekend meals were different. One day on the weekend — usually on Saturday night but sometimes Sunday night or even Sunday lunch after mass — even in the summer, there was a roast dinner which Dad loved especially and which Mum did well. Depending on the season there was always plenty of affordable lamb, mutton or hogget but beef was also used although pork was a rare treat. Regardless of the animal or the cut a roast of meat was always called a joint. Chicken, though

— which for some reason was sold by the fishmonger, not the butcher — was expensive 'pound for pound' (meaning the pound weight relative to the pound of money) and so was reserved as a special treat for Christmas day.

Cooking a joint was started by melting enough old fat or new dripping to half-fill a deep roasting dish. The meat to be roasted, whatever it was, was rubbed all over with salt and more especially on the skin of a real joint such as the leg or forequarter from a sheep, young or old. Mustard powder was also rubbed deep and hard into the flesh of a beef roast while pork, or at least the rubber-like skin, required special treatment, being cut through the fat to the flesh in a close diamond pattern and rubbed with salt to ensure, after cooking at a very high heat, it emerged as hard and blistered crackling. The meat was left to cook alone at first, longer and hotter than would be fashionable today, for an hour or more; only then would the oven be opened, the meat checked, turned and basted, and the vegetables added to the boiling fat. Pieces of peeled potato, kumara, pumpkin, parsnip, and onion cut through the equator, were all cooked with the meat. Mum made a rich gravy using the meat juices left in the pan, after the dripping had been poured away, with salty water strained from the boiled green vegetables, and thickened with corn flour. A serving of boiled vegetables complemented those from the roasting dish. Peas were my favourite with a roast, especially when flooded with Mum's thick, smooth and salty gravy. If the roast were lamb or mutton she also made a jug of fresh mint sauce using mint from the garden — mint grew in the garden like an invasive weed — finely chopped with vinegar, salt, brown sugar and water.

Once the roast was cooked, after a couple of hours or even more, the dripping, complete with bits of vegetables and meat which had broken away in the cooking process, now full of a strong meaty and salty flavour, was poured off through a sieve, before it set, to be used again and again during the coming week adding flavour to and gaining it from whatever else was cooked in it. Men of an older generation relished the cold dripping, flavoured by meals past, as a substitute for butter on bread but the taste and texture of bread and dripping was one which Dad didn't enjoy and which few of my generation acquired.

A cottage pie (made from left-over roast beef) or a shepherd's pie (made from left-over roast mutton) were not only economical but were ideal for a hot mid-winter tea. Despite their different names they were in fact the same dish. They were favourites of Dad and so they often turned up early in the weeks of winter after the weekend roast.

'Come on, Johnny, let's make a cottage pie,' said Mum knowing how much I enjoyed helping.

It was a simple process. First Mum got me to peel a few potatoes which she put on the stove to boil vigorously. Then she scrupulously stripped every shred of cooked flesh from the bones of the cold roast while I clamped the mincer to the kitchen bench, tight and secure. The cast iron mincer was standard equipment in every kitchen. It comprised a maw at the top which led to a wide horizontal tunnel within which a snugly-fitting corkscrew was turned by a long external handle. And so while Mum pressed the meat scraps into the maw and down into the tunnel I slowly turned the long handle. The meat scraps were thrust along the tunnel by my screwing action and forced through the holes in a fixed steel plate where they were met by another plate, this one being turned by the handle, whose holes were sharply edged. And so the meat was shredded and minced.

This minced and somewhat moist cold meat was then gently fried in fat with chopped onions, then mixed with diced carrots, and perhaps parsnip or Swede, and pressed firmly into a casserole dish. Mum then spread the surface with a sweet relish or HP sauce. When the potatoes were well cooked I strained them, mashed them to a creamy smoothness with butter and milk, spread them evenly over the waiting meat, and then enjoyed scoring a wavy pattern into the surface with the back of a fork. The uncovered dish was then put into a hot oven until the potato top had acquired a distinct crispiness by which time both the already-cooked meat and the potatoes would be hot and ready for serving.

Whatever the meal there were always plenty of vegetables, depending on the season, although not much variety, all boiled hard and long in heavily salted water; potatoes served whole, or mashed, mashed pumpkin, kumara served boiled or mashed, carrots, beans and peas — I enjoyed helping Mum slice the beans, French style, and shell the peas — silver beet and spinach from Dad's garden and plenty watery marrow and choko from Grandad Little's garden which I enjoyed with melted butter. There were also plenty of the vegetables I didn't like but was always made to eat: cabbage, cauliflower, Brussels sprouts and broad beans.

Summer though brought a change to the table. When the weather was hot we often had cold meat and salads. It was a change of diet that I welcomed and it must have been easier for Mum to prepare although I think it left Dad somewhat unsatisfied. Sliced ham and luncheon sausage were the staples although butcher's brawn, pressed tongue, corned beef and pickled pork were also popular prepared in advance and served cold. Sometimes Mum would make a bacon and egg pie in advance and serve it cold; I thought her cold bacon and egg pies — with sliced onions and tomatoes — were the most delicious in the world. But whatever the summer choice the cold meat would be served with new potatoes — tiny potatoes boiled with their skins on and served with melted butter — sometimes complemented with boiled corn cobs, more coarse and less sweet than those enjoyed in later years, also smothered in melted butter and salt, and salads.

Summer salads were simple and unvaried. They were based on a finely shredded iceberg lettuce, the only lettuce then available, to which was added tomatoes, spring onions, grated carrot, grated processed cheese — like most people then Mum preferred the Chesdale brand of processed cheese, bland and gluey, to New Zealand's real cheeses — and sliced or halved hard-boiled eggs. Exotic European-style salad dressings were unknown. Indeed, so conservative were tastes that if they had been known they would certainly have been rejected as oily and unpalatable and characterised, along with any other unfamiliar foods and food ideas, as 'foreign'. And while mayonnaise was familiar most people preferred their own home-made salad cream made with Highlander sweetened condensed milk.

Winter or summer, Monday to Sunday, whether tea was meat or fish, hot or cold, it was always followed by what was called pudding at forty-three and elsewhere, but sweets, dessert or afters at other places. Sometimes, in the winter especially, Mum made a true steamed pudding — much like Gramma Little's Christmas pudding but not as rich or ripe, and lacking alcohol — full of fruit and served with cream or hot custard made with corn flour or prepared custard powder. Or she made what she called a golden syrup pudding, heavy and coarse, rich and sweet, and covered with its own thick and sticky sauce. Rhubarb from the garden, or any other fruit, stewed with brown sugar and served with hot custard, was a special pudding favourite as was jam tart — I preferred mine cold — and the egg custard tarts, made with eggs, milk and brown sugar and sprinkled with nutmeg, which Mum made so well. Apple crumble was another standard and was especially popular at forty-three when desiccated coconut was added to the rolled oats, flour and butter, although the stewed apple could be replaced with any seasonal fruit.

But puddings didn't have to be complicated or cooked to be enjoyed: summer or winter it might have been as simple as tinned or bottled fruit — peaches, apricots, pears and pineapple were all popular — served with jelly, cream and, later, when we got a refrigerator, Tip Top ice cream sliced from a brick-sized carton and served with pink wafers. Jelly was always enjoyed; there were plenty of flavours and brands available but Mum preferred a brand called Lushus which came in a unique and oddly-shaped three-sided packet. She believed, perhaps as a result of advertising, that the so-called 'flavour bud' — a solid piece of brightly coloured and strongly flavoured confection, shaped much like a large acorn, hidden in the sugary ingredients — imparted a stronger and better flavour. I helped stir the jelly, watching the flavour bud melt away in the boiling water. Or she made summer pudding standards such as blancmange, Spanish cream and junket — dishes which are hardly known now but which I enjoyed without knowing what they were nor how they were made — or trifle, made with cubes of stale sponge cake mixed with jam, walnuts and cold custard to which Mum happily added port, the only time she ever used alcohol in her cooking.

And finally Tessa and I were encouraged but not made to finish our tea with a piece of fresh fruit from the bowl which stood on top of the china cabinet in the breakfast room and was always full. Depending on the season Dad was able to furnish heavy bunches of sweet black grapes, soft and fleshy figs full of rows of tiny pips, small magenta-coloured guavas with a tough skin and indigestible pips but a flesh as sweet and syrupy as nectar, and passion fruit, sweetest when the skin was brown and wrinkled. Grandad Little provided seasonal golden queen peaches, big and firm and furry-skinned, as well as nectarines and peacharines from his small but highly-productive back yard orchard. This seasonal and somewhat unreliable supply was topped up by Mum from Wongs' with apples — I preferred Granny Smiths above all others — pears, Australian navel oranges, bananas, Chinese gooseberries and the dark and tart tree tomatoes, later called tamarillos, which I enjoyed even though their acidy tartness stung my tongue and lips and made me shiver all over. We were allowed to leave the table to eat our fruit although asking the question: 'May I leave the table?'

was as obligatory as saying grace.

The end of tea marked the beginning of the rosary but by the end of July there was a distinct falling off in family enthusiasm for the evening ritual. Mum soldiered on bravely, urging us every night to join her on our knees in front of Our Lady's statue. Tessa followed her, more from loyalty than holiness, trying hard to hide her ennui, but I had never enjoyed the time-consuming and pointless ritual and was now attending only reluctantly.

'Don't forget what Father said,' said Mum, referring to Fat Pat's oft-repeated words about families that prayed together staying together, but it meant nothing to me; I simply couldn't imagine my family ever *not* staying together. Meanwhile Dad used every excuse to avoid the nightly business despite Mum's black looks which were meant only for him but which I could easily read. And anyway he often worked overtime, not getting home until eight o'clock by which time the rosary had been said and all he wanted was his tea.

Dad had only reluctantly accepted Mum's Marian year piety and by now, even on nights when he was home for tea, he simply stayed at the table, reading the *Star*, quietly declining to kneel down with us any more.

'What about Dad?' I asked Mum indignantly on the first wintry night we kneeled down without him.

She kissed her crucifix, as she always did, and sailed into the sign of the cross, answering me in the process.

'In the name of the Father and of the Son and of the Holy Ghost amen your father's too tired for Our Lady,' she said in one breath with a sideways glance at the table which Dad ignored.

'It's not fair,' I said glumly, receiving in reply my own glare from Mum.

Nothing was said after that, and no comment on the situation was welcome, but I could sense Mum's silent displeasure and Dad's quiet defiance. And so for the rest of the year Dad stayed at the table each evening after tea, sitting in front of the fire in the winter, reading the *Star*. By the end of the month I had made up my mind to join him.

'I don't want to say the rosary any more,' I said to Mum.

She looked surprised, shocked and puzzled.

'Johnny Boy?'

'Dad doesn't have to and I don't want to either,' I said. I thought it was a strong argument.

She said nothing. Didn't insist or argue. I suppose she knew that you can make people kneel down but you can't force them to be holy. But I saw tears in her eyes that night and knew that I had hurt her. I was somewhat ashamed, guilty even, and not brave enough to stay in the room as Dad did. And so, as she and Tessa kneeled down, each kissing a crucifix to signal the start of their rosary together, I went to my own room where I angrily broke the chain of my rosary, spilling the beads on the floor, and lay on my bed to read, alone and cold. I too was hurt, confused, but I had come to hate the rosary and now resented it for making me hurt Mum. A few minutes later Dad poked his head into my room. He was holding the *Star* open where he had left off reading. He didn't say anything. He just raised his eyebrows by way of enquiry.

'I'm not going to say the rosary any more.' I was compelled to answer his silent question.

'I know. I heard,' he said. 'But what about Mum?'

'She doesn't mind,' I lied.

'I think she does,' he said. Nothing more.

I don't think he hated the rosary as much as I did but he didn't love it either. He certainly wasn't as holy as Mum. And so almost every night for the rest of that Marian year, the year of Our Lady, only Mum and Tessa kneeled down in front of the little statue and said the rosary.

After that night Mum gradually became even more devout sufficient to sorely test Dad's tolerance and cause embarrassment to her own family and friends who, Marian year or not, simply continued to observe their religion in the same moderate manner that once was hers. What exactly brought about the increase in her godliness I didn't know. Dad's refusal to attend her nightly devotions, and my following his example, and my only mildly-disguised contempt for her beloved rosary, couldn't have helped, but there must have been more. Only years later could I imagine and understand the greatest worry of a devout young Catholic woman, and the stress it must have caused. Mum was only thirty-five then and much as she loved Tessa and me I know now that a new baby then would have been an almost unbearable burden in a home where there was always too much work and not enough money. Perhaps, in turning so devoutly to the rosary, she was seeking spiritual consolation for a marriage that was less than perfect and from which, as a Catholic woman with no way of supporting herself and her children alone, she could see no possible escape. That in her stress she turned to her religion, in fact the very cause of her female vulnerability, was paradoxical but not unusual.

Whatever the cause of her elevated holiness, I — just ten years old, selfish, self-centred, ignorant of the myriad worries that haunt grown-ups, and therefore uncaring — merely found her high-minded piety embarrassing. Above all I was glad I didn't have to say the rosary any more.

Despite his lower level of piety Dad was as active in the church as Mum. She belonged to a woman's sodality called the Legion of Mary, whose members sat together at mass once a month or so, while Dad belonged to both the Holy Name Society and the Saint Vincent de Paul Society. The members of both societies were the same set of men, Dad's friends. Members of the Holy Name Society vowed to defend the name of Jesus Christ and to never use it in vain. This, and their wider promise not to swear or curse in general, was hollow in Dad's case as he swore, cursed and blasphemed liberally whenever he was out of Mum's hearing. I knew intuitively that I should never mention his swearing to Mum — it was a matter between men — and he knew that I knew. One Sunday or so a month he sat not with us at mass but at the front of the church with a lot of other men wearing a special gold Holy Name medal on a blue ribbon. They all took communion together. On other Sundays after mass he went somewhere with the Saint Vincent de Paul Society doing whatever they did in the way of good works. He came home on those Sundays smelling of whisky so I supposed there was a sociable as well as a social purpose to the society's work.

While Dad's intentions were good he was not a saint. His mystical inclinations were few if any. He did what he did in his church activities partly to be with his friends but more to please Mum, and even that had its limits. With a child's ability to detect hypocrisy, unsullied by experience and wishful thinking, and intolerant of well-meant intentions, I secretly believed Dad was not even the moderately religious man he pretended to be. I didn't care but I did wish he would be more honest.

It was believed then that men of Dad's generation were somehow emotionally stunted by their experience of The Slump and the war which followed it and so were unable to express or display affection or love for their children. It was thought that they were isolated from their kids, removed from their upbringing, by war and then overwork, except for the application of physical punishment by hand or belt. And it was believed that Catholic men in particular drifted away from their wives who were thought to be frigid for fear of pregnancy. Such men, went the thinking, sought solace in other women and alcohol and so came home, drunk and belligerent, to beat their wives and thrash their children.

There might have been some truth in these beliefs. Dad was probably no better and sometimes somewhat worse than other men of his generation, Catholic and otherwise, in most respects except one: he was rarely angry or violent. Even when somewhat intoxicated, which he often was, or drunk, which he sometimes was, he never physically harmed or threatened to harm Mum. Nor did he hit me more than was normal for the times which admittedly was more that would be acceptable in later years. From Mum, though, I never received more than a light smack. Sometimes, in frustration, thinking a harsher punishment was called for, she would tell me to 'wait until your father gets home'. But her report to him at the end of the day was softened by time and his response was only half-hearted anyway. As a result I saw Dad as nothing more than a firm but benign and somewhat aloof figure of authority, less than perfect, happy when drunk and somewhat flawed by his religious hypocrisy, but worthy of my love and respect and utterly incapable of frightening me or hurting any of us.

Whatever his faults and limitations Dad always *tried* to do the right thing by us and it was no doubt in a misguided attempt to increase the family income, and so make life easier for Mum, that he allowed himself to be seduced by the promise of ill-gotten money. To my unsuspecting and unworldly mother — pious and preoccupied — the climax, when it came, later in the year, was sudden, surprising and shocking. A wiser wife, less trusting, innocent and naïve, might have read the signs earlier and realised that it, the coming climactic event which would shock us all, was in fact only the last chapter of a long tale that could have only one ending. At the time it left her angry and disillusioned, and temporarily blemished the purity of her Marian year. But it came late in the year and its telling must wait until then.

August

'YOU'RE A WICKED, WICKED BOY, TOMMY CRONK,' SAID
Sister Ursula to Tommy whom she had made to stand at the front of
the class for the strap. 'Your father's no better and no doubt you'll
both burn in hell.'

'Don't care,' said Tommy defiantly. 'And neither does my Dad.'

I liked it that he said that.

'You're a child of Satan himself,' said Sister Ursula, trembling with
anger. 'And the devil will have you in the end I'm sure. And your father
too.'

Angela James, a standard six girl, had overheard Tommy telling
another kid that Our Lady couldn't have gone up to heaven body and
soul.

'My Dad said it's impossible for human bodies to go up to heaven,'
said Tommy. 'Only souls can go to heaven, not bodies. And anyway
up there there's only stars.'

Angela told Sister Olivia who was outraged.

'It's an outrage,' she said to Angela.

'It's a heresy, Father,' she said when she told Fat Pat.

'You pulled the very words out of me own mouth there, Sister,' said
Fat Pat.

'So what'll we do, Father?'

'You'll have to strap the little pagan idiot in front of the whole
class.'

'Yes, Father.'

'Three times, mind.'

'Yes, Father.'

'And prepare the whole class for a special lesson.'

'Yes, Father.'

'Well done, Sister.'

'Yes, Father.'

So Sister Olivia told Sister Ursula to give Tommy Cronk the strap
three times in front of the whole class which she did first thing the
next morning. A cold morning. Tommy wasn't scared and he said it
didn't hurt much. He said that it was so cold that his hands were numb
anyway. When the strapping was finished Tommy sat down not the

slightest bit embarrassed and we all nervously awaited the arrival of Fat Pat. Sister Ursula said he was very angry and was going to give us a special lesson about the feast of the Assumption of Our Lady into heaven on August the fifteenth.

'The holy father,' said Fat Pat, pronouncing it, as usual, as 'da holy farter' which made us all snigger, 'has said that Our Lady, that's Our Lord's own earthly mother, of the immaculate conception, that means her soul was unstained by original sin, was assumed into heaven, that means taken up into heaven, body and soul, by god himself, to dwell with him and his son, Our Lord himself, and all the saints and apostles for ever and ever,' said Fat Pat with a mix of passion and anger. 'And His Holiness, as the vicar of Christ on earth, cannot make a mistake about such things. That means what? What is he, the holy father, the pope? You, Johnny Little?'

And there he was, in his black cassock and biretta, red-faced and white-haired, looking and pointing directly at me. I knew it was infallible or invincible. But which? I guessed.

'He's infallible, Father,' I said.

'Well done, son,' said Fat Pat.

To me. Well done. I couldn't believe it. Praise from Fat Pat. Praise or not, though, I really didn't care one way or another about the infallible pope or what he said about Our Lady being assumed into heaven body and soul. What I liked was that Sister Ursula had purposely strapped Tommy Cronk on the left hand thinking he could still work with his right hand not knowing that he was left-handed. I liked it that Tommy said he couldn't do any work all day because his hand was too sore and that Sister couldn't do anything about it. I liked it that she sent him home after catechism. I also liked it that Tommy said his father was going to drop Fat Pat but I don't think he did. I also liked it that, by a wonderful accident of the calendar that year, the feast of the Assumption, a holy day of obligation, fell on a Sunday which meant I wouldn't have to go to mass twice that week in August.

But what I liked most about August was the August holidays.

As usual Mum was busy, even in the school holidays, so it must have been hard for her to find ways to keep me and Tessa occupied, especially when the winter weather was at its worst in August and we had to spend so much time inside where it was dry and warm. I could keep myself occupied with my own toys, colouring in and reading, but

Mum found it hard to keep Tessa amused and occupied. She was a stubborn wee thing, not easily encouraged into games and play that seemed girlish to her compared to the much more interesting things I was up to. She was envious of my self-reliance and sometimes tried to join games which were not easily shared especially when most of my fun was the result of self absorption and imagination. She was therefore a worry to Mum and a pest to me, as younger siblings often are, and I was always glad when the day came — as it did in the second week of the holidays — for our big outing.

Meanwhile, if and when I became bored Mum encouraged me to help with the cooking and baking, getting a chair for me to stand on so I could help at the bench with the weighing and measuring, mixing and beating. In this way, standing on a chair at Mum's side, I learned the value of New Zealand's famous Edmond's cook book and the rudiments of mixing and baking the cakes and biscuits which Mum and her family made so well and enjoyed so much. I learned the importance of reading and understanding the recipe, of carefully and accurately measuring the ingredients and getting everything ready before we started; how to cream the butter and sugar by standing the mixing bowl in a sink of hot water, how to judge the consistency of the batter, to judge the heat of the oven, alternating the trays between the top and the bottom to compensate for the unevenness of the heat, how to do it all without getting burned, and above all, at a time when oven doors didn't have windows, ovens didn't have thermostats, and oven temperature gauges were unreliable, how to resist the temptation to peek; to be patient. Perhaps it was patience above all which I learned at Mum's side in the kitchen all those years ago.

'What'll we make today, Johnny Boy?' she asked, allowing me to choose from a fairly limited menu.

Scones and pikelets, Anzacs and queen cakes, peanut brownies and Afghans, even butterfly cakes, gems and sponges — complete with icing or filling as required — were all attempted with Mum's supervision and more or less success. I liked making the queen cakes best mainly because Mum gave me a free hand with colouring their icing and adding decorations such as hundreds and thousands, walnuts and preserved cherries. And even when a baking failure was obvious Mum was kind enough to praise my efforts and pretend to enjoy the results. And although she didn't include me in the preparation of tea — the evening meal not the drink — she sometimes let me make, or help to make, the hot pudding, perhaps an apple crumble, apple Charlotte, or a delicious steamed pudding or golden syrup pudding. And then, when the cooking and baking and steaming were done, when the hot, sweet and delicious-smelling result was removed from the hot stove-top or oven to rest and cool and send its sweet aromas through the house, I quickly and easily then, and always afterwards, understood the deep satisfaction which comes to anyone, anywhere, man or woman, deservedly, after any job well done.

Because she was a mother, naturally kind and gentle, she was happy to indulge me in this way, to put time aside for me on cold wet days during the August school holidays, and to put up with the mess I must have made and left. But she had no such time or patience when it came to preparing tea even though I might have made or helped to make the pudding. That was because Dad came home tired and hungry and intolerant of delay. Unlike Mum he didn't like to see me, his son, a male, doing in the kitchen what he considered to be woman's work.

'But, Dad,' I said once. 'The best cooks in the world are men.'

'They're not men,' he said contemptuously. 'They're French. Doesn't count.'

After his hot meat and vegetables dinner, plainly cooked just as he preferred, Dad enjoyed his pudding and his assumption that it had been cooked by Mum, as part of her wifely duties, was never disabused by her or her clever little assistant cook.

While Mum was tenderly fond of me, her growing boy, as all mothers are of all their sons, it shouldn't be inferred that she was over protective or that I was a mummy's boy. On the contrary she seemed to have an instinct for just exactly how much mothering I needed. Dad had no such instinct. He was not a good, patient or natural teacher and didn't understand the importance of passing on manly skills. Even when he did include me in his routine chores of household maintenance, plumbing or wiring, gardening, or even mechanical repairs and maintenance on his bicycle or lawn mower, willingly enough at first, and with the best of fatherly intentions, he soon became impatient, not understanding why I wasn't born with a natural aptitude for things mechanical, the manual dexterity necessary to handle mechanical- and wood-working tools, and the same intuitive understanding of the physical world which he had apparently always possessed. But even the most intuitive men, skilled and dextrous in their maturity with tools and machines, metal and wood, were not born fully developed in manly skills. Like all men they once needed, as boys, a push in the right direction, by the right man, to kick start their masculine understanding of things physical and mechanical which was parked somewhere in their developing male mind. As the proverb puts it: 'Tell me and I'll forget; show me and I might remember; but involve me and I'll understand.' Dad would never have had nor heard of such a thought.

I doubt Mum would have heard of it either but she acted on it naturally; a woman's intuition perhaps. And so she did her best to get me involved in manly occupations just as she had involved me in her cooking and baking. Knowing I was forbidden to use Dad's tools she made purposeful trips to O'Connell's, the hardware shop, at the beginning of each school holidays to buy me some small-sized but real tools. In this way I gradually accumulated a complete junior tool kit: a hammer, nail punches, a cross cut saw, a fret saw and hack saw, chisels and sharpening stones, hand drills and bits, spanners and pliers and screwdrivers. She collected scraps of wood and empty wooden boxes from somewhere and bought bags of tacks and nails of various types and sizes, and a variety of screws. She also found many pieces of thin plywood and showed me how to draw patterns and shapes with a pencil which I could cut out with my remarkable little fret saw. And so, working on my own, I made things, badly at first, and in the process learned more than ever I could have been taught by an impatient father. I discovered many simple but important principles of physics — involving balance and leverage, gravity and weight — and acquired the mental ability and agility necessary to visualise an object, list the materials required, and plan and follow through on its construction. And I unconsciously developed the ability to weigh and measure and balance things in my mind, to judge a material's strength and aptness. I cut myself sometimes, bruised my fingers and thumb with the hammer often, but slowly, sometimes with advice from a kind neighbour or an uncle or a big boy, I acquired the manual skills necessary to handle my tools and manipulate the raw materials of my work.

Mum bought me a large magnifying glass and showed me that if I sat with a piece of wood, the sun at my back, and moved the glass nearer to and farther from the wood until the sun's rays were focused on a bright point, and if I held it there long enough, I would soon be controlling the vast power of the sun to burn the surface of the wood and raise a tiny puff of smoke. Using paper, wood chips or sawdust I could even start a fire. From there it was a natural step to make patterns on the wood, like poker work, or to print my name, first drawn in pencil, which, with a steady hand, I could burn into a piece of wood, a pencil case or wooden ruler, or onto the flap of my leather schoolbag. Providing the sun was shining, even weakly in the wintry August holidays, that large and strong magnifying glass provided me with hours of fun.

Also during the holidays Mum acquired — somehow from somewhere — a large industrial magnet. It was beautifully and precisely made of steel in the shape of a large and thick U. Each of the two fingers of the U was about twenty-five centimetres long which meant it was particularly heavy and not a toy at all. She also acquired a large paper bag of fine iron filings which provided me with endless amusement and puzzlement about the intricate patterns. 'How does it work?' I asked her but she didn't know. She did know it was exactly the sort of thing to amuse and fascinate a curious ten-year-old boy. I soon tired of playing with the iron filings; they made an infinite variety of patterns but their behaviour was unpredictable and beyond understanding, and they were hard to control and collect and remove and put back in their bag. But I quickly discovered how much fun I could have with nails and screws and anything ferrous. And then how the attraction of the powerful magnet worked even through thick wood which meant I could move something metal on top of a table by moving the magnet about underneath it. That August the attraction of that magnet was powerful and irresistible in more ways than one.

For a young woman bringing up a boy, her first child, Mum was remarkably creative in the appropriate ways she found to keep my hands and mind busy. Once, when I was very young, before I had even started school, she had made me a sort of motor car using an upturned wooden apple box to one end of which, in the inside, she nailed a round tin lid through its centre. Sitting inside the box, using the round tin lid as a steering wheel, and adding my own engine noise, I could drive my four-year-old self, fast or slow, wherever I wished, entertained for hours and days with my very own car made from nothing but a wooden box and an old tin lid.

'Waste not, want not,' Mum used to say and she truly meant it. She had never known a time when something — more particularly money and food — was not in short supply. To throw away anything even remotely useful, or which might turn out to be useful one day, was to mock the experience of a lifetime and raise in her timid heart the spectre of The Slump which continued to haunt her and her generation. And so she carefully flattened, folded and stored every brown paper bag she brought home from the shops, collected used string and rubber bands, burned candles — which were essential when electricity was short and sometimes rationed — until they were no more that a flat pool of white wax, and sharpened and resharpened her pencils until they were no better than short stumps which could no longer be gripped or accurately steered over paper. Nothing was wasted: old clothing too worn-out to be passed on as hand-me-downs or given to charity was carefully unstitched — although all buttons were removed and saved in one of the button jars first — and the least worn parts cut into pieces about ten centimetres square. Women called these square pieces of cloth, sometimes no better than scraps of rag, Peggy squares or dolly squares which were collected and sewn together by some friend or relative who had an aptitude for sewing, and a sewing machine to match, and who made a hobby of such things, into a quilt of either random-coloured squares or in a planned pattern either of which was referred to as a patchwork quilt. Old sheets were 'turned' which meant they were cut in half and turned so that the unworn ends met in the middle and the divided thread-bare middle parts were hemmed to become the ends. Old towels were cut down to make face flannels, and old face flannels became cleaning rags. Nothing was wasted and in these and other ways Mum managed to save money.

Sometimes her collections could be put to good use as cheap toys and amusements. She always saved empty match boxes and Dad showed me how their outsides could be joined together using the inside slides. Junctions could be created as could circles and curves of remarkable strength, and the size and extent of an abstract or meaningful construction were limited only by the number of empty match boxes available. Dad was also skilled at folding empty cigarette packets — both the outers and the inners — into shapes resembling a variety of animals and birds, miniature folding wallets and purses that opened and closed like the real thing, even abstract and geometric shapes, managing to incorporate the small pieces of thin and delicate silver foil used to line the cigarette packets when full. He showed me the results, and I was suitably impressed, but unfortunately he didn't show me the process.

He did show me how to make what he called a tractor using an empty cotton reel, a short piece of candle, a thick rubber band — all drawn from Mum's collections — and two matchsticks, in a simple step-by-step process. First he used his red-handled pen knife, which he always carried, to cut notches around each of the raised outer rims of the wooden cotton reel; these were the equivalent of the heavy tread of a tractor tyre. Then he carefully bored a hole through the middle of the candle stump removing the remnant of the wick in the process; the waxy candle was to act as a lubricant. The rubber band was threaded through the hole in the candle and the hole in the cotton reel and held outside one end of the cotton reel by being looped over the middle of half a matchstick and outside the candle end by being looped over one extreme end of a complete matchstick; the rubber band was to provide the energy. He then held the rubber band in place at the half-matchstick end and turned it, using the whole matchstick as a winder, until it, the candle stump, was held tight against the side of the cotton reel. Eventually the rubber band was wound so tight inside the cotton reel that if released it would have spun the matchstick furiously, out of control, until all the pent up energy was released. But by winding it tight and then placing it on a gentle slope with a surface rough enough to provide some purchase for the 'tyre' — a carpet or rug was ideal — with the end of the long match resting on the down side of the slope, which provided resistance, the rubber band was unable to spin out of control but was forced to unwind slowly and so drive the little tractor up the hill.

Dad showed me a clever trick using a large button, an especially large and heavy example carefully chosen for the purpose from one of Mum's button jars, and a piece of strong thread twice the length my outstretched arms. The thread was put through one of the button's holes and turned back to return through the opposite hole where it was joined to its other end. I then put one or two fingers of each hand through each end of this long loop, opened my arms to almost full stretch and then manoeuvred the button until it was resting in the middle of the sagging cotton. Now, with practice, the button could be persuaded to spin in one direction. When it reached the limit of its spin in that direction I gently pulled the loop apart urging the two lines of cotton to straighten and so cause the button to reverse its spin until it had completely unwound the cotton and continued its spin to wind it tight in the opposite direction. After only a little practice and almost no effort — my arms moving in and out as the cotton loop wound and shortened, unwound and lengthened — the button would be made to spin at an unbelievable speed at which it was reduced to a blur creating a wonderful hum in the process.

Humming reminds me that Dad also showed us how to make a simple musical instrument using one of his thin cigarette papers folded around a plastic comb and held tightly in place by a finger and thumb at each end. Holding the paper of the little instrument against dry lips while humming a tune caused it, the very fine paper, to vibrate in sympathy with the sound and so make an amplified and buzzing noise the same as that made by a kazoo. Such a simple toy kept me and Tessa occupied for hours although surely the noise would have soon become irritating to a grown-up's ears.

For her part Mum showed us how to use an empty cotton reel to do what she called French knitting. First she hammered four short nails partly into one end of a wooden reel spaced evenly around the centre hole. The woollen thread was manipulated around these nails to make stitches that emerged in a continuous row of knitting from the hole on the other side of the cotton reel. She started and ended the knitting for us but I have no idea how she managed to do either. We used wools of different colours and thicknesses — left over from Mum's knitting projects — to create stripes and lend a visual interest. The result was a thin knitted tube of potentially infinite length that could in fact serve no practical purpose other than keeping our hands and minds busy during the rainy, stormy days of the August holidays when we were compelled to remain indoors.

On the first reasonably fine day of the holidays Mum took us to town on the tram. She made many such journeys alone — while we were at school — contrived perhaps as a pleasant and probably therapeutic break from routine, any change being as good as a well-needed rest. No doubt she saved a little housekeeping money and deferred a few simple purchases until she could justify her next little outing, but on this occasion we were going on an important mission for Tessa. And that made Tessa feel important. For me though it was more than just an outing, more even than a special trip for Tessa's sake. Going in the tram, into the hustle and bustle of Karangahape Road, was an adventure.

Getting off and on the tram in Karangahape Road was easier there, and in Queen Street and Symonds Street, than it was at home due to the tram zones built in the middle of those busy streets. The trams ran on steel rails set down in the middle of the main roads, in both directions, which meant that passengers getting on or off the tram had to cross the road to or from the footpath. Mum and Dad said that motorised traffic was required by law to come to a complete stop at tram stops whenever there were passengers crossing the road but there was too much traffic in Karangahape Road to allow for such delays and so tram zones were used instead. These raised constructions, slightly higher than the raised footpath and about as long as two trams, were located in the middle of the street, to the left of the lines of each direction, and were defined at each end by thick and curved concrete bulwarks designed to shield waiting passengers from rogue cars. These solid and bulky bulwarks were painted with silver reflective paint, sometimes striped with orange, and sometimes sporting a round and reflective orange light larger than a dinner plate. The idea was that passengers could wait on the tram zone in safety — alighting passengers could wait there too until it was safe to cross the road — protected from the traffic by the concrete bulwarks while the raised height of the zones made it easier for passengers to get on and off their tram.

'Press the bell now, Johnny Boy,' Mum said when we were near the Pitt Street intersection. Our mission for Tessa lay at the other end of Karangahape Road, towards the Ponsonby Road corner, which was referred to as the reservoir for the large water reservoir there. But Mum was drawn first to that part of Karangahape Road, both sides, which lay between the top of Pitt Street and the top of Queen Street. In this section stood her favourite shops: small department stores — mere babies compared with the Farmers' or the real department stores of Queen Street — where a working-class housewife with only a faded and unfashionable wardrobe, and a meagre purse, could feel comfortable. The multi-storied George Courts and Rendells were her favourites together with the sprawling Maple Furnishing farther up the road on the corner of Symonds Street, opposite Grafton Bridge and the Jewish cemetery. But she looked much and spent little at her favourites, spending more, but only a little more, and even then only on the essentials which were cheaply available at Woolworths — which she and everyone called Woolies — McKenzies and Melverns. I liked them all but Woolies was my favourite. From the street I liked the curved corner windows, at the two entrances, which distorted my reflection, making me especially tall and angular, although it puzzled me how and why grown-ups didn't notice or didn't care how odd I and they looked in these windows. Inside I liked the way the long, narrow store was so brightly lighted with strips of modern fluorescent tubes. Prices were clearly marked and cash registers were placed at regular intervals so the service at Woolworths seemed always to be prompt and efficient if not particularly friendly. I liked walking slowly down the narrow aisles, checking the counters to the left and right, and the way the goods were displayed on these counters which were low enough at the front for me to see into, and which sloped up to the back, to better present the goods, where, at a higher level, a serving person, usually a young woman in a plain black dress and a white blouse, perhaps with a lace-trimmed collar, served customers by leaning forward across the wide and sloping display counter to complete the transaction. From her elevated position, in a central aisle between two such counters, she could easily see what was happening up and down the aisles where her services might be required. Customers indicated their needs by holding out their purchases in front of themselves, over the counter, and if they thought they had been missed, or considered the service to be too slow, they drew attention to themselves by hitting the top of one of the counter bells which were installed at regular intervals. Impatient customers indicated their irritation by hitting the bell-tops hard and repeatedly to create a blur of jingling. Indeed, the sound of these counter bells combined with the ringing of the cash registers meant that Woolworths and McKenzies stores were full of the sound of bells which must have been music to the ears of their owners.

I was fascinated by how, on these sloping counters, the small items on display — such stores stocked all the miscellaneous necessities of life like pins and needles, hair clips and hair curlers, brushes and combs, buttons and bows, knives and scissors, and many other things now forgotten or obsolete — were separated from each other, each in its own square or rectangular space, by a system of glass dividers with bevelled and polished edges. These dividers, apparently available in an infinite variety of heights and lengths, were held together, in the required arrangement, by metal clips cleverly designed to be pressed down to grip and hold the glass dividers vertically and in place wherever and however they should meet or intersect. It was a technical and engineering marvel, allowing for versatility with precision, that appealed to my tidy mind.

I didn't mind Mum's dawdling through Woollies and the other shops but Tessa was getting impatient so before long we set off briskly — a little too briskly for Tessa's little legs — on the long walk to the reservoir.

'How far is it?' said poor little Tessa who was almost running to keep up with me and Mum.

'Not far now, Tess.'

'Where's Susan?'

'She's here in my bag, dear,' said Mum, patting the paper parcel in her string kit. 'Don't worry.'

Susan was Tessa's walkie-talkie doll. She had got it for Christmas but one of the arms had come away from its socket and so we were heading for the dolls' hospital. I was intrigued by the idea of a hospital for dolls, foolishly imagining rows of small cots, each holding its own sick doll, all being supervised by kind and caring nurses in white uniforms. But when we got there I was profoundly disappointed to find that the dolls' hospital wasn't a hospital at all but just a very big toy shop and that selling dolls, and mending broken ones, was only a small part of a large and heartless business.

I didn't care for dolls but I knew that girls did, and that Tessa cared deeply for her Susan, and I was horrified to discover that the man in the shop lacked any awareness of the way little girls felt about their dolls and was no more caring or sentimental about Tessa's broken Susan than he would be about my broken tricycle or Dad's broken lawn mower. As the shop man stood there, behind the counter, wearing not a white hospital gown but a greasy grey dust coat, inspecting Tessa's doll, turning it blithely this way and that, discussing the problem with Mum while a sad and solemn Tessa looked up and listened, a worried look on her frowning little face, I looked behind the counter. There I could see shelves loaded with dusty brown open-topped cardboard boxes of doll parts. There were hundreds of arms and legs, complete with tiny hands and feet, fingers and toes, all tossed in higgledy-piggledy; there were even heads of all shapes, sizes and styles, some bald, some with shiny, curly hair, many with only almond-shaped empty holes with sharp edges where there should have been eyes. And, worst of all, there were boxes and boxes of eyes, mostly bright blue with black pupils, many with curled eyelashes and, at the back, the dull metal levers and counterweights and other mechanical arrangements necessary to ensure that a doll's eyes would shut as they should when her little owner-cum-mother laid her down in a toy cot. It was, I thought, a shocking and ghoulish sight that Tessa, or any small girl, should not have to see.

'I wish I didn't have to leave Susan there,' said Tessa when we left. 'I didn't like that man.'

'Neither did I,' I said.

'He'll fix Susan's arm, Tess,' said Mum. 'That's the main thing isn't it?'

'S'pose so,' said Tessa.

The fifteenth of August, the notorious feast of the Assumption, came in the middle of the holidays. Because it was Our Lady's own holy day of obligation, and that it fell on a Sunday which meant we didn't have to go to mass twice, Mum persuaded Dad and me to join her and Tessa in saying the rosary at the end of the day.

'It's the least you can do for Our Lady on her special day,' she said. 'And, Johnny Boy,' she added. 'I bought you some new rosary beads specially for the occasion.'

Dad succumbed to her special request and so did I; I didn't have much choice. And so, for the first time in weeks, I knelt down at Mum's little shrine to Our Lady and said the rosary, with my new rosary beads, with as much spirituality as I could muster praying as hard as I could that Mum would take me and Tessa to the pictures in town one day before the holidays were over.

She did, so the rosary must have worked. She let me and Tessa choose our picture from the advertisements on the back page of the *Star* and we happily settled on the Regent partly because of the main picture that was showing, *Money From Home* starring Dean Martin and Jerry Lewis. But in truth she guided us in our choice, and we knew. She pretended to be influenced by the quality of the picture and the advertised shorts, which is what we called the supporting films that played in the first half of the programme, before the interval and the main feature. *The Regent's outstanding first half includes Latest News, Sportlight "Rough Ridin' Youngsters", and a Herman and Catnip cartoon "Drinks on the Mouse",* said the advertisement in the *Star*.

But we knew there was another reason to choose the Regent — I personally much preferred the Civic — and that was Aunty Irene.

Aunty Irene worked at the Regent, serving at the Nibble Nook, the ice cream and snack bar. She was Mum's youngest sister — I suppose she must then have been twenty-three or so — and she looked awfully glamorous and important in her stiff white uniform with a matching white cap, like a nurse's cap, serving the customers and giving change.

The Regent was an ornately designed theatre on the east side of Queen Street just a few doors down from Wellesley Street and hence almost diagonally opposite the Civic. It had a deceptively narrow frontage and a long narrow foyer leading to the box office. Still photographs were displayed in glass cabinets on the foyer walls and I liked to stare at them — at least those which weren't too high — to whet my appetite for the delicious treat that was in store inside the dark theatre. I liked the Regent for its cool, shiny, brown marble floors, and the elaborately designed plasterwork of the walls, and the way there was a palm court restaurant on the mezzanine floor — with thick carpets, large exotic plants, and huge concrete-based lead-light table lamps any one of which was bigger at its base than the whole of our breakfast table at home — from which I could look down on the people in the foyer.

Mum bought our tickets and then we went to see Aunty Irene at the Nibble Nook. When she had time to speak to us she seemed to know all about Dean Martin and Jerry Lewis, and the picture, how funny it was and what the customers were saying. It was, I thought, like having inside knowledge, and the fact that I had an aunty who worked at the Regent and knew all about the pictures was the next best thing to knowing a real film star, someone from Hollywood. And so I was always proud when Aunty Irene stopped what she doing to chat with us.

We saw Aunty Irene again at half time but she was so busy there was no time to chat. Tessa and I stood back while Mum went up to the counter to buy us all an ice cream. She was served by another lady but Aunty Irene saw her, looked about for us, saw us standing shyly in the background and so gave us a big smile and a wave. Some of the kids waiting to be served turned around to see who she was waving at. That made me proud all over again.

The picture was good — Jerry Lewis was really funny — but it was about horse racing and gambling and I could sense, even in the dark, that Mum didn't like it very much. She didn't say anything to me then or later but I could tell she was tense when we came out. She made us sit on a big leather couch.

'Do up your coats,' she said, 'while I go and say ta-ta to Aunty Irene. It's cold outside. And it's been raining.'

We buttoned up our coats as we were told. She soon came back, took us by the hand, and said we had to hurry.

'But what about Aunty Irene?'

'She's awfully busy, Johnny Boy.'

'Can't we say good-bye to her?'

'No. Not now. We've got to get home.'

Mum had us by the hand and was dragging us out of the theatre foyer.

'But why do we have to hurry?'

'I didn't know the picture would be so long,' she said. 'Come on. Dad'll be home soon and he'll want his tea.'

So the picture about race horses wasn't the only reason for her anxiety.

It *was* cold outside, on Queen Street, and getting dark. The Maori *Star* boy was calling out 'Star-oh' and the traffic seemed to be especially slow and noisy. The shops were all lit up and their lights — and the lights of all the cars, vans, trucks and trams — were reflected shimmeringly in the shiny black wet road. The trams had on their inside lights too so they looked like small ships gliding smoothly over a black sea. It was all so unfamiliar — being in town when it was almost night — and I liked it. I wanted to walk slowly, listen to the sounds of Queen Street, the grinding of all the trams in a line taking home all the workers, and the beeps and barps of all the cars; to watch everything — I especially liked the way all the lights were reflected in the wet road — and everyone, men and ladies, hurrying, hunched over against the cold and gripping the collars of their coats tight to their necks; to absorb and enjoy the hustle and bustle atmosphere. But Mum was anxious, walking fast, dragging us along behind, and we had to almost run to keep up. The footpath was crowded with people going home from work and the shops and it was hard for her and us to weave our way between them.

'Why do we have to hurry so much?' I called out.

'Look,' she said but I didn't know what to look at. 'Look at all the trams.'

Queen Street was jammed with trams, nose to tail in both

directions, as far as I could see.

'It'll be a slow trip home and Dad'll want his tea,' she said again. 'He'll be worried if we're not there when he gets home. And I think it's going to rain again.'

The tram home *was* crowded. And slow. A man on a sideways seat stood up for Mum. She thanked him nicely and drew us close and held us and tried to help us keep steady. I noticed that she kept looking anxiously at her little watch. It was drizzling by the time we got to Winstone Street and so we ran together all the way home. Mum was awfully relieved to get there before Dad. Tessa and I had to hang our coats in the wash house and put on our slippers. By the time we came back to the breakfast room Mum had lit the fire and was in the kitchen getting tea ready.

'Wasn't that fun,' she said.

Going to the pictures — often or rarely — required time and money that weren't always available and it was books that provided us with the most portable and inexpensive form of entertainment especially during the holidays. The public library, while free, wasn't the only source of reading material; there was Taylor's. This local shop — another family-owned business — served as a newsagent, bookshop, stationery shop and toyshop and was one of my favourites. Many people, perhaps most, took a regular magazine or two, weekly or monthly, including many newspapers and magazines sent by ship on a six-week journey from England. Their orders were held in a labelled pigeon hole at the back of the shop. Mum always took *The New Zealand Woman's Weekly* and arranged for me to get the monthly *Junior Digest* which was a small-format and somewhat earnest magazine published in New Zealand for New Zealand kids, especially boys, which concentrated on science and nature subjects. Sometimes I was allowed to buy one of the Disney comics, and I also liked the Classic comics which specialised in condensing literary classics and rendering them into colourful comic books. Mum imposed limits on my comic and magazine purchases but they were based not on matters of quality and taste but on her ability to pay. She knew I was a reader and so she took great pains to keep me supplied with anything readable including cheap comics especially when she discovered that reading them had no effect on my ability or desire to read proper and free books from the library.

Stationery was important too especially as Taylor's was the local supplier of school exercise books, note books, basic text books — like spelling books, dictionaries and atlases — as well as pencils, pencil sharpeners, rubbers and rulers that were the basic tools of a primary school pupil. And as the Taylors were Catholics they always had plenty of missals and prayer books. But there was much else on offer at Taylor's. It was the place to go for paper and string, rubber bands, Christmas decorations, knitting books and wool, scissors and pocket knives; a sort of general store where kids and grown-ups could find what they couldn't find anywhere else.

Although there was no better place for toys than the big toy department at Farmers' Taylor's did stock a miscellany of small toy items to keep children occupied and amused including jig-saw puzzles, marbles, assorted stamps, scrap books and the coloured and decorated 'scraps' that girls loved to collect. These scraps were old fashioned even then, printed on a thin shiny paper and depicting, in loud colours, boys and girls, men and women, in clothes and hats that were as distinctly Victorian as their hair, facial expressions, makeup and clothes. They were cut out, embossed, sprinkled with silver glitter, and girls collected them and pasted them in blank scrap books with an enthusiasm and for reasons which I never understood.

But I understood all about colouring books which Taylor's stocked in every size, thickness and theme together with the essential pencils, crayons and paint boxes. I enjoyed colouring in and was fussy about the books selected and the subjects they contained. The best colouring books were made of a thick, coarse, creamy paper, which must have been cheap but was by far the best surface for a fussy colourer, with rather simple drawings made with thick lines defining large flat planes which allowed room for the maximum artistic expression. Pastels were my favourite medium — they had the strongest colours, the widest palette, they could be blended together on the page for the most subtle effects, and they had the best coverage by far — but they were rarely available at Taylor's probably because they were expensive and so could be afforded only by real artists. Crayons, though, were cheap and almost as good although I despised coloured pencils, usually the Lakeland brand, for their lack of coverage and intensity of colour, the tendency for the leads to break, and the need to keep them constantly sharp. They came in beautifully printed flat tins of various sizes, containing a greater or lesser rainbow of colours, and were frequently given by well-meaning grown-ups probably because the tin packaging was so attractive. But it was a mystery to me how grown-ups were so easily fooled by the packaging, couldn't see the shortcoming of pencils, and didn't know that if they must give a set of coloured pencils then a pencil sharpener was an essential accessory to be provided at the same time.

Colouring books and crayons together provided a simple and inexpensive way to keep me quiet and amused for hours and it was a clever and knowing aunt, grandparent or family friend who kept a goodly supply of colouring books and crayons to be brought out for the visiting me. I was always grateful to such knowing grown-ups and would happily lie on the floor on my tummy, concentrating on a picture with great colouring potential — like a circus clown, a London bus with advertising slogans on the side, a fantastic jungle bird, a field of bland-looking cows whose breed would be determined by my choice of colours — choosing my colours with thought and filling the spaces with precise care, while Mum above chatted away to her hostess as they shared milky tea, buttered scones, gems or pikelets.

Many grown-ups believed, mistakenly, that I would enjoy using a paint box. Paint boxes were popular gifts but were always a disappointment. They were made in a variety of sizes — some tiny with only a few colours, some huge with perhaps a hundred colours or more arranged in shades of the primary colours — with lids printed to suggest the art of the great masters. The lids were pressed and moulded in such a way that, when open, they provided a series of shallows in which the young painter could mix his colours like a professional with a palette. The paints themselves were arranged in rows of hard little rectangular pellets — perhaps two by one centimetres and only a millimetre or two thick — recessed into a white tin tray that was itself set into the base of the shallow tin; below each small brick of hard paint was printed the name of the colour. A brush was supplied — it lay in its own recess — although it was usually poorly made, cheap, and incapable of accurate use. Two tumblers of water were required — one to wet the brush which was used to soften the bricks of paint and one to clean the brush of one colour before using it on the next — and a rag to dry the brush before applying it to a different colour. As usual though children were let down by grown-ups who didn't realise the shortcomings of the cheap water colour paint box. Water colours were useless for colouring in as the soft and grainy paper of the colouring books absorbed the watery colour causing the paper to wrinkle, the colours to run uncontrollably over the lines, and to blend in with the neighbouring colours. And the watery mess soaked through to the drawing on the other side of the page rendering it useless forever. Unlike pages coloured with pastels, crayons and pencils, which, once finished, could be left — conquered and forgotten — while I turned to the next page, or leafed through the book looking for a suitably challenging picture, a page coloured with water colours had to be left open and set aside to dry meaning no other page could be attempted for hours. Why, I wondered, did grown-ups not understand these simple things?

There was another sort of colouring book in which only plain water had to be applied to the pages, sections of which would immediately assume an appropriate if watery colour. Grass, for example, would turn green, the sea blue, buildings red, flowers yellow, and so on. It must have been a clever process but it demanded no skill or imagination from the user and, anyway, the colours were particularly insipid. I thought such colouring in books were a silly waste of money and time.

But even with the best tools, and the best colouring books with the most interesting pictures, I could spend only so much time colouring in before getting bored. The shopping trip to Karangahape Road, and the trip to the Regent to see Dean Martin, Jerry Lewis and Aunty Irene, together took up just two days of the two weeks holidays and most of the other days were spent inside, especially if it were raining as it did so often in August. So Mum and we were all glad when the rain stopped and Tessa and I could play outside. We weren't alone in our inside boredom and whenever it wasn't raining Winstone Street was crowded with neighbourhood kids looking for someone to play with. There was always plenty to do and if there were not then there was always plenty to watch.

Boys have always enjoyed watching men at work, especially if machines are involved, even or especially if the work is particularly routine, dirty and mundane. I loved watching the rubbish men on school holiday Thursdays and happily followed them up and down our street, Milton Street, Studio Street and adjacent streets, fascinated by what they did and how they did it.

Even the most dirty and mundane work requires its own set of unique and acquired skills and the rubbish men of the Auckland City Council were clearly proud of their particular skills and strength and the speed with which they made their progress. There was no concept of conservation or recycling. All packages bought had to be one day thrown away. All meal preparation created scraps and peelings and cores, and all meals finished left fat, skin, bones and shells. Some wise gardeners, keener and more accomplished and probably more enterprising than Dad, with more time, managed a proper compost heap at the bottom of their garden, but at forty-three, and most other houses I knew, all household rubbish, including food scraps and leftovers — whether animal, vegetable or mineral — were wrapped in a newspaper parcel after each meal and dropped, or, towards the end of the week, squashed, into the rubbish bin. Empty tins and unwanted bottles and jars, and anything else not wanted, for which space could be found, were also consigned to this bin.

There were three exceptions to this rubbish rule and each concerned glass. First, the large, long-necked beer bottles, standard at that time, were stacked on their sides under the house, or somewhere convenient — and out of sight for Mum's sake — until the day when the boy scouts arranged a neighbourhood fund-raising bottle drive. An entire summer Saturday — from early morning until well after dark — was spent by the volunteers, boys providing the labour to pack the bottles into the brewer's wooden crates and carry them to the street where a team of men, methodically cruising the streets with trailers hooked to their cars, loaded the now full crates into their trailers and carried them back to the scout den for sorting before returning them to the brewery for a cash benefit. The second exception was any empty soft drink bottle of the Innes company for which a tuppnee (tuppence or two pennies) deposit had been paid on purchase which could be redeemed, one at a time or in bulk, at any dairy. Mum allowed us to return empty soft drink bottles one or two at a time to the dairy and spend the small reward on a treat but some families saved the soft drink bottles for the inevitable annual bottle drive. And thirdly, any good and sizeable glass jars and bottles, perhaps but not necessarily with a screw top, were saved by Mum in a separate box, to ensure they didn't go out with the bottle drive, to be filled, during the year, with the seasonal fruit preserves, jams, jellies, pickles, relishes, chutneys and sauces which she and her sisters concocted from thrift and necessity before the advent of frozen food and the home freezer.

But the recycling of glass was the exception to the household rubbish rule. Everything else, mostly the paper parcels of moist and rotting food, including so much cooked and uncooked meat trimmings, fish bones and vegetable scraps, all confined for up to seven days in a bent and dented tin bin whose lid rarely fitted, soon became both smelly and fly blown, especially in the summer. Going to the rubbish bin, with yet another parcel of rubbish, was usually my after-tea job and as a result I was accustomed to both the rotting stench and the sight of masses of wriggling smooth and creamy maggots. By the time the rubbish was due for collection the bin was heavy and overflowing with a week's worth of newspaper-wrapped parcels. The bin had side handles and it was Dad's job to carry the heavy thing to the street — an especially unpleasant task when the overflowing top, with lid askew, was at face level when carried — where he left it on the grass verge for collection.

The rubbish truck was like a smelly, mobile rubbish dump escorted by squadrons of flies, amongst which the rubbish men worked five days a week, and squabbling seagulls. It was a conventional looking truck with moderately high sides the only concession to its purpose being a series of large curved lids, three each side, which could be rocked from one side to the other to leave open only one third of each side of the truck's tray at a time in which two men worked, one on each side. Below the open or closed doors was one common rectangular container in which all the rubbish, newly released from the loosely-wrapped newspaper parcels, formed one common sea of putridity. The men worked together with one or two on the top of the always-moving truck, literally standing ankle- or knee-deep in this stinking, slippery mess, while their colleagues ran ahead and behind the truck, tossing the lids aside and lifting the bins by one handle, one bin per hand, and throwing them, one at a time, in a graceful and well-judged arc, in such a way that the man standing on their side of the truck could catch it and turn it upside down in one action. Frequently the contents remained stubbornly inside — having been squashed in to fit — which meant the man standing in the rubbish had to use both hands and arms to beat and bash the bin against the truck's steel sides until it surrendered its compressed and rotten contents. Then, with the same elegance with which the bin was sent up to him was it sent down again to his colleague who returned the favour with yet another full bin while returning the empty bin to its place roughly outside its owner's gate, or at least within a few minutes walk of that gate, where its lid had lain since the beginning of the process.

I admired the rubbish men recognising easily that they weren't necessarily especially strong — although they must have been stronger and fitter than most — but highly skilled in what they did, working quickly as a team, knowing that, unlike men who worked an eight-hour day in a factory or office, they had a finite amount of work to do each day and when it was done they could go home. But the price of their speed and efficiency was the damage they inflicted on the rubbish bins which they handled so adroitly on the way up and down but so roughly at the top and bottom of each transfer.

'Go and find the bin for Dad,' said Mum every Thursday afternoon.

And so I went through the weekly ritual of walking up and down the street, identifying and retrieving our particular bin, and matching it with its lid found somewhere else, and returning it — complete with a lingering stink and a mass of wriggling maggots — to its place at the back of the house. There I laid the lid on the ground and sprayed the inside of the dented bin with deadly DDT from a manual spray pump kept in the wash house. Then I splashed it liberally with a strong disinfectant before doing my best to close the lid on it and the whole horrible procedure for another week.

The Walker's ice man was another regular visitor whom I liked to watch at work. I was fascinated by his gaily painted yellow and blue truck and especially by the way the big slab-like letters of the name *Walker's* were painted as though they were made of ice topped with soft white snow like that which I had seen on Christmas cards; snow that was overflowing its place on the top of the icy-looking name and falling softly and randomly down the front of the letters to suggest the cold. I admired the artist who could so cleverly suggest the hardness of ice, the softness of snow and the sensation of cold, with no more than a paint brush and some blue and white paint.

But the era of the ice box was almost over. Most houses in Winstone Street had managed to buy a refrigerator but there were still a few regular ice customers including the Hibberts.

'Today's the last day,' said Sally Hibbert, a boy in our street whose real name was Selwyn.

'What do you mean?'

'Getting a fridge next week,' he said. 'No more ice after this one.'

I was standing with Sally on the grass verge. Together we watched the driver open his truck's back freezer door, which had a mechanical handle the same as that on the butcher's cooler, from which clouds of vapour rolled out from the mysterious and icy inside, and down to the road where they mysteriously disappeared. Using a pair of giant tongs, shaped like opposing question marks, he pulled a huge, clear and blue-looking block of ice which he slung it over his oil-skin caped shoulder and carried it into Mrs Hibbert's kitchen.

Sally and I ran ahead, into the kitchen, where we watched the ice man put the block of shiny ice into the small ice box for the last time. There it would sit and gradually melt away over the next week or so until there was nothing in the compartment but a tray of stale water by which time it was to be replaced by a new refrigerator.

We didn't have an ice box or a refrigerator but like all houses of the time we had a special cupboard in the kitchen called a safe. The safe was about a metre high, wide and deep. Its door was flush with the inside wall of the kitchen while its body extended outside, on the south-facing wall where it received no sun, and was protected on top by a sloping tin roof. Large fretted openings in the sides, and wide slots in the floor, were covered inside with a fine steel gauze to encourage the movement of cooling air while keeping out flies and other pests (although cockroaches were unknown in those days). By this simple means food was kept cool and safe except in the very hottest weather.

But at the end of August Grandad Little bought us a refrigerator from Farmers'. I didn't see it being delivered, I didn't even know it was going to be delivered, it was just there when Tessa and I got home from school. It was standing, shiny and white, tall and rounded, its motor humming quietly, in the deep niche in the corner of the breakfast room. The old wooden console radio which it had displaced was standing in the middle of the room, drab and dusty and old-fashioned looking, where it had been moved and left by the Farmers' delivery men. Mum was sitting at the table, her chin resting in an upturned palm, staring at the new fridge in amazement and disbelief.

She look at us when we came in.

'Just look at what Grandad Little bought for us,' she said, indicating with her eyes to the big, white fridge.

It was the latest model *Leonard,* designed in a sort of rounded *art déco* style, with a chromed clip-lock door handle, like those on the ice man's truck and the butcher's cool room, but more streamlined. It looked huge although it had a less roomy interior than its bulk and size suggested because its walls and doors were so thick, thick for insulation, and because the lower third or more of its height was taken up by its motor. The inside storage was therefore quite limited. But it was a real refrigerator, constantly cold, and utterly sealed against flies, so making the kitchen safe redundant. It had to be installed in the breakfast room, in the corner where the big radio used to stand, because no provision for a refrigerator had been made in the kitchen of houses like ours.

Suddenly little blocks of ice were always available — providing the ice tray was refilled after use — and Tessa and I experimented with making flavoured ice blocks using lemonade and cordials and milky cocoa with saved TT2 sticks. And drinks, whether water, milk or soft drinks, or Dad's beer, were more refreshing when they were cold. And although the freezer compartment was tiny, just enough to accommodate the two ice trays and a little more, it meant that ice cream, packed in a pint brick, could be bought in advance and had for pudding, every day if we wanted. That was, I thought, an unbelievable luxury.

The new fridge should have been welcomed by Mum but she was less than entirely enthusiastic and once again somewhat resentful of Grandad Little's generosity. And she said that the regular defrosting of its freezer elements — a tedious rather than physically demanding task — just added something else to her long list of household chores. Its arrival also meant that there was now no place in the breakfast room for the big radio which was replaced, also by Grandad Little at the same time, by a little mantel model which stood high on a shelf in the kitchen. It was made of cream-coloured plastic and had only a small speaker with a distinctly tinny sound. No longer could Tessa and I lie on the carpet listening to the Sunday morning request session. Now we had to stand on a chair just to turn on the new little radio, and then sit below, on the cold lino floor of the kitchen, to listen to its distinctly inferior tone.

But it was worth it. Because we had a new fridge.

September

'DON'T STARE,' SAID MUM. SHE ALWAYS SAID THAT. BUT kids do stare, openly, without embarrassment, at anyone different; anyone who, for any reason, interests, fascinates, frightens or horrifies them.

Mr Elliott, who lived directly across the street from us, had only one leg and although I saw him almost every day I never got bored with staring at him and did so at every opportunity. I thought Mr Elliott was old then although he went to work every day and so probably wasn't really. He was a tall, thin man with a narrow, bony face and a yellow complexion. He wore a dark, pinstriped, double-breasted suit to work every day, and a dark hat with a little brightly-coloured feather in the band, and although he saw me once or twice every week-day, as he went to or from the tram stop, he never looked in my direction nor acknowledged me in any way.

The big boys said that Mr Elliott's leg was blown off when he stood on a bomb in the first world war. I didn't know whether or not to believe that, and although I knew about the recently-ended second world war I didn't know anything about the first world war except that it was a long time ago and that Grandad Little had been in it.

I liked it about Mr Elliott that every morning he — or someone in his family — carefully folded up the long but empty right leg of his trousers in deep, flat folds, and pinned it to the upper part of the trousers, below his waistcoat, using a large safety pin like men wear in kilts. I was fascinated by this arrangement and by the way this tall, thin and mysterious man, dressed in such an elegant but one-legged suit, swung rhythmically and rapidly along the road between his long, yellow-coloured wooden crutches, padded at the top, hitched under his arms.

One morning at the beginning of September I hid behind a hedge, peeking through a small gap, to watch him go swinging past and so see, up close, just how he managed to go so fast with just one leg and crutches. First he leaned forward on his single leg while, at the same time, he threw the end of his crutches outwards, like wings, and then far forward. By the time the black rubber ferrules of the crutches hit the ground he was leaning a long way forward. At that point, as the top end of his crutches began to arc upwards with his momentum, he allowed them to carry his full weight up and forward in a long swing until his long body was carried through the top of the arc. As it was then being swung forward and down the other side of the arc he swung on the pivot of his underarms, stretched out his single leg and aimed it at a distant point where, when it landed, he began the entire swinging process again. I was astonished by how much ground Mr Elliott could cover with each step, apparently with little effort, and by the elegant smoothness of his swinging and forward momentum.

I also learned that there were some things Mr Elliott couldn't do. Late that same afternoon, about the time I knew he would be coming home from work, I went to the tram stop and pretended to be waiting for someone; kids often waited at the tram stop for their fathers to come home. Right on time the tram arrived and I saw something strange which I didn't understand but would never forget. I saw the tram stop and I saw the one-legged Mr Elliott waiting at the top of the front steps. Then, as I watched, the conductor got off the tram at the back and came forward to wait on the street at the front door. At the same time the motorman left his cabin and stood beside Mr Elliott at the top of the steps, and waited while he set his crutches in place on the single step below, bending deeply to reach. And then, with the motorman's help from above and the conductor's help from the street below, Mr Elliott lowered himself onto the crutches until they were supporting his full weight under the arms and, gripping the handles tightly, leaned forward over the crutches and unfolded himself until his leg was on the lower step where it could take his full weight. It was a process that he, the motorman and the conductor had to repeat together again until he was on the street.

By then the motorman too was on the street, and he and the conductor waited, watching out for traffic — which had to stop to let passengers cross the street to get on or off the tram — while Mr Elliott adjusted his suit and arranged his crutches under his arm. Then he nodded silently to the motorman on his right and the conductor on his left, leaned into his crutches, and began the journey home in his unique, swinging and rhythmic style, looking neither right nor left but straight ahead with a grim look of concentration and determination. And whether Mr Elliott noticed it or not — and I don't know that he did — the motorman and the conductor remained on the street, at the foot of the tram steps, standing stiffly to attention, their flat right hands up to their caps in a full and respectful salute, until they could see that

Mr Elliott had safely reached the footpath.

Why did they do it? It was a mystery to me. I wanted to ask Mum but I couldn't without revealing that I had been hiding and watching — staring at — Mr Elliot. So I asked Dad one day when he was in the garage fixing his bike. Dad didn't care whom I stared at, when or why.

'But why did they salute him?' I asked.

'He was a hero in the war,' said Dad. 'The Great War.'

'The Great War? Why's it called that?'

'The war to end all wars they said,' he said.

'Is that why he's only got one leg? It got blown off by a bomb in the war'?

'Sort of, boy. Lost it at Gallipoli.'

'Where's that?'

Dad smiled which was nice. Usually he didn't like all my questions. 'The boy's too curious' I heard him say once to mum. His old black bike, which he rode to work every day, was upside down, resting on its saddle and handlebars. Now he was oiling the hubs and he spun the wheels with his hand. I watched the leather hoops, which he put around the hubs to keep them clean, go wobbling around. When he was satisfied with his work he stood up, wiping his hands on an oily rag.

'Turkey,' he said.

'Turkey?'

'Yes, Turkey,' he said again. 'Not the bird, boy, but the country.'

'Where the Half Man was born,' I said.

'What?'

Dad had forgotten the Half Man already.

'Doesn't matter,' I said. But I would never forget the Half Man.

'He might have lost his leg,' said Dad, 'but he came back with a special medal.'

'Did he?' I was impressed by that.

'Oh, yeah. A real hero he was.'

'Did you get a special medal from *your* war?'

Dad laughed and tousled my hair with a greasy hand. I knew, and he knew I knew, that he never — not ever — talked about the war.

'Come back with malaria, boy,' he said. 'Just malaria.'

Mr Lee was another old neighbour I longed to stare at. Another veteran of the first world war Mr Lee was different from Mr Elliott in almost every way. Mr Lee was tall too but he was well muscled and heavily build and unlike the unfriendly Mr Elliott — who was not exactly rude but reserved and private, perhaps with good reason — Mr Lee was jolly and friendly to everyone including me. He was a bit deaf and so wore a large pink hearing aid in one ear with a microphone pinned to his breast, and like most deaf people tended to speak louder than necessary. He had a complete pair of good legs, and so walked everywhere, usually with his two fat black Labradors, with an athletic briskness as if to celebrate having limbs to walk with. But Mr Lee had lost the lower part of one arm in the war and it was this disability which fascinated me.

Like Mr Elliott's empty trouser leg, the empty sleeve of Mr Lee's suit jacket — he always wore a dark pin-striped suit in the street but sometimes without a collar on his shirt, or a tie — was folded up and pinned in place at the top. He strode down the road with his overweight dogs running ahead, or falling behind for a sniff at this post or that hedge, or to leave their own scent in the doggy manner. He carried a short bamboo stick under the stump of his missing arm which he withdrew with his good hand to tap or prod his dogs if they stayed too long at one sniffing post. And as he made his progress he responded to every nod, wave and greeting with a jolly and loud 'cheerio' and a toothy smile and, if the person were known to him, would interrupt his walk for a short chat; he was always jolly with his friends, frequently throwing back his head for a loud laugh.

Whenever I passed Mr Lee in the street I wanted to stare at his stumpy arm. But whether I was with Mum or on my own I would hear her command. 'Johnny, don't stare,' she would say, aloud or in my head, and her moral authority easily overcame my desire to stare and I reluctantly turned away from the fascinating and somewhat famous Mr Lee. But if I were alone I said: 'Hullo, Mr Lee,' and he always chuckled and said 'Hullo there, laddie,' in reply.

I thought, almost knew for certain, that Mum's insistence that I should not stare at Mr Lee arose less from a desire to protect an old and disabled man from the rude and open stares of a child but from a dislike of the man himself, a dislike bordering on contempt. I didn't know why Mum and Dad, and all my family, and many other people at church, should feel that way towards such an apparently nice and jolly old man but my questions on the subject were brushed aside.

'He's a communist and a traitor and he hates Catholics,' said Mum.

I knew that there were wars against communists and that communists hated Catholics and that Fat Pat prayed for the conversion of Russia at every mass but it didn't make sense to me that Mr Lee was a 'red', one of *them*. He seemed so kind and friendly. I also knew, from listening to grown-up conversations, that Mr Lee used to be in parliament but that he was thrown out and that he was now an enemy of the party which in my family was almost as bad as being an enemy of the church. But Mr Lee's notoriety simply increased my interest in him and made me want to stare at him even more.

I liked it that Michael Sturgess didn't mind my staring at his polio leg. Sometimes I think he positively enjoyed the attention. His left leg was thin and withered, purple, limp and lifeless. He wore a steel calliper — a junior version of that worn by Miss Staines the elocution teacher — without which he would have been unable to get about at all.

That leg calliper alone was worth close inspection. It was made of vertical steel rods and bars, hinged at the knee, which supported the left side of his body and within which his withered leg was held by an elaborate arrangement of adjustable leather straps and buckles and which, at the foot, was fitted into the heel of an especially adapted shoe. I don't know when Michael got polio but I couldn't remember a time when he didn't wear a calliper. But my interest went beyond Michael's disability and his clumsy mechanical calliper. He was my age, not especially tall, but he had dignity and poise, even standing in his calliper, that would have been exceptional in any boy. His hair was dark and his face was square with perfect features — everything in ideal proportion — but, more importantly, he projected a sense of calm, composure, self-confidence and humour. His blue eyes looked directly and frankly into another's — whether a grown-up or a kid — and he was always smiling. He liked everyone and everyone liked him and he especially liked small children and animals upon whom he seemed to have a calming effect. One day, much to my astonishment, he showed me how he caught bees and held them, two or three at a time, buzzing, in his closed hand. Then he opened his hand and showed me the orange and black and hairy things crawling over his hand and arm. He was a constant player with the Winstone Street kids of all ages but I never knew him to say or do anything unkind to any person or thing.

Michael's parents were not Catholics but they sent him to Saint Michael's, and he was accepted, which could not then be taken for granted, because of his polio and because it was closer than the public school. But as far as I could see that was the only concession his family and he made to his disability. No doubt he had many problems to overcome, at home and elsewhere, but he never complained. He joined all our games and never asked for any allowance or consideration. He had a scooter and a tricycle and, later, a bicycle of his own, and he managed all of them with only a little difficulty. He could even run quite fast by throwing his braced leg forward and rolling his whole body over it and then pushing off again with his good leg.

But what I appreciated most about Michael Sturgess was that he let me and other kids stare at his leg as much as we liked. He let us play with his calliper and would even take it off and let us wear it, adjust it, and walk about with it while he was left helpless on the ground. He let us touch his withered leg, squeeze it and pinch it and watch the pinched bit go white, and happily talked about his handicap without any embarrassment, and about the Crippled Children's Society, where he went every week or so, making it sound so desirable, so much fun, that I became envious that I wasn't crippled and so didn't qualify for membership. And whether or not he planned it, our natural but morbid curiosity about his handicap and his mechanical calliper — our innocent desire to stare — evaporated in the presence of his guilelessness.

There were plenty of other people worth staring at. People I didn't know. Ancient witch-like crones with pinched faces no better than a mass of wrinkles. Tiny old people with deformed hands and crooked fingers bandy legs and hunched backs; little grown-ups so hunched over that they could hardly walk and when they did they looked only at the ground and I wondered how they didn't bump into things. There were women who were almost or completely bald. Or very hairy. There was one lady in a grocer's shop who had a proper goatee beard.

'Don't stare,' said mum.

Bearded long-haired men were moderately stare-worthy but at least they were clean. There were tramps in town that were really filthy. Filthy men with filthy hair and filthy sticky beards and hands and feet that were black with grime. They wore filthy clothes. Their filthy trousers were held up with a twine belt with string bow yangs below their knees; and they carried dirty coal sacks over their shoulders. I longed to have a really good stare at them but mum crossed the street to avoid them which made staring hard.

People in wheel chairs were worth a good stare as were blind people. I liked to stare at blind people with empty eyes which to me, when I dared look, seemed shrivelled; and the white and coloured parts seemed to be blurred and mixed together. And they were always 'looking' up. I liked to watch them tapping their thin white sticks ahead of and beside themselves as they walked.

'Don't stare,' said mum.

'But they can't see me staring,' I said. 'They can't see anything.'

'It doesn't matter if they can see you or not,' she said. 'Never stare at people less fortunate than yourself. Remember, Johnny Boy, there but for the grace of god,' she added.

I remembered but I didn't know what she meant.

Fat people, men and women, were also very stare-worthy. I wondered where they got their clothes huge from.

'Don't stare,' said mum.

It was so frustrating being me; being ten years old and wanting to stare and not being allowed.

'They deserve pity not staring,' said mum. 'They've got something wrong with their glands.'

'What are glands?'

'Never mind.' I don't think she knew what glands were either. 'Just don't stare, that's all.'

I knew without understanding that pregnant women — especially those whose pregnancy was advanced — were not really fat but I didn't know what they were instead. I could see for myself that truly fat people were fat everywhere but that pregnant women were fat only in their stomachs. And even though I received the standard 'don't stare' from Mum I sensed there was something different about the fatness of pregnant women because apart from their great size, and the funny leaning-back way they walked with their legs apart, they didn't seem to be unhappy or handicapped or disabled in any way. There was of course no shortage of pregnant women to stare at — we were at the beginning of what came to be called the baby boom — but I preferred to see one at a distance, across the street or in the tram or in a shop, so I could get a better overall appreciation of her strange shape and watch how she walked. To the extent that I could safely stare from a distance I did but when I was with Mum, and she stopped in the street to talk to one she knew so that the swollen stomach was almost directly in front of me, just above my eye level, I found it too close for comfort. For while I wanted to have a really good close stare, especially as, above me, beyond the swollen stomach, my chatting mother was too preoccupied to notice whether or not I was staring, I was frustrated by the lady's closeness because I couldn't get an overall appreciation of her great size and strange shape.

'Don't stare at the mongols,' said mum. Often. Because there were a lot of them about to stare at.

As usual her command was a demand that stood alone, without explanation, and I was left to wonder why there were so many of those oversized loud-mouthed kids who looked, sounded and acted alike, like brothers and sisters. They all had the same short limbs, thick necks, the same dry skin, stiff hair, slanting eyes, too-big tongues, drooling mouths and slurred speech. I longed to stare at them, to understand them, even to talk to them, but I wasn't allowed.

Public kids — that's what we called kids who went to the primary school — always wanted to stare at the religious sisters of Saint Michael's. I understood their curiosity because the sisters' clothes — their habits — looked like nothing else within a protestant child's experience. They wore thick, heavy, brown dresses which fell, in deep vertical folds, directly to the ground, like the heavy curtains at the pictures, with stiff and brightly-white headpieces which covered the forehead, the sides of the head and the neck, leaving only the face showing. And their heads were topped off with a heavy and elaborately folded triangular wimple, in the same brown material as the dress, that fell down the back.

I also knew that public kids, uninitiated in the mysteries of the rosary, were awestruck by the long chains of large beads that hung from a wide and thick black leather belt with a huge silver buckle — more like man's belt — into which was thrust at an angle, like a dagger, a large wood and brass crucifix with a gruesome metal figure of Jesus in his last agonies of execution. This oversized string of beads swung and clattered as the sisters, always in pairs, walked — but without visible feet seemed to glide — around the shopping centre drawing odd looks from cynical and frequently contemptuous grown-ups. But seeing these sisters up close every day, being familiar with them as women, old and young, and finding them to be almost universally irritable and unkind, meant that they had absolutely no staring value to me.

Something odd and unexpected happened at school in September, immediately after the August holidays. All of sudden, without warning, all the kids at school started playing a new game. Actually it wasn't a new game but a very old game but it was new to me, to everyone at school, and it caught on like wildfire. At first I thought it was only a fad, a passing fashion, confined to Saint Michael's, but I learned that it was a nation-wide craze, and for two or three years it changed everything about play times before, during and after school.

Suddenly the playgrounds were eerily quiet and empty at play time and lunch time, as well as during the normally busy hour or so before school, as hundreds of energetic kids stopped their noisy and boisterous running and playing and instead sat all around the playground in small circles of four or five players, seeking the shade if necessary, concentrating deeply, watching each other closely, taking turns to complete a fixed set of manoeuvres with their knuckle bones. Playground accidents were suddenly eliminated and playground supervision became especially easy for the duty sister.

It's hard now to understand the attraction of such a simple game. Five identical pieces — each made of shiny steel in the approximate shape of an animal's knuckle bone — were used and although the game must have once been played with real knuckle bones, and some kids played with plastic pieces, each one a different and very dark colour, steel pieces were preferred because they were smaller than real or plastic knuckle bones, better suited to small hands, while their extra weight meant they behaved more predictably because they landed heavily and didn't bounce.

The principle of knuckle bones was simple: the player had to throw one of the pieces — the jack — in the air and quickly complete the required movement or handling of the other four pieces on the ground, using one or both hands depending on the move being made, before catching the falling jack with the same hand with which it was launched into the air only a second or two before. To not complete the move in time, or to complete it but fail to catch the falling jack, meant passing to the next player and resuming the series only when others too had stalled and it was one's turn again. There were a number of moves — some quite complex — but the game always started easily enough with onesies, where the player set four knuckle bones on the ground, threw the fifth in the air, quickly picked up one knuckle bone and held it firmly while turning his hand to catch the one in the air by now falling to earth. Obviously this manoeuvre had to be repeated three more times before moving on to twosies, threesies and foursies, which required two sets of two, one set of three and then one, and then all four together, to be scooped from the ground and held in the hand while catching the falling jack. Aside from the skill, which most kids acquired quickly and easily with only a little practice, holding five knuckle bones in a small hand was not easy. The game then moved on to scatters in which the pieces had to be picked up in the standard manner having first been scattered onto the ground from the hand rather than being clustered together. Scooping up and holding four widely dispersed knuckle bones — scatters four — while the fifth was in the air, and then catching the fifth in the same hand, required a good eye and dexterity both of which most kids seemed to have in abundance. Next came overhand scatters in which the player tossed all five pieces in the air and caught as many of them as possible on the back of his hand and spread fingers. Those caught were again tossed in the air from the back of the hand while the player had to scoop up those he had missed and then turn his hand again to catch those now returning to earth. And so it went on with the moves becoming more complex and difficult. There were moves called clicks and no clicks (in which the pieces had to or had not to make an audible click in the hand as they were collected and caught), juggles (in which the picked-up piece had to be juggled once with the jack), catching flies (which required the player to catch the pieces overhand, from the top), over the jump (which required the player to set his non-throwing hand vertically on the ground, like a hurdle, and lift the pieces from one side of it to the other) and in the stable (where the fingers of the non-throwing hand were spread on the ground to make four openings through each of which the player had to push one piece). In these as in all other stages of the game the manoeuvre had to be completed in the assigned manner while the jack was in the air.

The knuckle bones craze went on for many years after my Marian year to become an all-consuming obsession with children and at schools throughout the country. But there were still many other games and past-times for boys at school, some moving in and out of fashion for no discernible reason while others, marbles in particular, were ageless and perennial. We could play marbles uninterrupted for hours.

Boys called both their marbles and the games they played with them alleys. They kept and carried their big or small collection of alleys in a cloth bag they called their alley bag which all mothers were obliged to make for their sons. An alley bag was made from a piece of scrap material, carefully chosen for its masculine look, and closed at the top with a draw string. Alley bags therefore came in a variety of colours and patterns — Mum made mine from a piece of brown corduroy — which made it easy for boys to quickly recognise their own. A full alley bag could be strung from the belt and incidentally made a formidable weapon when held by the draw string and swung at the head or limbs.

Playing marbles at school was usually for keeps or 'keepsies' meaning winners took and kept the marbles they won, some boys amassing a huge and varied collection. Not playing for keeps but in a friendly fashion, purely as it were for the fun of it, was called 'funsies' but to play funsies at school, in public, was to invite ridicule from older boys and bullies. As a result funsies was played only secretly with friends and family who could be trusted not to tell.

All marbles were perfectly spherical and of a roughly standard size, about as big as a cherry, although every boy had at least one over-sized marble, somewhat smaller than a golf ball, called a bonzer. Most marbles were made of clear glass — called glassies — within which was locked a swirling form of seemingly random colour or colours, but there were in fact an infinite variety of coloured and patterned glass marbles including some of a solid colour, some with no colour at all, and some being spheres of clear glass full of tiny air bubbles. Many other materials were also used, from ceramics — we called them clayies — which were usually of a drab colour, unpatterned, and too lightweight for most games and so only slightly regarded, to pure and shiny steel — called steelies — which were in fact industrial ball bearings of just the right size. Steelies were hard and heavy and these qualities, together with their scarcity, made them especially valuable and cherished.

Marbles were projected forward as accurately as possible and with more or less force depending on the game being played. A reasonably accurate player, skilled at both power and distance, was at an advantage in most games. The most popular method of playing was to hold the marble firmly but not tightly in the crook of the forefinger with the bent thumb resting behind it. The angle of attack could be varied by raising or lowering the hand, although many plays were made with the back of the forefinger actually resting on the playing surface, while the direction and aim was determined by kneeling on one knee, resting the shooting hand just forward of the other foot, making fine adjustments to the aim at the wrist, and then flicking the thumb forward through the crooked forefinger and so firing the marble out with just the desired speed and power. Some players were especially adept at another form of marble projection in which the firing hand was turned palm outwards towards the target and the marble was held, by the thumb and forefinger of the other hand, in front of the last part of the open hand's middle finger which was then drawn back and released with a flick that sent the loosed marble on its way with more power and speed than could be achieved by conventional means. To be effective this method required a lot of practice and skill and was usually employed only by very serious big boys playing keepsies on large rings. Sometimes a bonza was used in this way in the hope, or even with the intention, that the target glass marble would be cracked, broken or even shattered. If and when that happened, and it did only rarely, all the players, even the loser, and all the observers — there were always plenty of younger observers at these ruthless events — whooped and shouted with callous delight before moving in to closely inspect and pick over the ruined marble's remains.

There were many variations of marble games, at Saint Michael's and everywhere, including one called holeys which was probably based on golf or may have itself been the ancient basis of golf. Holeys required a more or less permanent course of small hills and valleys, hazards and obstacles, around which were any number of scraped-out sloping-sided holes into each of which, and in the correct order, each player had to land his marble before moving on. But the most popular game by far required nothing more than a patch of fine gravel or dry earth into the surface of which was scratched a small circle — there was no standard size — and sometimes a large outer circle to define the outer boundary of the game. In rings, as this game was loosely called, the players took turns to knock the other players' marbles — in effect the stake — out of the inner circle from any position outside it. But the rules of this and all marble games were many and varied and impossible for me to describe here only because they were made up on the spot by the players concerned. Once the game's rules were set they were strictly applied for the duration of that game but would rarely be used again in quite the same form or even remembered.

At that time New Zealand was a small, conservative and homogenous nation and it was important to conform, to follow the rules, even for kids playing marbles. The New Zealanders' view of the world — an especially narrow view I think — was formed largely by the newspapers and their blurry black and white 'pictures by wire'. There was a daily news bulletin from the BBC in London but the quality of the short-wave reception was usually poor and, anyway, most people considered their radio a source of entertainment not information. It was more than five years before television was to come to New Zealand but Hollywood's latest films were always on show in town and, after a time, at the local cinema.

My first experience at the pictures was Walt Disney's *Bambi* which I saw at the Civic, with my aunts and cousins, when I was six. Despite Aunty Irene and the attractions of the Regent I thought that the Civic was by far the grandest picture theatre in the world. It was designed as if it were an open courtyard in an ornate Indian palace. The walls were intricately modelled and decorated with gold, with heavy velvet curtains of crimson with gold fringing, and tall turrets and towers with open windows from which came the mysterious glow of green and red and purple lights. There were cavities in the walls in which stood statues of strange Indian gods and goddesses with glowing eyes, and snakes and elephants, and vast tapestry wall-hangings depicting Indian princes and maharajahs wearing white robes and turbans, bedecked with jewels, and riding on the heads of elephants who were similarly draped in lavishly embroidered mantles. There was a roof of course but it was so designed to look like a dark-blue evening sky falling away, in a wonderful illusion, far beyond the free-standing walls, turrets and towers; you felt as if you were sitting in the courtyard at dusk. And at the front the proscenium formed a huge arch as ornately decorated as the rest of the interior. It was guarded by two lions — one at each side of the stage — who sat, with their front feet outstretched, looking sideways into the audience with eyes of red light.

I suppose Mum took us to the Civic once a year or so. If we were seated early enough we would see a man, dressed in a dinner suit, seated with layers of organ keyboards and stops and controls seemingly wrapped around him, rise up in a slow turn from below the stage to stand high in the air, at least half way up the height of the proscenium, as he played the organ. But this was an organ like none other, a special *Wurlitzer* organ, for which the organ pipes as well as bells and xylophones, cymbals and skulls, and all variety of strange and remarkable musical inventions, were arranged around the theatre, in the balconies of the towers to the left and right, where the audience could see the hammers working, playing the tune, in response to the keyboard commands of the organist so far distant from the sounds he was controlling. And then, at last, the organist stopped and, with a wave to the audience, disappeared below, whence he had come. Now, in the darkening sky, which was the ceiling, came a million stars that twinkled and blinked, just like those in the real sky, throughout the picture. This was the Civic moment I loved best of all. It was, to me at least, the most beautiful and magical sight in the world.

It's hard now, impossible even, to properly convey the cinema's importance at that time, and not just in New Zealand. It was, without doubt, the single most valuable and influential medium of entertainment in the world, central to the lives of many people, making going to the pictures at least a weekly event for most people. Gramma Fahey and Aunty Irene had a permanent commitment to the Saturday night pictures at one of their local theatres — they had four or five to choose from including the Astor, the Princess, the Capitol, the Mayfair and the Crystal Palace — and happily (and undiscerningly) went off to see whatever was showing.

Saturday night at the pictures was indeed an important occasion. Even though socialising was possible only before and after the programme and during the intermission — when the foyer and the street outside would be filled with people smoking, eating ice creams and talking noisily — it was for many people the social and recreational highlight of the week. They were well-dressed people too; on Saturday nights men wore their best suits and women their best ensemble, even their furs, hats, gloves and jewellery, to sit in the dark picture theatre, unseen.

New pictures ran four times a day but only at the downtown theatres — of which there were many — preceded by one or two trivial short films, the 'shorts', and trailers of upcoming features. Of the shorts I liked the cartoons best — *Tom & Jerry* and *Bugs Bunny* were particular favourites but there were many others — and as soon as the title of a cartoon appeared on the screen the theatre would be filled with the uninhibited cheers of all the kids present. There were also newsreels featuring important world events, and short humorous films, usually American, neither of which appealed to me or any kids. Then there was an intermission before the feature film.

Only when the potential of new films was exhausted, when downtown patronage began falling off, were they moved to the suburbs to attract customers who would never have gone to town to go to the pictures, even to see a new and popular release. Many people considered it extravagant to go to a cinema in town when for a much smaller sum the suburban cinemas showed a 'double feature' meaning two big pictures on the same programme, but no shorts, separated by an intermission. But the quality of the suburban theatres varied widely, depending I suppose on the theatre's ownership and management, and most people knew the good from the bad. Some theatres had obviously old and unreliable equipment which frequently broke down and interrupted the film. Seating was important as was the quality of the flooring — many theatres had carpet only on the aisles with the seats fixed to bare and dusty floorboards — and some theatres, even in town, were reputed to house vermin in the seats, carpets and draperies. Going to such a theatre was referred to as going to the bug house.

Whether good or bad, in town or in the suburbs, all pictures theatres were large buildings, some were downright huge, elaborately and extravagantly decorated inside as if to conform to the fantasy and glamour of the movies, with imported marble, sumptuous velvet curtains and drapes, and ornate chandeliers. They were furnished with what were once luxurious and comfortable seats imported in the booming nineteen-twenties well before The Slump. This illusion of glamorous elegance and Hollywood style was carefully maintained in most of the downtown cinemas but in suburban theatres the glamour had long faded. The marble was dull, the velvet drapes were limp and dusty, the chandeliers were missing many bulbs, and many of the seats had broken springs and torn upholstery.

All exhibitions in all theatres began with the lights being dimmed for the playing of a sound recording of *God Save The Queen* which was then considered New Zealand's national anthem. The audience stood in respectful and loyal silence until the last note had faded. Only then did they reach back to lower their seat, take their place, adjust their clothing for comfort before concentrating their hopeful gaze on the flickering images that came to life on the large almost-square screen in front of them, caring not whether the picture was colour or black-and-white, American or English, comedy or drama, a play or a musical, but looking forward to nothing more than a couple of hours of pleasant and undemanding entertainment, perhaps with some musical numbers and romance thrown in and an ice cream at half time.

Movie stars were as famous and well-known in New Zealand as they were all over the world and their lives and careers were followed assiduously, in newspapers and magazines and more especially in specialist movie magazines, by Mum and her sisters. Indeed, the cinema, as I knew it then — with sound and colour — was still a new phenomenon. The novelty of sound had been introduced only fifteen years before I was born while colour was common but formerly rare, and the wide screen was only a couple of years old.

By my Marian year Tessa and I were allowed to go to the pictures alone, together with hundreds of other local kids, not to the Civic or Regent or any other cinema in town but to the smaller and more modest theatre in the shopping centre for the Saturday matinee. We went whenever we could, whenever we were allowed, whenever Mum and Dad had nothing else planned, summer or winter, to see whatever was playing. It cost us ninepence each to get in and Mum always gave us a shilling each meaning we each had three pence to buy an ice cream at half time. I must have gone to what was called the two o'clocks a hundred or more times over the next few years but the many separate experiences have merged into one memory. There was the constant noise made by hundreds of excited children who could have heard nothing of the dialogue and have had no idea of the story unfolding on the big screen in front of them. There was a serial, usually a western story with cowboys and whooping Indians in constant pursuit, one of the other, ending each week in such an exciting fashion that the audience would be compelled to return to see the outcome. I especially liked the serial called *The Durango Kid* although it bothered me — as it did in all cowboy pictures — that the wagon wheels appeared to spin sometimes forward and then sometimes in reverse. It was an illusion that annoyed my tidy mind and left me wondering why the grown-ups who made the pictures weren't clever enough to solve a problem which must have annoyed them as much as it annoyed me.

There was something odd about going to the Saturday matinee, or rather coming out when the picture was finished. Every time I came out of the pictures on a Saturday afternoon I was reminded of *Bambi* and my first movie experience at the Civic. That story, of a young deer growing up in the forest to become a leader, a handsome and haughty stag with great spreading antlers like his father, thrilled me to bits then and made the six-year-old me and my little cousins cry with fright and then with joy and relief. The shared relief was so real and so great that neither I nor my cousins felt even slightly embarrassed to be standing together with our mothers in the bright daylight, outside the Civic on the busy corner of Queen Street and Wellesley Street, sobbing and sniffing and smiling with joy that the beautiful Bambi had survived so heroically. I looked about at the big intersection — of Queen Street and Wellesley Street — which was so busy and noisy and smelly, with people and cars and trucks and trams all being directed from the middle by a policeman with white gauntlets, and wondering how everything could be so normal. I wondered how the people around me, going about their business, whatever it might be, could be so unaware of the drama and tragedy that I had just seen unfold so wonderfully, magically, realistically and believably, inside the Civic, under the big clock, right in the middle of Auckland. How, I wondered, could so many people care so little about Bambi and his life?

It was the same when I came out of the local theatre on Saturday afternoons. Not only were my eyes shocked by the relative brightness of even a gloomy day but my mind was shocked and surprised to discover yet again that the mundane world in which I lived was still there. I had to remind myself that it had continued, in my absence, to go about its normal humdrum Saturday afternoon business unaware of the marvellous adventures which had been playing out on the big screen in the dark theatre behind me. It, the theatre, had stood in the middle of the shopping centre far longer than I had been alive and must have shown thousands of pictures — silent and sound, black and white and colour, small screen and Cinemascope — to hundreds of thousands of people before me. It exercised and challenged my mind to remember that every day and every night other pictures were playing in other picture theatres all over Auckland, all around the world, and that other people were being entertained, excited, frightened and amused just as I, ignorant of their experiences, was going about my own life in my own little world. I tried to remember that every time I went past a picture theatre — any picture theatre — but it wasn't easy.

'How was the picture, dear?' Mum asked after the Saturday flicks. It was usually after four o'clock when I got home.

'Was good,' I always said, and it always was good even if it were not.

'What was it called?'

'I don't know,' I said, and I didn't. 'But it was good.'

Late one Saturday afternoon in September, after the fun and excitement of the two o'clocks, I was touched again, as I was occasionally but without warning, by a strange almost cosmic sadness. At home everything seemed so eerily normal. Mum was in the kitchen making tea so there was the smell of something cooking. The radio was playing softly in the background. Dad, having mowed the lawns and finished in the garden, was sitting on the back step having a glass of beer and a cigarette. His glass was standing on the grey-painted and somewhat uneven tongue-and-groove porch floor and I could see a film of yellow foam slipping slowly down its inside to meet the rising bubbles. A tall-necked brown bottle of DB Draught beer stood beside it together with a green soft packet of cigarettes on its side and a yellow match box. It was nearly dark and the air was cool but Dad was hot from his work. There were complex mixed smells outside: of burning wood and coal from home fires, of freshly-mown grass, hoppy beer and acrid tobacco smoke. I noticed how blue and smooth the cigarette smoke looked rising in the cool still air. Dad didn't say anything but he winked at me. I wondered if he knew what I was feeling. I looked up. The winter sky was broad and flat and grey and cold looking, and streaked with thin, distant and unmoving clouds touched with pink. A flock of starlings — black dots against the western sky — whirled and turned frantically for a reason I didn't understand. And then, high above them, a formation of ducks, their wings set far back on their bodies, their heads thrust forward, flapped steadily and determinedly westward towards the misty-blue shape of the Waitakeres behind which the sun would soon be setting.

The end of Saturday. After the pictures. It was so quiet. And then I heard a dog barking from far away, a perfectly normal suburban sound that somehow, for some reason, sounded poignant and melancholy. All, in fact, was perfectly normal and yet that day, and at other such moments — they came fleetingly, randomly but often — I felt inexplicably sad. It was a feeling that passed soon enough although the lingering memory of such deep juvenile sadness is even now almost as sad as the sadness itself.

October

ONE DAY AT THE BEGINNING OF OCTOBER I WAS
called to the front of the class by Sister Ursula and given a sealed white
envelope. 'Don't open it now, young man,' she said. 'Take it home and
give it straight to your mother.'

I didn't have to open the envelope to know what was in it. I had
received such an envelope before and I knew it contained only dreadful
news. I returned to my desk in shock, feeling physically sick. The
lessons of the day were wasted on me.

According to the notice in the envelope I was required to attend
the murder house at such-and-such a time on such-and-such a date
later in the month. The murder house was in fact a dental clinic staffed
by a government-employed female dental nurse who had received
special but limited training sufficient to provide free dental treatment
to the nation's children, including the filling of cavities and the
extraction of lost causes. All state primary schools had a dental clinic
but Saint Michael's didn't — no Catholic school did — so I had to go
to the dental clinic at the public school.

Some times over the next two weeks, perhaps engrossed in my
work or play, I would momentarily forget the murder house notice
until, for no particular reason and from some deep recess in my
frightened mind, the thought of the pending appointment would
return. Back came the familiar feelings of murder house dread
accompanied by tummy-flies that would not go away.

At last, inevitably, the appointed time arrived. Simply going to that
school, the home of the public school bullies, was an ordeal. But to
have to enter the grounds of a place which was not merely protestant
but actually heathen — where no religion was taught or allowed — felt
like heresy. I thought Mum would hate it — she had to take me — but
she seemed utterly unconcerned, nonchalant, when she picked me up
from school and took me to that wicked place on the tram. Before long
I found myself walking with her through the ungodly state school
gates, along a short avenue of heathen pohutukawa, to the pagan dental
clinic building built, like the profane school, from wooden
weatherboards painted cream and with a roof of terra cotta tiles.

I sat nervously in the waiting room with Mum, listening to the
buzzing drill from behind the clinic's closed door and, frequently, to

the unmistakeable sound of a child crying. Then, much sooner than I ever would have wished and hoped, and yet glad it would be soon over, I found myself sitting alone in the white enamelled chair especially designed for kids, a strong light in my eyes, in an atmosphere that smelled of methylated spirits, ether and cloves and generally of a hospital, with a white-uniformed and white-capped nurse standing beside me, looking into my open mouth, picking about with sharp and pointed steel instruments. I was surrounded by all the apparatus of a dentist including the tall and menacing drill standing to attention with its single but many-elbowed arm and its wheels and cords, all designed to whirr and grind a dull drill slowly, noisily and hotly into my innocent teeth.

I sat terrified and open-mouthed in that awful chair for ages imagining with horror that when the visit was over she, the dental nurse, would walk out to the waiting room with me to tell my waiting but uncaring mother that there was something wrong with my teeth which would require drilling and filling on a return visit. Mum would receive the news calmly and would work with the nurse, with clinical, businesslike and uncaring efficiency, to make a return appointment while I would have to stand to one side, meek and helpless, overcome with disappointment at this dreadful setback. Did that young dental nurse ever know the fear she struck into the thumping hearts of her nervous little patients?

But, oh, when it was over, the wonderful and overwhelming relief; the lifting of a great burden.

'Everything's fine, Mrs Little,' said the nurse. 'John here has excellent teeth. Nothing to worry about.'

'See, Johnny Boy,' said Mum. 'I told you.'

'I expect you'll take him to Mr Steiner next year.' Mr Steiner was the real dentist in the shopping centre.

'Yes,' said Mum. 'Marist next year.'

'They grow up so fast, don't they.'

'Oh, they do. It's terrible.'

So there was no awful news. No need for an injection; for drilling and filling. No need to wait while Mum made another appointment. No need at all for a return visit. Ever. Instead I was a given a bright new leaflet on shiny paper about the dangers of Bertie Germ and the importance of eating fresh fruit, otherwise having endured no worse than a routine inspection and a stiff reminder about the proper brushing of my teeth after every meal.

This little lecture, which I had heard many times and would hear many times again, seemed to me to be another example of grown-ups ignoring a reality that was obvious to kids: that the brushing of teeth after every meal was simply impossible when we never took a toothbrush or toothpaste to school with which to brush our teeth, properly or otherwise, after play time or lunch. But Mum dismissed this incongruity believing from experience that any teeth-brushing was better than none. Like many if not most grown-ups, in my world at least, she wore upper and lower dentures — with bright pink gums and unnaturally white and obviously artificial teeth — being herself the childhood victim of The Slump and its attendant poverty, poor diet and widespread ignorance of dental health. Indeed most people — certainly all my aunts, uncles and grandparents, Dad being the only exception — finding in their early grown-uphood that they were unable or unwilling to pay for expensive, painful, primitive and ongoing dentistry, chose the one-off pain and expense of extracting a mouthful of teeth, not all of them bad, to be replaced by dentures, as the lesser and less expensive of two evils. Mum said it was a decision she regretted for the rest of her life.

'You thank Our Lord you've got good teeth, Johnny Boy,' she said, often, especially when I said I couldn't be bothered brushing my teeth. 'Take care of them now and you'll never be sorry.'

Mum was a big supporter of the government's dental health policies for children, and of the dental clinic and dental nurse which were their agents. Wisely she chose to disregard my childish fears in the hope that with the help of the free dental nurse service I would avoid the lifelong burden of dentures which she, and so many people she knew, had mistakenly chosen to carry.

I didn't know any of that. I knew only the chilling fear that came with the compulsory annual visit to the murder house and the relief when the ordeal was over. Then I quickly dismissed the dental nurse's lectures — about fresh fruit and regular brushing — and the posters at school, and the brochures about Bertie Germ, and brushed my teeth, carelessly and reluctantly, morning and night, only because Mum made sure I did.

The free milk programme, through which all schools received a daily delivery of government-supplied milk, was another part of the state's post-war drive for the health of the nation's children. The milk was delivered overnight by the local milkman in wire crates of stubby, wide-necked half-pint bottles one of which every kid was compelled to drink before play time. The crates were stored in a small wooden shed — the milk shed — which stood at the school gates for the express purpose of storing milk in the shade until it was needed. The necks of these half-pint bottles, which were available only through schools — half pint bottles were otherwise used only for cream — were sealed with a waxy cardboard top, pressed into the opening, which had a semi-perforated hole, set slightly off centre, which we broke through with a finger or thumb to insert a paper straw. Older kids, and kids from the states who thought straws were for sissies, preferred to remove the cardboard seal altogether and drink directly from the bottle.

Despite its designed purpose the milk shed at Saint Michael's did a poor job of shading the milk. Its walls and door were clad with widely-spaced vertical palings for ventilation through which the corrupting fingers of the morning sun easily reached. That meant that, except for the coldest days in winter, the milk was inevitably warm, even sour-smelling and -tasting, by the time it was delivered to class. Milk monitors — usually strong standard four boys from the states — were assigned the task of leaving class before play time to collect the milk from the milk shed and deliver the crates containing the assigned number of bottles to the door of each classroom. Before we were allowed out at play time we had to sit at our desks and drink our bottle of unpleasantly warm and sour-tasting milk, and were not allowed to leave the room until our bottle was empty. I didn't like the warm milk but I managed to drink it each day although some kids hated the taste to the point of retching. But there were no exceptions to the rule. All kids had to drink their half-pint of milk every day, whether they liked it or not, and had to show Sister their empty bottle before they dropped it in the crate on the way out to the playground. Many kids reacted badly to the warm, sour milk and were surely put off drinking milk for the rest of their lives.

During play time the milk monitors returned the crates of empty bottles to the milk shed, each bottle now lined with an opaque and milky slime, many with a crushed and torn cardboard lid on the bottom, and most with a soggy straw resting limply inside. The empty bottles remained in the shed, in this fly-attracting condition, until they were picked up and replaced by the milkman during the following night. As a result by the end of the day the odious smell of sour milk from the milk shed was overwhelming and was reinforced five nights a week during school term until it became a permanent smell that lingered forever around the milk shed.

Meanwhile, having consumed our warm milk, we were allowed outside for play time, a quarter of an hour in which to eat our morning play lunch. I enjoyed my play lunch because Mum liked to indulge me with tasty treats. A snack of cake or biscuit, a piece of chocolate, perhaps a piece of fruit, or a piece of pie left over from the previous night's tea, were all welcome at play time and I enjoyed making a new discovery each morning. But there was no lingering over the eating of play lunch as I was anxious to resume the pre-school games which had been so rudely and inconveniently interrupted by the start of lessons at nine o'clock.

A milkman called at forty-three every day, or rather every night, including Sundays. He delivered the same milk order each night, picking up the washed empty bottles left out by Mum or Dad before they went to bed and replacing them with bottles of fresh milk in a purpose-built cupboard, open at the back, which was part of the letter box. So inflexible was this delivery system, the milkman carrying only exactly what he needed, that the regular order could be varied only in advance by leaving a note rolled up and standing in one of the empty bottles. A record of deliveries and payments was kept on a printed card and every two weeks on a Saturday someone, I assume it wasn't the milkman who must have slept all day, called to collect the money and mark off the card with a squiggle by way of a receipt.

The milkmen worked from small battery-powered doorless little trucks — called floats — with a flat bed and roof but without sides. Electricity was used for these wagons because it was as silent as the Farmers' electric trolley bus although the rattling and clinking of the empty glass bottles in their wire crates made enough noise to often disturb my sleep in the early hours of the morning. These little electric floats started the night fully charged although their speed was limited by the heavy weight of their load. In a self regulating process the gradual lightening of their load — as heavy full bottles were replaced with lightweight empties — was matched by the gradual running down of their battery power which meant, full or empty, their speed potential, never very great anyway, remained at a reasonably constant slow.

So slow, steady and reliable was the milk float that the milkman could leave it moving while he ran to and fro, replacing empty bottles with full, as it carried itself silently and smoothly down the middle of a dark and always empty road. The milkman had to make only an occasional steering adjustment.

'Same when I was a kid and the milky used a horse,' said Dad. 'Horses were used a lot then.'

According to Dad the milkman's horse would know the route, would walk on, in the middle of the road, without instructions or guidance, would instinctively know the pace best suited to the milkman, and would even wait patiently, head down, if he got ahead of his master. It made me wish horses were used more. The only horses I knew were old Robbie, who lived at the end of Gramma Fahey's street, and the racehorses which lived in Andersons' paddock. Although I knew dear old Robbie well I only ever saw Andersons' horses from a distance, or on an open horse float as they went to or from some race meeting, and Dad said it was best to avoid thoroughbreds anyway.

Like the horses they replaced, milk floats needed a rest and recharge and so by the end of the night's work, in the morning, the float's batteries were almost exhausted. I rarely saw our milkman at work but I saw him each morning, as I made my way to school, by which time his little cart's power was so reduced that I could easily walk with it as he returned slowly — slower even than a tired horse — to the main road depot. His progress was signalled by the clinking and clanking of the empty glass bottles in their wiry crates while he, the tired driver, sat patiently in his doorless cabin, resting forward on the steering wheel, his foot pressed to the floor, having a quiet smoke as he returned his float and its load of empties to the depot.

It must have a been a lucrative and steady business being a milkman because there was no family I knew that didn't take a quart or more of milk each day. Perhaps many people over-ordered — although my thrifty mother didn't — knowing that milk was cheap, that come morning a fresh supply would be waiting at the gate courtesy of the faithful milkman and his electric cart, and that if required extra supplies were always available from the dairy for just fourpence a pint.

Unlike any other shop the dairy was open early and remained open late, seven days a week. Of course it wasn't a dairy at all but a small, family-owned and operated general store — the family lived above or behind the premises — crammed to the ceiling with all sorts of stock in a remarkably successful attempt to be all things to all people at all hours of every day including weekends and holidays. Dairies had been allowed to evolve, and to keep their own hours, despite regulation, as a matter of public health. Before household refrigerators were common the dairy was the only place convenient where fresh milk — in the beginning raw, unhomogenised and unpasteurised — could be safely stored in a refrigerated state to be passed on to the customer without delay. And because fresh milk was seen to be essential to family health, more especially the health of their infants and growing children, shopping regulations and rules were waived for dairies so that milk (and just about anything else as it turned out) should be freely available outside normal trading and shopping hours. And it should be affordable which was why milk was heavily subsidised by the government. Fourpence (less than four cents) for a pint of milk was, even then, a ridiculously small amount.

Our dairy, at the bottom of Winstone Street, opposite the bakery on the main road, was always open, from early morning until late at night, and was the place to go for ice cream cones and ice blocks. Watery ice blocks on a stick — factory-made in a variety of weak flavours by the Tip Top ice cream people — were a new and popular innovation. They were called TT2s although nobody seemed to know whether there was ever a TT1. The dairy was also the only place where a vast choice of lollies were sold to kids by the penny-worth. A mouth-watering and colourful selection of loose unwrapped sweets was contained in a long row of open-backed glass compartments which sat on a high counter. Mr and Mrs Drake, the dairy owners, were kind and patient enough to let us kiddie customers make a mixed selection, using their fingers to put each lolly, one at a time, into a small white paper bag as we hummed and hahed our way through our selection.

There was also a three-tiered display of Wrigley's chewing gum on the counter. Wrigley's was the only chewing gum available then and we called it chuddy. There were just three flavours: Spearmint, PK and Juicy Fruit. Each tiny packet cost tuppence (two pennies) and contained just four white-coated pellets. Mum thought chewing gum looked 'common' although she discouraged it rather than forbade it and acknowledged that it was not only cheap but lasted a lot longer in the mouth than most chewing or sucking lollies. But I thought the flavour — I preferred Juicy Fruit — disappeared too quickly and discovered that the enjoyment of the grey and tasteless gum could be extended by dipping and rolling it in the sugar bowl, a technique of flavour enhancement that did not have Mum's approval. Nor for that matter did my habit of sticking the exhausted grey and tasteless wad in a hiding place, behind the head of my bed for example, to be retrieved, reflavoured by sugar, and enjoyed again at a later date.

Below the lolly cases were the dairy's chillers for the milk, cream, butter and cheese, and the ice cream freezers. Most dairies sold ice creams in cones — packaged ice cream came only later when the home ownership of refrigerators with a small freezer cabinet made its storage possible — offering only one size of cone and a small variety of flavours although some offered miniature cones for small children. Double cones too were available at some dairies, although not at Drake's, but Mum thought they were excessive and extravagant. When an ice cream cone was required Mr or Mrs Drake — they were the only people who served in the shop — would lift and put aside the freezer's large and rubber-edged insulation lid, bend forward to plunge an arm into the depths of the freezer to scoop the ice cream from a big cardboard barrel. They used a metal scoop, designed for the purpose, to collect a roll of ice cream which they transferred to the empty cone held in the other bare hand. Then the scoop was turned over and used to tap the ice cream securely into place. Drakes also offered to dip the finished ice cream cone upside down in a fast-setting liquid chocolate. A chocolate dip ice cream cost a penny extra and was therefore a special treat. Mrs Drake was more practised and accomplished than her husband at the ice cream rolling process, and more generous, which meant that Tessa and I always hoped to be served by her.

Milk shakes too were a special dairy favourite, especially in the summer when Drake's milk was ice cold, much colder than at home, and so especially refreshing. Bulk milk was held in a large vat, in the same chiller as the bottled milk and cream, adjacent to the freezer. Once again it was Mrs Drake who made the better milk shake. She would raise or set aside the chiller lid and lean down to reach deep into the cabinet to fill the especially-shaped aluminium milk shake container — which had fluted sides to assist the mixing process — using a tin ladle with a hooked handle. There were plenty of colourful and syrupy flavours to choose from, on display behind the counter, and ice cream could be added for an extra penny or two. The dairy's milk shake machines —designed to take two, three or even four containers at a time — were fast, powerful and noisy electric models onto which the milk shake holders were clipped for a couple of minutes of thorough mixing. Some dairies then poured the cold and frothy mixture into another tall glass, thick and heavy-based, although Drake's served their milk shakes in the fluted aluminium mixing container to be drank on the premises. The drinking straws, necessarily thicker than the straws used for soft drinks, stood upright in a tall closed chromium-plated barrel which itself stood on the high stainless steel counter near the chillers. Mum had to get our straws for us which she did by lifting the barrel's lid with one hand which raised the floor of the barrel upon which the upright straws were resting and so presented a spray of cream-coloured straws from which she, using the other hand, could take one or two. Drinking straws were made from a thick waxed paper and they soon became limp and soggy if I drank my milk shake slowly or used them to stir the drink or otherwise delay consumption.

Cigarettes and tobacco were a big part of the dairy's business. On many Saturday nights Dad sent me off to Drake's to buy a packet of cigarettes and an *8 o'clock*.

'You know the story, boy,' he said. 'An eight o'clock, a packet of fags, and thruppence for yourself.'

He sent me off to save himself the trouble of getting there early and waiting in line for his precious paper which quickly sold out every Saturday night.

'Grey's as usual?'

'Twenty Grey's as usual.'

I earned my Saturday night thruppence by waiting outside Drake's for the paper truck to arrive and then braving the rush of men to the counter. Few men would tolerate me, a small boy, beating them to the counter but even if I did the Drakes found it easy to ignore a small boy while they served their impatient grown-up men customers. They often purposely and conveniently overlooked me until the rush was over. But I didn't mind. I had already taken a copy of the *8 O'Clock* from the pile and I gripped it tightly until I was eventually served.

These days it's unlawful to sell cigarettes and tobacco products to children but there were no such restrictions then and grown-ups — whether in dairies, barbers, tobacconists or grocers — had no hesitation in giving me what was obviously ordered by my father for his own use. Cigarettes then were thick, short, stubby and unfiltered — filter tips and the so-called king size brands came later — and Dad preferred his Grey's brand, two shillings (twenty cents) for a packet of twenty, which were packed in a soft silver foil pouch wrapped in a green paper label featuring a Scots soldier in a bearskin busby, presumably a member of the regiment of Royal Scots Greys. (There was also a Grey's brand of rolling tobacco and I was intrigued that the slogan for the cigarettes was 'Grey's are Great' while that for the tobacco was 'Grey's is Great', commercial confirmation of a valuable school lesson in subject-verb agreement.) The military theme was popular in the cigarette and tobacco business with cigarette brands such as Capstan, whose blue packet featured a naval capstan, (slogan: 'Time for a Capstan'); Player's ('Player's, Please') whose packet featured a portrait of a bearded sailor, who looked distinctly old fashioned even then, framed by a rope-braided life-saving buoy; and Army Club and Senior Service referring directly to the army — presumably the British army — and the royal navy. Rothmans, Pall Mall, De Reske, du Maurier and Matinee brands were also popular although there were many, many others. The popular rolling tobacco brands without a cigarette version included Kauri (in a tin), Park Drive, Pocket Edition and Three Castles as well as Grey's.

Few men didn't smoke and drink then although both must have been expensive habits especially for poor families. But for men at least, and for some women — Mum smoked lightly but never drank alcohol — smoking and drinking were ingrained and established behaviours considered no less normal or necessary than eating or breathing. And in cases where money was especially short the men modified their behaviour by buying draught beer in half-gallon glass flagons instead of in bottles, filled at the pub for home consumption, and rolling their own cigarettes instead of buying the more expensive factory-made cigarettes referred to as tailors (for tailor-made). Men who rolled their own cigarettes rationed themselves to make a two-ounce packet of tobacco last from one pay day to the next which meant that by the end of the week their cigarettes were rolled so thin that they contained no more that a few stringy threads of weed.

Rolling a cigarette wasn't hard. Dad taught me so I could roll him a fag when his hands were otherwise occupied, dirty or greasy. But rolling a neat cigarette — one that looked tidy and smoked evenly without going out — called for a great deal more skill especially when it was done one-handed as it was by many busy men. Pre-packed tobacco was bought by the two-ounces in either a box with a sliding inner, much like a large match box, or a lidded packet or tin, in both cases lined with a thick waxed paper. Whether cardboard or tin the containers were sturdy enough but many men transferred their tobacco to a rubber-lined pouch with a zipper top of the style more often used by pipe smokers (whose tobacco was darker, damper and more coarsely shredded). Especially-fine cigarette papers, tipped with glue at one long edge, were bought in a small flat packet. They were branded Zig Zag for the way the flimsy folded papers were so interleaved that the drawing out of one paper from its little slit — there were two such slits in each packet — delivered the next ready for use.

To roll Dad a cigarette I opened the paper down its length and held it with the glued inner edge farther from me. Then I pulled a tiny ball of tobacco from the packet and teased it into a thin line of tangled strands along the middle crease of paper until I was satisfied that it was neatly and evenly distributed along the paper's length. Using my two forefingers I folded back the plain unglued edge of the paper across and slightly under the line of tobacco at the back at which point I began rolling the small cylinder backwards and forwards, quickly and repeatedly, between my thumbs and forefingers — a clever one-handed maker would use just one thumb and forefinger — until I was satisfied with the even distribution of the tobacco within the rolled paper and the overall neat appearance of my new cigarette. At that point the back edge of the paper was standing up to present the glue-tipped edge forward which I would then bring to and run along the wet tip of my slightly extended tongue one way and then the other. Then I carefully rolled down the wetted gummed edge of the paper to stick to the dry paper and so complete the containment of the tobacco. But the manufacture wasn't complete until I had carefully, delicately, torn off the few loose strands of tobacco inevitably left hanging from each end of the paper tube and returned them to the packet. This last act was essential: loose strands at the soon-to-be-lighted end would catch fire and fall away dangerously into Dad's lap while those at the soon-to-be-sucked end would come away in his mouth to be quickly spat out. Tobacco had a dreadfully offensive taste on the tongue which was why smokers of tailor-made cigarettes tapped one end of their unlighted cigarette against something hard to drive the loose tobacco away from the end they were about to put into their mouth. This remained an essential act until the introduction of filter cigarettes which, when they arrived, were regarded by Dad and his friends as suitable only for women.

While cigarette lighters were familiar and common — most were the Ronson brand — Dad didn't use one. For one thing they were expensive to buy but they were also expensive and mechanically troublesome to run as replacement wicks, tiny flints and expensive lighter fluid were all required at hand. Dad and most smokers used wooden safety matches and were skilled at striking a brown-ended match off the edge of the box and holding it and the box in their cupped hands, sheltering the flame from the wind, which they did from habit even if the air was still. But before being lit the end of all plain cigarettes, whether tailor-made or hand-rolled, was carefully wetted in the mouth so that the dry paper didn't stick to the lip. Failure to wet the end in this way resulted, when the smoker drew the burning cigarette away from the mouth between his first and second fingers, in either the painful tearing away of a layer of skin from the lip, or the fingers sliding down the smooth papery length of the cigarette and tearing out the burning end which fell on the floor or in the smoker's lap or somewhere else equally dangerous.

The dairy and perhaps the petrol station were the only exceptions to the highly organised and regulated world of shopping. The dairy, as we have seen, filled an essential need while petrol stations could have somewhat extended hours only because motorists might need petrol — what was then commonly called benzene — in an emergency. But there were strict limits to what a petrol station might sell which, as well as benzene and oil, was limited to motoring-related accessories such as lubricating grease, tyres, batteries, lamps, spark plugs, fuses, gaskets, fan belts and such things necessary for emergency repairs by the home mechanic. There was only one all-night emergency petrol station in the entire city, in Grey's Avenue.

The only other shopping concession was the so-called late night shopping law which permitted shopping centres to remain open until nine-o'clock on Friday nights. Otherwise shops were simply not permitted to open at all on nights or weekends. It was a system designed to protect the sales assistants who worked in the shops from exploitation in the same way that industrial regulations enforced the eight-hour day, forty-hour week for factory workers. But it ignored reality and created many inconveniences. For example it meant that all shops were closed during the only times — nights and weekends — when factory workers such as Dad, and the shop-workers themselves, had time to shop. Husbands and wives therefore had only a couple of hours on Friday nights to make shared shopping choices about anything they needed which meant almost all the household shopping was left to the housewives. And the rules, designed to protect employees from exploitation by employers, ignored the fact that only department stores and large chain stores were real employers. All our local retail shops — East brothers' Four Square store, the Wongs' fruit shop, the Pellow brothers' butchery, Mr Olsen's chemist shop, Mr Ineson's bike shop, Mr Nicholls's shoe shop, Mr and Mrs Taylor's book shop, O'Connell's Hardware and many more not mentioned — were owned by the people who worked in them, hardly exploiters of shop labour but owner-operators who were willing, with the help of their families, to open longer hours, nights and weekends, to provide a better and more convenient service to their customers and so increase their turnover. But they were forbidden by law to do so.

Mum and Dad didn't complain about their shopping opportunities being so limited and their lives being so controlled and regulated. Having experienced so much privation in the past they were comforted by the certainties provided by a regulatory and protective government ruling over them — an homogenous and egalitarian populace sharing a mildly puritan ethic — with a firm but gentle hand.

It was more than a mild puritanism that made hotels and bars close at six o'clock in the evening, Monday to Saturday, and remain closed completely on Sundays. This strange arrangement — a hang-over from the days when alcohol was considered a social evil — meant that hotels were closing for the day just as their thirsty working class customers were finishing their hard day's work. This led to the famous six o'clock swill when New Zealand men were compelled to consume as much beer as they could in the short time between their arrival at the pub after work and the six o'clock call for time. The moral forces of the time — including the government — thought it was better that the working men of New Zealand be allowed only a limited time in the pub, drinking beer with their mates at the end of their working day, on the assumption that when the pubs closed they would go home to their wives and children, whether or not they wanted to, whether or not they were happy there.

Hotel licences were strictly limited. At each general election the New Zealand public had the opportunity to vote for prohibition in their constituency. The result was that large tracts of Auckland were dry (unlicensed). That didn't mean that local grown-ups didn't drink — they did, much and often — but that they, as voters, and perhaps the women more than the men, didn't want a pub in their neighbourhood. And so, when I smelled alcohol on Dad's breath, which I often did, I knew that he had detoured a long way from home to have a drink. His favourite pubs were the Ponsonby Club, The Suffolk, The Star and The Rising Sun. The Ponsonby Club stood on the corner of Ponsonby and Jervois Roads, a place known since Victorian Times as the Three Lamps Corner, or more simply as Three Lamps, for the three gas lamps on a single standard which once stood in the middle of the intersection with Saint Mary's Bay Road and College Hill Road. It, the pub, was better known as the Gluepot because it was believed that once inside men became stuck, finding it impossible to free themselves from its clutches. The Suffolk, half way down College Hill Road, on the corner of Wood Street, was an old wooden pub typical of the urban pubs of Victorian Auckland. The Star Hotel was a large and more modern building on the eastern corner of Karangahape and Newton Roads while the Rising Sun was half way along Karangahape Road towards Pitt Street.

There were, of course, numerous other hotels — in Queen Street, Karangahape Road, Pitt Street, Hobson Street, Parnell, Symonds Street and Newmarket — to which Dad, his colleagues and friends, could and did go after work and on Saturdays. One of Dad's colleagues called Ray Masters even managed to get a drink on Sunday mornings by driving into town in his pyjamas, dressing gown and slippers, slipping into the house bar of the Royal International and posing as a guest entitled to service there even on Sunday mornings. Evidently it was not an uncommon ruse.

Trips to town with Mum made me familiar with all the wonderful pub names designed to conjure up visions of the romantic past of the British Empire: The Naval and Family, The Queen's Head, The Coburg, The Queen's Ferry, The Exchange, The Edinburgh Castle, The Windsor Castle, The Carpenter's Arms, The King's Arms, The Shakespeare, The Rob Roy, The Albion, The Royal George, The

Carlton, The Astor and others. Pompous and portentous names, reflecting the Victorian birth of Auckland, which I never forgot. But they were only names to me; I never saw the inside of even one of their pubs.

Only men were allowed in a hotel's public bar although it was generally agreed that no decent woman would want to drink in such a place anyway. However most or perhaps all pubs had what was then called a private bar or a club bar where women could sit down for a quiet drink, with their male or female friends, away from the noise and degradation of the public bar.

In the public bar — which was invariably noisy and smoky — men ordered their sweet draught beer at the bar where, in the interest of efficiency and speed, taking the beer to the glass rather than the glass to the beer, it was poured from a tap on the end of a long and conveniently flexible hose into their twelve ounce glasses. If there were a group of them their glasses were carried to and from the bar in wire carriers, much like small milk crates, from which they were distributed around the party with no concern for which glass was last used by whom. Often, even usually, the men kept their glasses and poured their beer from large glass jugs which, again in the interests of a speedy delivery, were refilled by a barman patrolling behind the bar with a long and flexible delivery hose, his finger rarely off the trigger.

There was of course only limited room at the bar itself and most men stood with their friends around one of the tall tables arranged around the room. These specially made tall tables had a tin cup of sorts sunk into the centre of the top into which, on their arrival, one of the party would tip a splash of beer and into which they all would drop their burning cigarette ends. These ash 'trays' soon became full — men who drank beer inevitably smoked as well — while the floor, sometimes carpeted but more usually covered in linoleum, soon became wet and sticky with spilled beer.

Men took their turn to shout a round which meant leaving the party, carrying the empty glasses or jugs, elbowing one's way to the bar, gaining the barman's attention — barmaids were unheard of — getting and paying for the refills, and returning to the table with the replenished supply held high to avoid being jostled and bumped in such a way that the precious amber fluid would be spilled. This obligation to shout made its own contribution to the six o'clock swill by putting moral pressure on each member of the party to take his turn at shouting and, equally, for all the other members to consume every glass that was served. A good time was had by all until they were all thrown out at closing time. By a quarter past six the streets of Auckland were suddenly full of drunk men often needing to empty both their stomachs and their bladders as soon as they conveniently or inconveniently could.

When it came to smoking and drinking Dad did both, often to excess. Mum thought he drank too much — it was the only opinion about him which she never hid from me and Tessa — but it was a moral issue for her not a matter of manners, behaviour or even economics. Indeed, as far as I knew the cost of Dad's drinking and smoking was never questioned by Mum whose duty it was to run the entire household, including shopping for food, on what was left of Dad's pay packet after he had taken out enough for his own pleasures and expenses.

October, which had started badly for me with the compulsory visit to the murder house, ended happily with the annual visit to Saint Michael's of the fun doctor. We were given a note of his pending visit a week in advance and were required to bring along sixpence each on the day to pay for entry to his show. Only two or three classes at a time could fit into the school hall so there must have been three or four shows on the assigned day. We sat on the dusty wooden floor of the hall while the fun doctor stood at the front — there was no stage — beside the school's old upright piano and entertained us from there for an hour. He did simple magic tricks that drew gasps of amazement from kids too young to be cynical; he juggled balls and skittles and hoops, whose bright colours were faded and chipped, starting with three or four and adding more to the tumbling circle, which he skilfully kept whirling through the air in a blur of colour while making it look hard, or pretending to nearly drop something before recovering just in time, while keeping up a innocent patter of silly jokes mostly at his own expense. Nothing brought more laughter and joy to the audience than his playing the mouth organ with his nose while playing a banjo, or playing a simple and familiar air on the piano with one hand, juggling a few soft balls with the other, whirling a couple of hoops on an extended leg, and occasionally bending forward to the keyboard, still juggling his balls and whirling his hoops, and picking out a note or two with his nose. Despite the fact that the fun doctor's routine was exactly the same as it had been the year before, I enjoyed his visit immensely, gasping at the same tricks and laughing at the same silly hats and the same jokes.

The fun doctor was a tall and somewhat sad old man, with wispy grey hair that was long for the times and covered, when he wasn't performing, by a soft felt hat. He always wore an old, dusty and baggy grey suit from which he seemed to draw so much of his magical paraphernalia while larger pieces of his equipment were carried in a couple of boxes painted in bright circus-style colours that were faded and chipped. He must have had a real name but no one seemed to know it and his assumed persona — as a doctor of fun — seemed to be especially appropriate: his visit to Saint Michael's was a therapeutic tonic and I felt happy for the entire day after his visit. I thought even the sisters were amused by the old fellow and certainly gave every sign of liking him as a person as well as a clown. But who he really was, how and where he first learned and then performed his clownish music hall tricks, and how he came, so late in life, to be on an endless and gruelling circuit which must have extended well beyond the limits of the schools of Auckland, I never knew. He was, like all the best entertainers, an enigma.

November

DOWN IN ANDERSONS' PADDOCKS A HUGE BONFIRE
was being assembled by the Andersons themselves and by their
neighbours in Anderson Avenue, Winstone Street and Milton Street.
Kids collected the dead and dry branches that had fallen from the
macrocarpas and pine trees which defined the boundaries of the
Anderson property while their parents took the opportunity to get rid
of unwanted timber and old wooden furniture. Indeed almost anything
that would burn was added to the mountain of junk destined to be set
alight on Guy Fawkes' night which we kids, ignorant of the event's
history and meaning, and the role of the man after whom it was named,
called Guy *Fox* night. It was also known widely as bonfire night, the
fifth of November.

Now my mind, and the minds of all the kids I knew, turned to the
coming excitement. 'Remember, remember, the fifth of November'
went the rhyme although it was no more than a ragged remnant of a
much longer and macabre poem about the 'gunpowder treason and
plot that never should be forgot.' The poem and the plot, and the
reason for the treason, were long forgotten in New Zealand but the
name of the French man Guy Fawkes lingered as an historical excuse
for setting off fireworks.

A limited range of fireworks was available and the most and best
were sold by Wongs'. But there was no limit to where, when and to
whom fireworks could be sold and so kids young and old, but more
especially the big boys, did everything they could to raise money to buy
fireworks. A few big boys went to a lot of trouble to make a Guy, an
effigy made by stuffing a man's old suit with paper and rags, fashioning
a head of sorts and topping it with an old hat. They sat him in one of
their iron-wheeled trolleys, holding a crudely-made cardboard sign
which traditionally begged the public for 'a penny for the Guy', and
traipsed around the shopping centre seeking contributions to their
fireworks fund. Some of the big boys from Milton Street, including
Roger Machynlleth, had got together a guy. Unlike many big boys
Roger would always talk to me so I asked him how much money they
made from their after-school begging.

'Lots,' is all he said. It must have been plenty because he was able
to buy plenty of fireworks including the expensive cannons and sky

rockets which were the big boys' favourites.

Andersons' welcomed everyone in the neighbourhood to their Guy Fawkes night party and Roger's guy was destined to be burned upon their huge bonfire in accordance with tradition. But in fact big bonfires like the Andersons' were rare in suburban Auckland in the nineteen-fifties and even the tradition of the Guy was dying out. But Guy Fawkes' night itself and the letting off of fireworks were still hugely popular and there was a remarkable level of grown-up tolerance for the weeks of noise and nuisance leading up to the big night.

Even so, some enterprising, curious and foolhardy big boys, including Roger Machynlleth but more particularly his audacious friend Eddie Roberts, were notorious for the Guy Fawkes trouble they caused. They used to break open the tubular bodies of their big fireworks to extract and collect gunpowder which they packed into hollow old keys and iron pipes. Nothing and no one was safe from these inventive and intrepid boys who literally risked life and limb in the making and exploding of these home-made devices which were more like ordnance than fireworks.

Zany, naughty, clever, creative Eddie Roberts — already famous for his madcap ways — gained lifelong notoriety that year, and got his picture in the *Star*, when he seriously injured his right hand while playing with gunpowder in his father's workshop. I knew about the accident but didn't say anything to Mum or Dad but they saw it in the paper one night after tea. Mum was shocked.

'What about this boy Eddie Roberts, Johnnie Boy?' she asked me. 'It says here he lives in Milton Street.'

Even then I could hear firecrackers going off outside, on the street, and wanted to go out and watch.

'Not a family I know at all,' she continued. 'Do you know them, Fraser?'

Dad shook his head.

'No, they're not Catholics,' I said. 'Eddie Roberts is Roger's friend but he goes to college.'

'And do you play with him too?'

'Lately I have been,' I fibbed. 'If he's with Roger I do.'

Knowing that Mum wouldn't like it — that I might be coming under the influence of an obviously naughty and unruly non-Catholic big boy — made me fudge about my friendship with Eddie Roberts. In fact I avoided him whenever I could; his crazy zaniness terrified me and even Roger Machynlleth was wary of his friend's wild ways.

'Catholic boys make better friends,' said Mum. 'You know that, Johnny Boy. But what an awful thing to happen. Even to a proddy. His poor mother.'

Unconcerned by all the fuss about the influence of non-Catholic boys, and Eddie's dreadful and disfiguring accident, Dad reached across to look at the item in the paper.

'After all, Leen,' he said, 'boys will be boys. Could've just as easily been Roger. Or even our boy.'

'Really, Fraser. Don't even think it.'

Evidently Eddie Roberts's injuries were even more serious than we knew then. Roger told me later that Eddie had completely lost the thumb and first finger of his right hand. As a result he was out of circulation for weeks afterwards which was a great pity as there was so much we wanted to ask him like where did the finger and thumb go and did he keep them in a jar or something? Unfortunately, even when he was seen again, playing with the other big boys, his hand was heavily bandaged and it wasn't until school started in nineteen-fifty-five that they took off the bandages and he was able to show off his incomplete hand. It was a gruesome, shiny, three-fingered sight and I wasn't alone in wanting to touch it and have a good stare.

In the meantime Eddie's accident didn't stop Roger and the other big boys who continued to make their own fireworks which they used, in the weeks before Guy Fawkes' proper, to blow up and so destroy the letter boxes, trees, flower beds and anything else they could think of belonging to unpopular neighbours, usually grumpy old men or crotchety old women, or anyone they judged for any reason to be eccentric or unlikeable. It was a lot of fun for them but I was no more than a timid observer of these escapades, standing back, my head turned to one side and so watching from the corner of my eyes, fascinated but afraid. No doubt the big boys enjoyed showing how brave and clever they were but I had no pocket money and no way to buy fireworks of my own and so I had to wait patiently for the real night. It came at last. A Friday night, fish and chips night, November the fifth.

Like all Catholic homes — and many non-Catholic homes as well — Friday nights at forty-three were always fish and chips nights because the church forbade the eating of meat on Fridays. I didn't know why meat was forbidden on Fridays, no one ever told me perhaps because no one actually knew, but I think it was meant to be some sort of punishment or sacrifice. But it wasn't a hardship to me. I liked it because I loved fish and chips. Sometimes Mum bought fresh fish, usually snapper fillets or whole flounder, fried it in dripping in her own thin batter, and served it with Wattie's tomato sauce, her own hot chips, and slices of heavily-buttered white bread. But on this particular Friday night — Guy Fawkes' night — Dad bought cooked fish and chips from the local fish shop which was always especially busy on Friday nights. The cooked fish and chips they served, fried in animal fat, was the only food on their menu and, except for meat pies, was the only form of hot take-away food then available. Despite the growing influence of American culture, fostered by war and the war-time presence in Auckland of American troops, there was no American-style hamburgers or hot dogs available anywhere that I knew. Even Coca Cola, which was not unknown, had never been tasted by anyone I knew and I never tried it or anything like it until nineteen fifty-five when I went to Marist. If Mum bought soft drinks at all, which she did only rarely, they were always the lemonade or ginger ale of the Innes brand.

As well as selling fish it was the fishmonger, and not the butcher, who sold poultry. Even though the inside of Pellows' butcher shop was painted with amateurish-looking murals featuring fat white hens and strutting roosters, golden and red, with huge showy tails, and pheasants and quail and other game birds, even rabbits, as well as the friendly and benign-looking farmyard animals that were their stock in trade, butchers in fact never sold poultry or game of any kind. The fish shop too had murals although theirs were painted on the inside of the shop's front windows and on the internal mirrors, of which there were many, and they were more elaborate, more naturally accurate, much more sharply- and beautifully-rendered and altogether more professional looking than those painted at Pellows'. Fish, of course, was the featured creature of the fishmonger's murals but there was always a bird mural somewhere depicting beautiful, brightly-coloured cock and hen pheasants flying low over an English-looking water meadow, as well as moor grouse, tiny grassland quail, even large drakes and ducks, turkeys and geese.

Varied as were the game and poultry depicted at the fishmonger's I never saw the domestic fowl pictured in a mural even though it was in fact the only bird sold there. The word chicken as used now was never used then in connection with food; it meant only the tiny, fluffy, yellow and unfledged young, not long hatched, of the domestic hen which was raised at many homes, in chook runs, more for their eggs than their meat, by a third or more households. The fowls sold by the fishmonger were never young; indeed, most fowls were merely laying hens at the end their productive lives. Even the word fowl was rarely heard outside the shop itself; most people referred to the birds, whether hens, fowls or tough old roosters, as chooks, and their meat as chook.

'Enjoyed a delicious roast chook for Christmas dinner,' was always heard but no one ever referred to eating or enjoying chicken.

However, because frozen foods were rare, and frozen chicken unheard of, the chooks sold by the fishmonger, while almost certainly old birds, hens or roosters, were at least fresh. And if none was in stock the customer could place an order which presumably meant a death sentence for some ageing fowl happily clucking and scratching on a poultry farm somewhere on the fringes of the city. And chook meat – whether bought from the fishmonger or given by a neighbour — had a very much stronger and more gamey flavour and texture than the bland but tender chickens of today.

Chooks were raised at home by many people and the Machynlleth family was just one I knew that raised their own. Over bare earth in his back yard Mr Machynlleth had built a chook run of framed timber covered in a wire netting aptly called chicken wire. At the end of the run was the hen house, with a raised wooden floor, walls and a roof, high and low roosts, and boxes filled with hay or straw, dry grass or shredded newspaper, where the hens could seek shelter from the weather and lay their eggs. Mrs Machynlleth was responsible for the daily feeding of the birds, a chore she sometimes delegated to Roger which meant I could sometimes help. As well as the grain of some sort, which was cast on the lawn every day, the chooks also feed on kitchen food scraps.

The Machynlleths' chooks were tame and trusting — like most domestic hens — and were allowed to range free around the yard and the neighbourhood. In this way they got the fresh air and exercise which was thought to be good for their laying health as well as being able to augment their diet with whatever insects, seeds and grit they could scratch from the earth, lawns and gardens of their range. And wherever and however far they roamed they always came back to their own house well before dark, dogs permitting.

Nobody had to go inside the chook house as it was fitted with waist-high hatches over the roosts which could be raised from the outside for the comfortable collecting of fresh eggs without having to frighten the birds. Every now and then Mrs Machynlleth kept aside some fertilized eggs to provide another generation of layers while a bird which had stopped laying was culled for her meat, a slaughtering job for Mr Machynlleth. Sometimes a quick and skilful twist of the neck was all that was required but the more usual method of execution was by chopping off the head using the same small axe on the same wooden block used to cut the household kindling.

'It's good,' said Roger when he learned I'd never seen a chook execution. 'Come and watch.' Evidently Mr Machynlleth was about to kill three of his chooks.

'One's for us,' said Roger, 'one's for Father Yeates and one's for the convent. Come on.'

Perhaps I was naïve; I was familiar enough with stories of slaughtered hens running around blindly without their heads — and with the metaphorical reference to a person in a panic 'running around like a chook with his head cut off' — but when I witnessed the real thing I was horrified. The sight of that headless white hen running frantically if briefly around the edge of Machynlleths' back yard, not bumping into anything, while hot blood spurted rhythmically from the stump of its neck, staining its pure white feathers with a dark stickiness and leaving drops of thick congealing blood on the lawn and the hedge, haunted me for years. All the same I stayed to watch the other two chooks get the chop because they were black which meant the blood didn't show so much.

The horror I experienced at the executions was mixed with boyish fascination when Mr Machynlleth cut off one of the dead bird's feet and Roger showed me how, by holding the bony leg in the fingers of one hand and pulling a piece of tough sinew with the other the yellow-scaled claws would open and close mechanically in exactly the manner they had when the leg was so recently attached to its late owner. Roger let me keep the mechanical foot but when I showed it to Mum she was horrified and made me throw it away. Once the birds were truly dead they became Mrs Machynlleth's responsibility. It was her job, as the lady of the house, to pluck them and clean them ready for cooking.

Even though we didn't keep chooks occasionally one generous

neighbour or another, or a kindly uncle, would present Mum with a plucked and dressed fowl and we would enjoy the rare luxury of a tasty roast chook complete with home-made stuffing and gravy. Otherwise, whether called fowl, hen, chicken or chook, it was an expensive meat to buy and was reserved for special occasions, none more special than Christmas day. And because our Christmas dinner was eaten at Gramma and Grandad Little's the taste of roast chicken came to be permanently associated in my mind with Christmas and Gramma Little who was an especially good cook.

Evidently, though, I have strayed from my subject; Gramma Little's Christmas dinner of delicious roast chook must wait while we return to the fish shop, the retail source of chook meat and, more importantly, of our fish and chips tea on Guy Fawkes night. Our fish shop was owned and operated by the Dragesovich family, a family of what were then commonly referred to as Dallies, immigrants from the Adriatic coastal province of Dalmatia. These always-devout Catholic families — large, jolly, hard working and sweaty — were the descendants of immigrant gum-diggers, winemakers and fishermen, and while some of them owned orchards and vineyards in west Auckland, in the Henderson and Lincoln Valley countryside, many of the descendants of the fishing folk became fish retailers. The selling of fresh fish in New Zealand inevitably meant becoming a fully-fledged fish and chip shop, English-style, where, in an especially un-Mediterranean process which must have been learned only as a means of business survival, thickly-chopped potatoes and a limited choice of cheap fish fillets dipped in floury batter were deep-fried in used dripping, drained, heavily salted and wrapped in printed newspaper while still hot. The Guy Fawkes' night task of picking up the fish and chips fell to Dad because he could call into the shop after work and get them home quickly on his bike while they were still steaming hot. I much preferred these hot chips bought from the fish shop, and brought quickly home, not only because they were longer and thicker than those made by Mum but because they were limp and soggy by the time they were served having been virtually steamed in their inky newspaper wrapping. Everyone enjoyed and preferred their chips this way and the idea that chips in 'the old days' were enjoyed golden and crisp is a modern advertising fiction. The chips we liked then — in 'the old days' — were pale, limp, moist, salty and delicious and we would have had them no other way. Indeed, crisp chips were considered inedible and so were discarded without hesitation. I liked to roll my limp, soggy and salty chips in a slice of buttery bread and eat the lot from my hands, the melting butter running down my chin.

Right after work on Guy Fawkes' night, nineteen fifty-four, Dad called into Dragesovich's after work and soon arrived home with the big, hot, steaming newspaper package stuffed down his shirt. He also had an unpromising brown paper bag of assorted crackers and fireworks, two thin skyrocket sticks protruding from the top, which he bought from Wongs' at the last moment at a sale price. This confirmed what I already knew: that we would not be going to the bonfire party at Andersons but would be staying home for our own humble little Guy Fawkes celebrations.

Tessa and I ate our fish and chips and buttery bread with our fingers while we waited patiently for it to get dark. Mum and Dad showed no impatience at all. In fact they seemed barely interested in Guy Fawkes. But at last they decided it was late enough and dark enough so we went out into the gloomy back yard with our little bag of fireworks which Dad let off without fuss or ceremony, allowing me to hold only the sparklers, which I thought were silly and girlish, and light only the occasional tiny Tom Thumb cracker — I preferred the bigger double happies, which the big boys let off by the string lot, and the even bigger cannons — or an unimpressive pretty display. Meanwhile Mum sat watching from a safe distance with Tessa beside her, wrapped in a warm rug.

So, after weeks of anticipation, seeing fireworks for sale everywhere, and watching the big boys letting off their double happies and cannons as well as their own creations, bonfire night in our back yard, with a mother and father who clearly lacked enthusiasm for the occasion, was an awful let down to me and I went to bed feeling inexplicably sad.

Even though Guy Fawkes night was over for me I was still able to share in the fun of other people. Once alone in my room I kneeled on my bed, which stood against the window, pushed the window wide open, let up the blind, and rested my elbows on the window sill. For as long as I could stay awake I watched the red and pulsing glow in the western sky that I knew was the Andersons' bonfire and listened to our nearer neighbours in Winstone Street, Milton Street, Studio Street and beyond, having fun, shouting and laughing. I heard the hissing and whizzing, crackling and banging of their fireworks, and saw the waxing and waning of red and yellow and blue and green colours that glowed now here and then there in the smoky air. And I looked up and tracked the fiery progress of skyrockets whooshing high into the black sky.

Lamenting our pathetic little back yard show of the night before I spent the next morning, Saturday, wandering around the neighbourhood collecting the blackened, spent and now useless bodies of the biggest skyrockets, with their wooden pointed heads and their long thick sticks, that were far more impressive than anything Dad had bought, wondering why he and Mum had been so indifferent to the whole idea of Guy Fawkes. And I realised then that, even though I and all the kids I knew were excited about it from the very October day when the vast and obvious displays of fireworks appeared in the shops, neither Guy Fawkes the person nor the event was ever referred to or discussed at forty-three or at school, that year or any year. At first I thought that Mum and Dad's indifference was due to a shortage of money or a reluctance to waste money.

'An awful waste,' said Mum, even as Dad was lighting a Roman Candle or a Mount Vesuvius. 'I hate seeing good money go up in smoke.'

Maybe parsimony was the reason for Mum and Dad's lack of interest in the celebration of Guy Fawkes night although I later learned that the real Guy Fawkes was a Catholic who was caught trying to blow up the protestant English King and his parliament with gunpowder. Evidently he committed suicide before he could be disembowelled alive which was his sentence. Protestant England clearly had more reason to celebrate the death of Guy Fawkes than had the members of the Catholic church in faraway New Zealand, including my mother and father.

Soon after Guy Fawkes the excitement of that night was overshadowed by something much more dramatic, the most remarkable event of my entire Marian year. By this time, towards the end of the year, and for a reason I didn't know, Dad had gotten into the Saturday habit of taking us for a long drive in Grandad Little's big Chevrolet, not returning home until late in the afternoon. I never enjoyed those drives — there was always so much I wanted to do at home — but Dad insisted. Mum seemed to enjoy the outings — no doubt they were a welcome and cost-free change from routine —

although I sensed a growing tension about them not only between Mum and Dad but between Mum and Grandad Little. It wasn't just the usual difference of religious opinion, or Mum's simmering resentment of Grandad Little's generosity, but something else: something about leaving Grandad Little alone in our house while we went for a drive in his big Chevrolet. I didn't get it at all. And then late one Saturday afternoon in the middle of November we arrived home from such an outing to find a policeman standing at our open front door.

'Run, Fraser,' said Mum to Dad, getting quickly out of the big Chevrolet. 'Something's must have happened to your father.'

Up the path we all ran, and up the porch steps, but the policeman stopped us from going any farther.

'Oh, I'd keep the kiddies back if I were you, Mrs Little,' he said. It was Mr Thomsette, the local policeman whom Mum and Dad knew well.

'Fraser?' Mum didn't understand.

'You better go in, Fraser,' said Mr Thomsette. 'Detective branch done that.' He was nodding at our smashed in front door.

The door's lead-light window had been smashed in and there was broken coloured glass and bent strips of lead on and around the step but more particularly inside on the carpet of the wide foyer.

'Righto. Mind out, Leen,' said Dad urgently, pushing Mum, me and Tessa back with his arms, rudely I thought, behind Mr Thomsette.

I saw then what Dad must have seen: a grim-looking Grandad Little, his head bowed, walking slowly up the hall, towards us, with another policeman and a man in a suit and hat who must have been a detective.

'Hell's bells, Dad,' said Dad.

'Turn away, you two,' said Mum. 'Don't look.'

Nothing or nobody could have made me *not* look at that moment. Grandad Little was obviously under arrest. He looked up, embarrassed, when he saw me. I'd never seen him look like that before. He didn't say anything but he smiled weakly and winked and rubbed my head as he went past and I wondered why he wasn't handcuffed. He didn't say anything to Mum and Dad either but was led away by the policeman and the detective to a black Humber Super Snipe which was parked in front of his own big Chevrolet.

'Oh, holy mother of god,' said Mum, crossing herself. 'Don't you kids ever say anything about this. Ever. To anyone. Understand?'

Tessa and I nodded dumbly but we knew instinctively that there were some family things that were never discussed with other people and this was obviously one of those things. Mum was crying a bit as she took Tessa and me inside. We had to tip-toe over all the broken glass which made a horrible crunchy, squeaky noise when we walked on it. Dad stayed on the porch talking to Mr Thomsette.

Luckily I had an idea of what had happened which was just as well because Tessa and I received no explanations. I tried to explain it to Tessa when Mum left us in the breakfast room to go back to the front door to clean up the broken glass. I knew, because Dad had told me before, that Grandad Little *used* to be a bookmaker. At first I took that to mean that he used to make books for his job but Dad explained that he used to be a bookmaker, not a bookbinder, and that as a bookmaker he was involved in running illegal gambling on horse racing. But now, obviously, as I explained to little Tessa, who listened wide-eyed and frightened to her clever and knowledgeable big brother, there was no 'used to be' about it. He was breaking the law and had been arrested and although Tessa said she understood I'm not sure even now that she did.

On that cool, cloudy, still, quiet and melancholy Saturday spring afternoon in November, while we were at Cornwall Park to see the lambs, Grandad Little had been caught in the act of taking bets on the phone at our house with his books open on the table. Evidently he had already been caught in this way at his own home in Sandringham — his telephone had been tapped by the police — and so on recent busy Saturdays he had come to our house to use our phone, which he was paying for anyway, and in return gave Dad the use of the big Chevrolet as a way of getting us all out of the house. Dad must have known what was going on but did Mum? Did Dad tell her? I don't know but I don't think so. I'm sure if Dad had told Mum she would never have agreed. But surely she must have suspected something. Perhaps she did. But perhaps she was too naïve to know or understand about bookmaking. Perhaps the chance of a family outing was too hard to resist. Or perhaps she felt somewhat indebted to Grandad Little for helping her and Dad to get their own nice house, so they didn't have to live in the states, and for the washing machine and the fridge and all the other things he bought for us and for all the money he spent to make life easier for her and us. In fact I didn't really know what she thought or knew.

But I did know that she resented Grandad Little's generosity as much as she appreciated it and, probably instinctively, suspected his motives. Whatever she knew or thought or felt beforehand, whether she protested to Dad or not, Mum was ashamed and humiliated by the whole affair.

'Please,' she almost begged Tessa and me, again and again. 'Please don't you ever, *ever*, talk about this to anyone.'

It seems that, more than anything else, Mum was ashamed that the front door of our house had been smashed in so obviously and loudly and that Grandad Little had been taken away by the police in broad daylight for everyone in the street to see.

'Leen,' I heard Dad say just once. 'I'm just so sorry,'

'I'm just so ashamed,' said Mum.

How did my mother, so innocent and law abiding, cope with such shame? For her — she, who went to confession every Saturday, mass every Sunday and holy day of obligation, who took communion at every mass, who said the rosary every day, who was kind and charitable, who worried about what people thought of her and her family, and whose ingenuous mind did not easily accommodate the unpleasant realities of life — that event on that Saturday afternoon in that November of that holy Marian year of nineteen fifty-four was a complete disgrace that brought shame on her and her innocent family; she believed it was a scandal that would never be forgotten and which she would never live down.

Perhaps she would have once been right to worry but in the nineteen-fifties illegal bookmaking was remarkably common and the arrest of another harmless old bookie was merely routine to the police and was hardly noticed by our Winstone Street neighbours. Bookies like Grandad Little existed only because there was still a demand for their services. In nineteen-forty-six — only eight years earlier, when Grandad Little would have been at the peak of his bookmaking career — the New Zealand police estimated that there were seven-hundred-and-sixty-three bookmakers in New Zealand handling, between them, twenty-four million pounds a year which was not only a vast amount of money then but, significantly, was four million pounds more than had passed through the legal government-owned on-course totalisators. It also meant that in nineteen-forty-six bookies, including

Grandad Little, were handling an average of more than thirty-one thousand pounds a year. Even if Grandad Little had netted only ten per cent of that a year — say three thousand pounds — he would have been making ten times the average New Zealand wage of just over three hundred pounds a year. No wonder he had a nice big Chevrolet and could so easily afford to help Mum and Dad with expensive gifts.

That my mother was naïve in such matters is an understatement. Her simple, innocent and trusting view of the world and its people was the direct result of her upbringing by an simple, untutored and superstitious widow in a houseful of ingenuous girls. With no experience of the healthy cynicism and curiosity that drives all boys and men to question everything and everyone, to take nothing at face value, and to test and stretch the rules whatever they may be, she — and her sisters for that matter — entered adulthood, marriage and motherhood full of romantic ideals but ill-equipped for the harsh realities of those stations. She was born in a poverty-stricken neighbourhood of nineteenth century terrace houses across the river Clyde from Glasgow. It was dirty, derelict and poor, a Dickensian example of the worst sort of Victorian working class slum. But the ship-building folk who lived there then didn't see themselves as slum-dwellers nor as particularly poor. They accepted their lot — as tiny cogs in the great gear wheel of industrial Britain — without question or complaint, only vaguely aware that people in other parts of the kingdom and empire lived better, ate better and dressed better. Without cinema, television or radio, and with only a rudimentary education, they led narrow lives with bare experience of the outside world and even less curiosity. They lived in ignorance as generations of working class Britons had lived before them, in the same villages and towns and cities, in the same hovels, cottages and tenements, working in the same mills and mines and shipyards, with rarely a thought to what happened beyond the end of their cobbled street, across the canal or beyond the river mouth. They were able to read and write sufficient only to their needs, and to add up to the last farthing the cost of their weekly rent and food, and, for the men, a few pence for baccy and a pint of ale, and to deduct the total from their wages to see how much, a few pence, could be put away for a rainy day. What curiosity had existed in the generation before Mum's, when millions of undernourished and unfit young British men dashed off to war, seeking free travel and adventure on the European continent — a place as remote and mysterious to them as the moon is to us — had been cruelly extinguished in the mud and blood of the western front, at Somme, Passchendaele and Ypres. Those who didn't perish in that war returned in broken health, enfeebled by poisonous gas, lacking limbs, deafened by ordnance, their minds deranged by what they had seen, convinced by personal experience that the mean cobbled streets of home, the comfort of family and friends, the warmth of their pub, a smoke and a drink, were infinitely more desirable than the swashbuckling adventures of a foreign war.

Right into the heart of this post-war misery of Greenock my mother was born. She survived, although two baby brothers didn't, and five years later she and three of her sisters were brought to New Zealand by their parents — the other two sisters, Kathleen and Irene, were born later, in New Zealand — on a New Zealand-government-assisted immigration scheme that cost poor Britons nothing but a few pounds. What induced her parents, my Grandad and Gramma Fahey, to leave Scotland I shall never know but they set off blindly for a land about which they knew next to nothing and from which they would never be able to afford to return, while New Zealand made promises about conditions, housing and employment which it was unable to keep. The experience of Grandad Fahey was probably typical. He was a tradesman shipbuilder, a skilled riveter, for Harland & Wolff, a vast and famous shipyard on the Clyde. He had worked on the *Titanic,* which the company had built at its works in Belfast, and had put his name to two of that doomed ship's lifeboats. But there were no steel ships being built in New Zealand, probably none were being built in the southern hemisphere, so he came to a new country where he was unable to work at his trade. As a result, and as a typical British tradesman of the time, trained in only a narrow discipline and lacking the education, experience and initiative to adapt to new ideas and circumstances, he was unemployed, underemployed or wrongly employed for most of his short life in New Zealand, never finding the prosperity and security he was seeking for himself and his family. What he thought of being so misled, and of the poverty and circumstances in which he found himself, at the other end of the world, with never a chance to return to his homeland, must remain a mystery as he died well before I was born. By then the country, and the Fahey's of Mount Roskill, were in the grip of The Slump; Grandad Fahey died suddenly, without warning, dropping dead in the back yard of the same Mount

Roskill house, a rental house provided to immigrants by the government, that Gramma Fahey lived in until the day she died many years later. At the time of her father's death Mum was just fifteen and had been working as a domestic servant for a wealthy family in Epsom since she was twelve years old, then the earliest possible school-leaving age. In the years that followed Gramma Fahey sanctified her husband's memory much as the maudlin widow Queen Victoria sanctified the memory of her Prince Albert. As a result she, Gramma Fahey, imposed on her young daughters an unrealistic and idealised view of their father as saint-like and perfect. Her daughters, young and impressionable, received and readily accepted their mother's image of their father as the ideal man, so perfect, so above reproach in all things, including morals. They never saw him, through grown-up eyes, grow old and make mistakes, and fail in ordinary things, being only a man, surely no better or worse than any other. Could any young man, seeking to marry one of his gentle, genteel but somewhat immature daughters, ever have matched the saintly qualities of her late father? Certainly not my father.

Even as a boy Dad was thought to be clever and cunning, charming and deceitful. But he had learned it all the hard way. Growing up in the nineteen-twenties he was taunted and teased by other kids for being a tar baby, 'touched by the tar brush' as they used to so crudely say. That was before the second great Maori migration, from the country to the city, and well before the even greater migration to Auckland from the Pacific Islands. So dark-skinned children like the young Fraser Nassau Little were considered different and unusual, especially in Auckland's then conservative working-class neighbourhoods of Mount Roskill, Sandringham and Balmoral. And children, even more then than now, were merciless in their treatment of those who were somehow different. During his primary school years, beginning in nineteen twenty-four, Gramma Little moved him from this school to that — Brixton Road, Mount Eden, Newton Central, Saint Benedict's — to protect him from racially-based bullying. 'Tell them your father is Spanish,' she said, worried and protective. He did, but it made no difference. And it wasn't until he was a grown-up, perhaps after spending so much time in the Pacific Islands, that Dad acquired pride in his brownness, the history of the Ngapuhi, and the heritage he had received from his father's mother and was to bequeath to his grateful children.

But in her motherly wish to protect her son from bullies and teasers

Gramma Little succeeded only in shielding him from the real world, reinforcing his already well-developed idea of his own importance, and inevitably damaging his education in the process. With abundant intelligence but a less-than-perfect schooling, and a family life that was far from normal, based as it was on the fringes of crime, the young Fraser Little discovered and developed his own boyish cunning and charm. A girl cousin, writing later of their childhood together, referred to him as a handsome little fellow with courtly manners and eyes like blue stars. She believed he had been 'born old, demonic and sophisticated', that he understood grown-ups better than most children, and could manipulate them and situations to suit his own purposes. This, then, was my father: sophisticated and manipulative, even as a boy. And as a man, a husband and father with many responsibilities, not much money, and a flexible moral code, he was easily seduced by the prospect of easy money, and the use of a big Chevrolet, into allowing Grandad Little to turn our home into a bookmaker's parlour.

Of how Dad managed the whole affair with Mum I had and have no idea. I assume he was contrite. I assume he apologised. They may have had rows about it, I'm sure they did, but I heard nothing in the way of arguments and little by way of apologies or explanations. And what happened to Grandad Little? Did he go to prison? Or pay a fine? I don't know, didn't ask and was never told. Mum got over the shame of it all when she discovered that none of the neighbours seemed to have noticed anything strange that Saturday afternoon in November, and if they did — how could they have not heard the shouting of policemen and the smashing in of the leadlight door? — they didn't mention it to her or Dad. Nothing was said by Fat Pat or her church friends and although there was a small line in *Truth* Mum didn't know and nobody we knew openly read that newspaper anyway. She was plainly angry with Grandad Little but that softened later when he — happily in time for Christmas — apologised to her, renounced his wicked ways, and returned to the church, confessing everything to his priest and becoming an active, practising Catholic again, so repairing relations between them. I was glad because I loved Gramma and Grandad Little almost as much as I loved Mum.

Regrettably, though, there was one thing that Grandad Little couldn't fix. The thing that affected Mum the most and which she found the hardest to accept — and forgive — despite the now repaired and downright cordial relations between her and Grandad. Now, in accordance with the law on these matters, the Post Office disconnected our phone, condemning Mum to using the phone box at the end of the Winstone Street and cutting her off for the next ten years from the easy and immediate communication with her mother and sisters. It was her punishment for a sin she didn't even commit.

December

AT SCHOOL THE OBLIGATORY END-OF-YEAR TESTS
were sat at the beginning of December but they weren't taken
particularly seriously by us, the sisters or our parents. Reports were
prepared based somewhat on the tests but more likely on Sister's
insights supported by her year-long experience of the innocent
subjects of her judgement; they were always mild in both their praise
and criticism and most parents took little notice of them.

But Mum did. She studied my report carefully although Dad merely
glanced at the grades and dismissed the standard, non-committal and
sometimes saccharine comments of a sister for whom he had a
scarcely-concealed contempt. But I didn't need my report to tell me
what I already knew: that I was naturally good at spelling, reading,
comprehension and composition, quite good at nature studies and art,
but that I had no aptitude whatsoever for arithmetic. Above all I knew
in my heart that which could not be marked or reported: I didn't like
school at all.

Once the tests were over the last week of the school year passed
slowly because there was nothing left to do. And so, under Sister's
supervision, we spent most of those days tidying up the classroom and
making it ready for nineteen-fifty-five. Paintings and posters were
taken down from the walls, nature study projects disposed of,
blackboards washed, and all the dusters taken out to the field to have
all the chalk dust beaten out of them. Windows were cleaned from the
inside, and the chairs and desks were pushed noisily to one side so that
half the floor at a time could be swept cleaner than it had been swept
all year, and then polished by teams of boys and girls with rags tied to
their feet, hands and knees, who managed to turn a chore into a game
as children can and do. The small assembly hall came next for the
standard fours with the same effort of spring cleaning — sweeping and
washing and polishing — supervised by two aproned sisters with their
sleeves rolled up.

When I told Dad what we were doing at school he didn't like it.

'They make the kids do what they have six weeks to do, Leen,' he
said over his shoulder to Mum in the kitchen. 'They should be teaching
them up till the last day. That's their job isn't it?'

'Fraser,' said Mum from the kitchen. 'Shush.'

'Well, what've they got to do for six weeks? Go sunbathing at the bloody beach? I don't think so.'

We were sitting in the breakfast room after tea. It was hot and humid. Dad had taken off his shirt. Mum was doing the dishes in the kitchen.

'Fraser,' called Mum, sounding exasperated. 'Don't worry about things so much. I'm sure the sisters are busy all holidays getting ready for next year.'

'You can thank your lucky stars you're leaving there, boy,' said Dad. 'Men next year. Be a different story then I bet.'

Dad sounded uncharacteristically interested in my schooling.

'Marist. Those brothers'll make you work. Not like those lazy nuns.'

'Fraser!' said Mum from the kitchen. She was obviously annoyed.

'He'll be better off being taught by men, Leen,' Dad shouted back. 'They'll toughen you up, boy. You see.'

'Don't frighten him,' said Mum. She came into the breakfast room drying her hands on her apron. 'It'll be all right at Marist, Johnny Boy,' she said to me. 'Don't worry about it, son.'

At last my last day at Saint Michael's came although it wasn't a day but a half-day. And when the bell went at noon for home time, and we had finished saying the angelus, crossing ourselves quickly and impatiently for the last time that year, the high-pitched noise we made together, bursting out of our classrooms and swarming across the hot playgrounds to the gate, was one of uninhibited childish joy. Yet even at its strident loudest our combined squealing and shouting did nothing to properly express our inexpressible and overwhelming happiness knowing we were free from the prison of school for the approaching Christmas and summer holiday. A wonderful long holiday which would last, uninterrupted, until the new school year began at the beginning of February. And that was more than six weeks away.

The first week of the holidays turned out to be an anti-climax; it didn't seem like holidays at all. Dad had to go to work as usual and Mum was preoccupied with Christmas preparations. There were Christmas cards to write and post, gifts to be bought and wrapped, food to be prepared, and plans to be made for the big day. Dad brought home a Christmas tree although I was disappointed that it wasn't a proper Christmas tree, so perfectly symmetrically triangular, of the type I saw at the pictures or on Christmas cards, but just the top cut off an ordinary old pine tree from Andersons' paddocks. And I hated how Dad just stood it — the alleged tree — in a tin bucket which he made no attempt to disguise.

'It doesn't look right to me,' I said.

'Whaddaya talking about, boy. It looks beaut, doesn't it, Tess?'

And Tessa agreed. Of course.

Mum was in charge of the decorations and although she encouraged me and Tessa to join in decorating the tree and the breakfast room I was disappointed that our tree, its decorations, and the streamers around the room, all looked drab, inadequate and unimaginative — that there was too much cheap crepe paper, faded and stained, and tired-looking tinsel and no lights — and I didn't understand why. And worst of all Mum brought out a shoe box from the press containing all the cast and components of a nativity scene which she had collected and added to over the years. The stable, assembled from thick cardboard printed to look like planks of wood with patches of snow on the gabled roof, was set out on a little table in the breakfast room, beside Our Lady's shrine, and arranged with hollow plastic models of Mary and Joseph, a tiny pink and plastic Baby Jesus lying semi-naked in a plastic manger, men in strange robes standing around looking wise, holy and eastern, all surrounded by model donkeys and cows and sheep. There were cardboard cut-out angels, tall and elegant and winged, glued to the roof, together with one or two ugly and tubby cherubs as well as a childish representation of a faded shooting star with a curved rainbow of a tail sprinkled with glitter. Tessa helped Mum enthusiastically, spreading cotton wool about the front of the stable to represent snow, and dry sand on the interior floor, and constantly adjusting the position of the people in the tableau. But I despised the whole thing not because of its religiosity but because all the elements were clearly out of proportion with each other which offended my sense of taste and style but of which my devout and undiscerning mother and sister seemed unaware.

'It doesn't matter, dear,' said Mum patiently when I pointed out that the cow was too big or the wise men too small. Meanwhile Dad was indifferent to the whole business quietly thinking it silly and childish.

Despite my disapproval and disappointments, despite wishing that our Christmas tree were a better shape, that it had blinking lights, and that it and our house were decorated more lavishly, and even having a vague wish there could be snow, I couldn't help being carried along by the general jolliness and infectious enthusiasm for Christmas which were abroad in December. All the shopkeepers decorated the inside of their shops with tinsel and Christmas bunting and had a colourful if somewhat standard Christmas message painted on their windows in green and red topped off with white to represent snow. *A Merry Christmas and a Happy New Year* was the basic idea with some adding *...to all our valued customers* or another important commercial sentiment such as *Order your Christmas ham now!,* and decorated, according to the size of their window and their budget, with portraits of a fat and jolly red-suited Santa Claus, a sleigh being pulled lightly and speedily through a starry space by reindeers, golden Christmas bells and red bows and green holly and snowy borders. There were other designs and messages including some with a biblical flavour of a decorative star with elongated points and a silhouette of the three kings on tall, long-legged camels with the message *Peace on earth and goodwill to all men.* That verse always annoyed Mum who insisted it should say: *Peace on earth to men of goodwill.*

'There is an important difference, Johnny Boy,' she said indignantly. 'And don't you forget it.'

And I never have.

Early December brought the big and famous Farmers' Christmas parade down Queen Street and up Hobson Street, with large and lavishly decorated floats, and marching bands and marching girls, with Santa Claus, seated on a grand throne, and surrounded by fairies and elves, on the last, largest and grandest float of all. But I had to be satisfied with the much more modest parade through the shopping centre, sponsored by the businessmen's association, held on a Friday night, early in the month, when the shops were open late. Many of the shops had a simple float but it was the sports teams which provided the most colour and interest. There was a blue-suited silver band in the parade, and later, standing in a circle in the shopping centre, to play Christmas carols, and I enjoyed standing with Mum in the balmy warmth of that early-summer evening, watching and listening as they played all the old favourites about snow and ice and snowmen and silent nights. And then, in the week immediately before Christmas, the Salvation Army band, sitting on forms on the back of a truck, drove up Winstone Street, stopping every fifty metres or so, under a street light if it was dark, to play their Christmas carols while other uniformed members of the church called into each house to collect donations which were always given cheerfully, willingly and generously, even at forty-three.

'Here come the Sallies again,' said Mum brightly when she first heard the lovely evocative Christmas music coming across from Milton Street and so joined in the refrain of *Hark! The Herald Angels Sing; Silent Night; Good King Wenceslas; Oh Come, All Ye Faithful*, or another of the old and familiar tunes she had known since her own childhood. And as she willingly fetched a sixpence or two from her purse, ready for the collection, Tessa and I dashed out into the twilight to wait for the Sallies to arrive. Then we stood beside the truck to watch and listen, and even to follow the truck to its next stop, until it got dark and we were compelled to go home.

And then at last it was Christmas Eve. A Friday night. Mum and Dad were busy wrapping last-minute gifts and getting ready for Christmas day but they interrupted their work to help Tessa and me set out a plate of Christmas cake and a glass of horrible-smelling whisky on the shiny brick breakfast room hearth for Santa. I knew that Santa Claus didn't really come down the chimney and that it wasn't he who drank the whisky and ate the cake, purposely leaving so many crumbs on the plate, '…because he's always in such a hurry,' said Mum, but I maintained the fiction for Tessa's sake.

Instead of hanging out stockings for Santa Claus Mum helped us fix a pair of Dad's long grey woollen socks to the mantelpiece with a drawing pin. In fact the hanging of stockings was another Christmas mystery which annoyed my tidy mind. As far as I was concerned stockings were those long nylon things which Mum and other women wore. Why, I wondered, should they be hanging out such filmy, flimsy and transparent things at all. No wonder, I thought, Mum preferred to use Dad's socks. Only later I learned that the word stockings was once used to describe the long woollen socks worn by men, women and children in cold climates. Not for the first time I wondered why grown-ups in New Zealand persisted in using a word that was obviously foreign and obsolete and, if they did, why didn't they explain it to kids.

But the hanging of the stockings — Dad's socks — was only a tradition. We knew that the real Christmas present would be found in the pillow cases Mum gave us. I laid mine, empty and limp, across the end of my bed on Christmas eve. I knew that in the morning it would contain something more than the trifles I would find in Dad's sock. I also knew it would be Dad not Santa Claus who would fill the pillow case some time during the night, when '…all through the house, not a creature was stirring, not even a mouse', but although I tried to stay awake to catch him in the act I was soon overcome by sleep.

What I wanted for Christmas, more than anything else in the world, was a new bicycle and for weeks before Christmas I thought, believed, that if I wished hard enough for one — closing my eyes unnaturally tight and thinking about a bike intensely every night before going to sleep, when I should have been saying my prayers — I would find it waiting for me, standing at the end of my bed, on Christmas morning.

My dream of bicycle owning was fuelled by the secret visits I paid to Mr Ineson's bike shop, before and after school, where I loved to breathe in the dirty, earthy smell of oil and grease. An aisle ran up the centre of the long narrow shop to the counter beyond which was a dark and dusty dirt-floor workshop littered with broken bikes, frames, greasy chains, and tools, with tyres and tubes, some patched, hanging randomly on nails and hooks. There was a workshop bench against one side wall, lit by the natural light which fell through a barred and dirty window, which was cluttered with Mr Ineson's tools. I longed to go behind the counter and explore that workshop but I had to be satisfied with what I could see peering over and around the counter.

'Yes, son?'

The greasy Mr Ineson, in his woolly hat, greasy khaki overalls and heavy greasy boots, was busy at the bench in his workshop. He wore rimless glasses and he looked back and over them at me, at the counter in the shop, reluctant to leave his work for a young boy whom he guessed, correctly, was only looking.

'I just want to look at the boys' bikes,' I said timidly.

'Look away, son,' he said.

'Can I try the brakes?'

'Do whatever you like, son, as long as you don't knock 'em over.'

And so I had permission to linger there, in the wonderful showroom of bikes. And from then on, whenever I visited his shop, Mr Ineson merely looked up briefly from his work and silently nodded his permission for me to inspect his stock at leisure.

To the left and right of the central aisle stood hundreds — at least it seemed to me that there were hundreds — of brand new brightly-painted shiny bicycles leaning on their stands in orderly rows. I ignored those bikes standing on the right of the shop as they were of the step-through style for girls, with chain guards, netting over the back wheel to protect dresses and skirts, and a wicker basket on the front fixed to the handlebars. Such bicycles, without a bar, with girlish safeguards and a wicker basket, deserved and received only contempt from me and all boys. I looked only at those bikes on the left side of the shop, the boys' side, walking slowly up and down the rows, trying the hand grips, testing the brakes and gears and admiring the mirror-like chrome and bright paintwork.

My only experience of the two-wheeled marvel was the old, black and heavy pre-war model that Dad rode to work. Unlike Dad's bicycle, big and heavy with large wheels and thick tyres, Mr Ineson's new English bikes — everything then was 'Made in England' — from Phillips and Raleigh, Rudge, Humber and Royal Enfield, for men and women, boys and girls, looked light and slim, sprightly and streamlined. And instead of being a dull black they were painted brightly in red and blue and green and yellow and gold, with chromium handlebars and embellishments, white rubber hand-grips especially moulded to fit the fingers, white mud-guards, front and rear hand brakes that were vastly more effective that the old-fashioned foot brakes, and saddles padded with foam. The lucky buyer could also choose from a range of wonderful accessories such as retractable stands, white-walled tyres, flared mud flaps, electric dynamos that powered streamlined and adjustable headlights and tail lights, battery-powered horns instead of old-fashioned bells, three- and sometimes four-speed Sturmey-Archer gears built into the hub and changed using a small lever on the handle bars, spring-loaded carriers that doubled as a pillion seat, and saddle bags to match the saddle.

Most cyclists repaired their own punctures then, and managed their own running repairs, so new bicycles came with a small leather bag hung from the back of the saddle containing a few basic tools and a puncture repair outfit in its own hinged tin.

Dad had his own tyre levers and puncture outfit but they weren't in a special tin and anyway I wasn't allowed to touch anything to do with his bike. He always said his bike was his work transport and he couldn't afford to have anything go wrong with it. Roger Machynlleth had a new Phillips with a complete puncture repair kit in a special tin which he stored in his saddle bag. Sometimes he let me help him mend a puncture on his bike so I knew that the little tin that came with every one of Mr Ineson's new bikes contained everything necessary to repair a puncture: a tube of strong-smelling rubber cement, a selection of rubber patches pre-cut to various sizes, a piece of shiny tin pierced with numerous holes — much like a kitchen grater — to roughen the rubber inner-tube around the puncture hole and so provide a better gripping surface for the glue, and a piece of fine chalk, like tailor's chalk, to rub over and so neutralise the sticky residue of glue so it wouldn't stick the tube to the inside of the tyre. Roger even showed me how to find a puncture by removing the tube, pumping it up and submersing it in a bucket of water; a rising stream of bubbles would quickly give away the site of the puncture hole.

A pump was standard equipment held on the bike's frame between two small and round arrow-heads fixed to the frame and facing each other at a distance just slightly less that the length of the pump at rest. A flexible and fabric-covered rubber tube, used to carry air from the pump to the inner tube, was housed in the pump's hollow handle. This tube was withdrawn when needed, screwed into the business end of the pump while other end was screwed around the protruding valve of the tube.

Ownership of one of Mr Ineson's new, brightly coloured and streamlined bicycles, with front and rear hand brakes, three-speed gears, an electric dynamo and lamps, and a stand, was all I dreamed of in those weeks before Christmas. It was, I suppose, a form of positive thinking although I had never heard that term and doubt that even the concept existed then. Or perhaps it was a form of praying. Whichever it was, it didn't work.

Tessa and I woke early on Christmas morning, full of excitement, forcing Mum and Dad to wake up, get up and join in. There was no time for washing or dressing, or for the brushing of hair or teeth, no time for breakfast. There was nothing to be done but open our presents.

Of course there was no bicycle waiting for me at the end of my bed. I was only briefly disappointed knowing in my heart that such an expense was beyond Mum and Dad and that anyway if a new bicycle could have been afforded it would have been bought for Dad not me. And I learned, or perhaps I already knew, that wishing is a waste of time. And so the fanciful and unrealistic dream of a new bicycle was quickly dismissed as I eyed the pillow case which now bulged with what was obviously a large box.

It was a wonderful gift, never to be forgotten, called a Magic Robot. The large, flat, rectangular box contained a number of sheets of paper, each printed on one half with questions set out in a circle and the other half set out similarly with answers. Each sheet contained questions of a certain category, drawn from science, nature and history, of the sort that would interest boys. But the real interest lay not in the rather routine questions and answers but in the robot's apparent cleverness. This eerily-green metallic-looking and slightly luminous figure, reminiscent in its modelling of the well-known movie Oscar, was five or six centimetres tall standing on a weighted and slightly convex base. He held a golden metal wand in his right hand that pointed down to the paper surface, at an angle of forty-five degrees, to the questions and answers. I liked the way you pressed the robot into place in its housing the centre of the questions circle, being sure to engage the little cog in the robot's rotating base with the matching notch in the housing, and turned the robot in the housing so that the wand pointed directly to the question I or anyone wanted to ask. Having established the question you then lifted the robot from its housing and stood it on the round mirror which was set in the centre of the answers circle. The little green robot man would then spin around until, moving this way and that, wavering over an answer as if slightly uncertain, until it stopped, its mind made up, so that the wand was pointed directly to an answer. And the answer it chose was always, magically, correct. A magic robot indeed.

Although I was immediately enchanted by my Magic Robot it didn't take long to figure out how it worked based on my experience with my magnet: that a magnet concealed in the base of the robot was always attracted to a magnet concealed in a fixed position under the mirror in the middle of the answers circle, that the answer to any question was always in the same relative place in the question circle, and that the turning of the robot and its wand to a question was incidental to the constant position of the robot's concealed magnet permanently positioned relative to the notch in the housing. Once I understood the principle I was able to predict the answer to any question with an infallibility that baffled my friends and angered Tessa who could and never would understand how her big brother could be so terribly clever.

But that was later. Meanwhile the pillow case also held a new, large, brown and stiff leather schoolbag which itself contained some other small but unwelcome reminders of school in the form of a wooden pencil case, a rainbow pencil with a rubber on the end, a plastic pencil sharpener and a new two-ended rubber one end of which was dark and hard and suitable for rubbing out mistakes in ink. The ink rubber reminded me not only of school but that I would soon have to go to a new school and face new teachers, male teachers, and new challenges including writing with real ink. They were unpleasant thoughts and reminders that were not welcome on Christmas morning and so I dismissed them all immediately.

Meanwhile, having unwrapped our 'big' present Tessa and I ran to the breakfast room to discover the small, inexpensive treats we knew Dad's socks would contain. In mine I found a box of crayons, a small clockwork car, a small bar of Cadbury dairy milk chocolate and an orange both of which I put aside to eat for breakfast when we got home from mass.

By now it was nearly half-past-six. Knowing that we would soon have to set off for mass — Christmas day being another holy day of obligation — we rushed out into the hot summery morning to find a sunny Winstone Street full of joyous kids (and their long shadows), many of them, like us, in their pyjamas or nighties, trying out their new tricycles, bicycles, scooters, roller skates or trolleys, being watched by bleary-eyed, tousled-haired but patient parents in dressing gowns, standing at their gate, or on their front porch, happy to see the playthings they had chosen so carefully, and paid for so dearly, being appreciated so obviously by their kids, and lending as much encouragement as they could manage so early in the morning.

Before long we had to return inside and get ready for the rest of the day. And what a day it would be. Christmas day was one of the most important family events of the year and so, to start it properly, Mum made sure that we were as smartly turned out as possible for mass. Unfortunately it was a Saturday which meant, I knew, that I would have to attend mass the next day, Sunday, as well. Mum and Dad wore their newest and best clothes on this most important day. And as every family did the same the procession of families arriving and leaving church on that hot Christmas morning had the appearance of a family fashion parade, a ritualised pageant with not a little of both pride and envy.

To even the most devout Catholic going to mass on Christmas morning was a bit of nuisance as it delayed the launching of what was the busiest and most important family day of the year. There was, after all, so much to do: whether the family was staying home or going somewhere else for Christmas dinner, there was so much food to be prepared. And yet going to holy communion on Christmas morning meant fasting from midnight on Christmas eve and that meant breakfast had to be delayed until after mass, not easy for anyone but especially hard for Tessa and me who knew we had a chocolate treat waiting for us at home. And then getting especially dressed-up for mass meant everyone had to get undressed, as it were, changing into clothes that were more suitable for the hot day ahead, for the orgy of eating which was the promise of Christmas day, and, for Tessa and me, for the rough and tumble of games we would play when we got together with our Fahey cousins.

It was a hectic few hours after mass during which I wanted only to be left alone to play with my new Magic Robot while Mum wanted only that I should get changed, put aside my toys, have something to eat for breakfast, and generally get ready for the day ahead.

At last it was time to go and it was with some reluctance that I left my Magic Robot behind. I was consoled by the certainty that we would receive a Christmas toy from each of our grandparents, and our aunts and uncles, and that we would return home late that night, tired and cross but happy, with more toys than we could easily carry. And so, having been well lectured about our behaviour, we walked to the main road where we caught the tram to Gramma and Grandad Little's in Sandringham for Christmas lunch.

Uncle Cliff was waiting for us at the Sandringham tram stop in his brand new Vanguard. He was very proud of his new car and anxious to show it off. Dad was very impressed — and understandably a little envious — but Mum was bored. Dad sat in the front with Uncle Cliff while Mum sat in the back with Tessa and me. We set off but Uncle Cliff took us to Gramma and Grandad Little's house by a roundabout route only partly for the purpose of skiting about his car; he also wanted to talk. While he was driving he stretched back and to one side to include Mum in the conversation.

'He's a new man after that,' he said.

'I know,' said Mum.

'Been to Good Shepherd, talked to Father Sheehan, confession, the whole blimmin lot.'

'I know,' said Mum again.

I knew whom and what they were talking about.

'They both went to mass and communion this morning,' said Uncle Cliff.

'That's good,' said Dad. 'After all these years.'

'It was a blessing in disguise,' said Mum, and she crossed herself silently. I knew she was talking about the police and our smashed in front door.

'Something had to happen,' said Uncle Cliff. 'He couldn't have carried on like that. Not any more. Not these days. At his age too.'

'He told Leen he was sort of forced into it to oblige his old customers,' said Dad.

Uncle Cliff shrugged. 'Who knows,' he said rhetorically.

'A blessing in disguise,' said Mum again.

Uncle Cliff, unconvinced, shrugged again.

'It *is*,' insisted Mum. 'A sign to us all. A thank you from Our Lady for our efforts during her Marian year.'

I knew she was talking about saying the rosary every night. Uncle Cliff looked sideways at Dad and shrugged again. I couldn't see his face, nor Dad's, but I knew they were both rolling their eyes.

'To have them back in the faith. It's made everything worth while,' said Mum.

When we pulled into the drive Gramma and Grandad Little were waiting for us together with Aunty May and Sandra. Gramma and Grandad Little were each wearing a frilly apron — no doubt Grandad was helping in the kitchen — and when we got out of Uncle Cliff's Vanguard all the grown-ups hugged and shook hands and said 'merry Christmas' and 'compliments of the season'. I noticed that Grandad and Mum looked deeply into each others eyes and hugged a little harder and longer than anyone else and I saw Mum's mouth say a quiet 'thank you' in Grandad's ear.

We went inside and straight to the lounge. It was a hot day but the room was light and airy because Gramma Little had pulled up the Venetian blinds and opened the windows and the lace curtains were billowing slightly and softly into the room on a gentle, cooling breeze. Tessa, Sandra and I sat on the floor knowing it would soon be time for presents which were lying in a random pile under the Christmas tree. It was a wonderful looking tree; not only was it the proper shape for a Christmas tree but it was a real bright green dusted with artificial snow and properly decorated with expensive baubles — not the cheap crepe and tinsel decorations we had to use and reuse at home — and proper blinking lights. And I liked it that Gramma and Grandad's presents were carefully wrapped, each in its own differently designed bright and expensive Christmas paper, with a small Christmassy card, attached by golden string, upon which was a simple sentiment. My card said: 'To dear John with love from Gramma and Grandad. Xmas 1954'.

Grandad took off his apron and poured a lemonade for me, Tessa and Sandra, sherry for the ladies — even Mum took one for the occasion — and beer for himself, Dad and Uncle Cliff from the long-necked bottle in which all beer was packaged at that time. It was of course DB beer; all the men in our family drank only DB beer — from Dominion Breweries — because, they said, it was brewed in Auckland and that Sir Henry Kelliher, the founder of the brewery, was a good Catholic who employed only Catholics and gave a lot of money to the church. Whether any or all of this was true I don't know but I heard it said often enough and knew at least two of Dad's friends in the Holy Name Society who worked at DB so there might have been something in it.

And then, when we had all raised our glasses and said merry Christmas to each other again, and settled down with our drinks, the gift-giving and –receiving began. Presents were exchanged between the grown-ups first while we kids waited impatiently. Gramma and Grandad had something for each of the grown-ups of both families while our two families each had something each for the other and for Gramma and Grandad. Then at last we kids received our presents: something each from Gramma and Grandad together and our respective uncle and aunt together. It was an orgy of gift-giving arising for the grown-ups from memories of harder times, a celebration that things were better now, as well as from the novelty of having a new generation of bright, healthy and eager children — grandchildren, nieces and nephews — to indulge with love and generosity. No doubt it gave the grown-ups much pleasure to give, to be able to afford to give as well as having kids to give to, but it must have been time consuming and expensive to choose, buy and wrap so many gifts.

But what were all the presents given and received that day? I remember none but my own, especially the number four Meccano set I got from Gramma and Grandad Little. It easily eclipsed my Magic Robot and turned out to be the longest-lived, most played with and appreciated gift I ever received, that or any other year. In the years that followed that marvellous and infinitely expandable construction toy, of green and red steel, and hundreds of tiny brass nuts and bolts, a toy of truly unlimited potential, was the focus of all my spare leisure time in the evenings, weekends and holidays to the point of becoming an obsession. Of all my other more simple and inexpensive presents — and there were many — I especially enjoyed the balsa wood kitset glider which I got later that day from Aunty Kathleen and Uncle Dick. It took only a few minutes to press out the glider pieces — a simple fuselage with the cockpit windows and the outline of the pilot's head blurrily printed in blue ink on one side only, the wings and tail, similarly printed with pseudo-military insignia — and put them together (no glue was required) and add a small piece of modelling plasticine to the nose. I experimented with the shape and size of the plasticine, and tried throwing the almost weightless little thing into the air from the ground at first and then from all sorts of elevated spots, retrieving it from roofs and trees. In fact that simple and inexpensive little toy gave me many weeks of solitary fun well beyond the end of the year until at last it was so patched and broken that it would fly no more and was permanently grounded on the tallboy in my bedroom.

After the excitement in the lounge, exchanging gifts around the properly shaped and decorated Christmas tree, Gramma Little went off to the kitchen to serve Christmas dinner — a hot lunch in the middle of the day — while Tessa and I were jollied by Mum, with a rather exaggerated concern, into helping Grandad pick up all the torn paper and ribbons and packaging that littered the floor. I didn't mind. In fact it was fun to be chasing around on the floor on my hands and knees, picking up all the rubbish, with Grandad making a game of it. He enjoyed it too and it was obvious to me now that any tension between Mum and Grandad, which rubbed off on Dad, Gramma and me, was gone forever.

I was glad because I thought Gramma and Grandad Little were wonderful. Grandad Little, a thoroughly urbanised Aucklander but with long and deep roots into the Ngapuhi north, was large and round and brown and jolly and kind and always smiling. And he always dressed so smartly, and his big Chevrolet was the biggest, roomiest, most luxurious and smoothest-riding car I had ever ridden in. And Gramma Little, tall and thin and always so elegantly dressed — even as a kid I could see that — with wavy silvery-blue hair, was a true New

Zealander with a New Zealand accent and an utterly New Zealand attitude to everything, an attitude I understood completely, with no strange accent and no memories of or longings for 'home' like Gramma Fahey. And unlike Gramma Fahey she was never cross. She plainly and openly loved everything and everyone including Grandad, her big black cat Monty, her home and kitchen, her neighbours, her many sisters, her sons and their wives and especially us: me, Tessa and Sandra. When she spoke to us she kneeled on the floor and looked deeply into our eyes, frowning with concentration, to really *listen* to what we had to say. And like Grandad she was always ready to laugh and smile in a way that gave me a feeling of being appreciated and loved. Gramma and Grandad Little obviously and openly loved me and I always loved them in return. And I knew that Mum now loved them as much as I did and I was glad.

Grandad sat at the head of the table with Gramma at the other end, nearest the kitchen, the four grown-ups on the side to her right, their backs to the windows, and we three kids opposite to Gramma's left. Christmas crackers were pulled and the silly toys and jokes were quickly discarded in favour of the paper party hats. I thought Grandad Little looked handsome and dignified even in his pink party hat — his big round brown face, open and stress free, beamed a constant and benign smile over his whanau — while Gramma and the other grown-ups looked just silly. So we all laughed at each other, and ourselves, and I loved it that there was nothing in the laughter but love and joy and good-natured fun.

Gramma and Grandad Little didn't used to say grace but this time Grandad Little happily took the lead, with a wink to Mum who laughed, and we all crossed ourselves and bowed our heads while Grandad said the standard if somewhat graceless Catholic grace, slowly and properly as if he meant every word.

'Bless us, oh Lord, and these thy gifts, which of thy bounty we are about to receive, through Christ Our Lord, Amen,' he said.

And we all said 'Amen' together. Then we all crossed ourselves again, Gramma and Grandad Little included, the first time I had ever seen them do it. It was Christmas day and our little Christmas dinner in Sandringham at the end of nineteen-fifty-four was clearly blessed with the happiness and joy that Christmas is meant to bring to families everywhere.

Despite Christmas coming in the summer Christmas dinner was

still a traditional British-style winter affair. It was a hot meal taken in the middle of the day and everyone dressed up in their Sunday best despite the hot and humid weather. The main course was chook, a rare treat served only on special occasions and surely there was no occasion more special than Christmas. Gramma made a delicious savoury stuffing for the chicken, and a salty gravy, and I loved every mouthful. There were vegetables too — roast potato, kumara and pumpkin which were Grandad's favourites, and fresh runner beans from his own garden, he was a good gardener — but the most important thing to me was definitely Gramma's roast chook, stuffing and gravy.

There were nine of us at the table so there must have been two chooks because not only did everyone get a wing or a thigh or a drumstick but there were two wishbones. Getting served a wishbone was considered lucky and the fact that one was discovered by Tessa and the other by Sandra was probably contrived by Grandad who was responsible for carving and serving the meat. After Tessa had sucked the meat off hers Mum took it from her and wrapped it carefully in a piece of sandwich wrap and put it in her handbag. When we got home, at the end of the day, I knew it would be stood up on the mantelpiece for a few weeks, in front of the chiming clock, until it was dry and brittle. Only then would we be allowed to take it down for the wishbone ritual. Tessa and I knew exactly what to do. With the open arms of the wishbone pointing down, we would each wrap the little finger of our right hand around one of the arms, make a silent and secret wish, and pull gently until the wishbone snapped. The Y-shaped bone didn't break exactly in half; one of the arms broke away from the thickened centre and it was said that the person left holding the arm with the thickened join piece would have his wish come true.

The traditions of Christmas and Christmas dinner meant that as well as the roast chook, the Christmas crackers and the silly hats, we had to end the celebratory meal with a traditional English-style Christmas pudding. It was called for some reason a plum duff although I didn't know what a duff was and I knew for sure it didn't contain any plums. Gramma was somewhat famous for her plum duffs. She had prepared them weeks or even months in advance, making a number of them at the same time. One or two were kept for our family Christmas dinner while the others were given as Christmas gifts to her family of sisters. She prepared the mixture — the traditional dry ingredients of flour, dried fruit such as raisins, currants, sultanas and peel, nuts and spices, and sugar, all made wet with eggs and milk — in a large preserving basin in her small wash house. She stood the mixing basin in one of the wooden tubs, presumably to catch any of the mixture that might spill, and got Grandad to help with the stirring. And she cleverly engaged me and Tessa in the process, whenever we were visiting, by demanding that we stand on a chair to reach into the tub and so help stir the mixture. Getting kids to help in this way, even if we could hardly manage to move a paddle through the thick, gluey mixture, was said to bring luck to the family at Christmas and throughout the coming year.

Once we had had our last lucky stir Gramma added the shredded suet, the sickly rich yellow fat taken from around animal kidneys, and plenty of it, and plenty of port wine and brandy. Finally, numerous silver coins — sixpenny and threepenny bits which she had sterilised in boiling water — were mixed evenly through the sticky batter which was then ladled equally into ten or so cloth bags which were tied tightly with string at the top and taken to the kitchen where they were steamed for hours in large pots of boiling water. On subsequent visits we were taken to the wash house to view the bagged puddings which were hanging like big grey pumpkins, round and fat and discoloured, from the ceiling. Gramma had a wooden contraption of racks in the wash house which could be raised and lowered, using ropes and pulleys, on which, during wet winter weather, washing was hung to dry slowly in the air. But for a few weeks before Christmas — when it wasn't needed for its primary purpose — the drying rack was used to hang the Christmas puddings in the air, away from rats and mice and prying grandchildren, where they could be regularly lowered for inspection, and for the adding of more liquor which not only added immensely to the richness of flavour but helped preserve them for many weeks after Christmas, and otherwise left to slowly ripen and mature until the big day.

And so, when the chicken course was finished and the men had been served another glass of beer, and when all the grown-ups except Gramma had smoked a cigarette, it was time for the plum duff. It had, of course, been steaming and rattling away in the kitchen during lunch and now it was ready. Gramma and Grandad both went to the kitchen to prepare it and we kids were allowed to leave the table to watch. The string around the gathered-in neck had been looped over a wooden stick which rested on the edge of the pot suspending the bagged pudding in the boiling water. It was Grandad who carefully lifted the bagged pudding from the pot, holding the two ends of the stick, and carried it to the bench where Gramma was waiting with a wooden board. Then, with great and probably exaggerated ceremony the string was loosed and untied and the top of the bag pulled away gently to reveal the smooth and fatty suet skin of the hot, steaming and sweet-smelling pudding; a shiny light-brown skin which, after so many weeks, had taken on the impression of the bag's creases and folds especially at the top. Now the gorgeous looking and beautifully formed thing, still giving off steam from the top, was fully revealed. Its bag, its home for so long, now lay around it on the board, wet and limp and stained, no better than a useless rag. It had a few damp crumbs and flecks attached, torn away from the pudding in the unveiling process, which we were allowed to pick off and taste, but otherwise it had served its purpose. Now it remained only for Gramma to carefully lift the pudding's bottom clear of the now unneeded bag, using her hands and a clean cloth, and place it in the middle of the large, flat serving dish of best china. Then we were told to run back to the table and await the pudding's ceremonial arrival. When we were seated and ready, and the grown-ups were ready too, Grandad came in with the wonderful big thing which now seemed to be on fire. He had, of course, in the kitchen, doused it generously with brandy which he lit just before bringing it to the table. The flames weren't big or dangerous, in fact I thought them rather pale and thin, but it was, nevertheless, an impressive way to bring any pudding to any table at any time in any country.

The arrival of the Christmas pudding brought obligatory groans from the grown-ups — although not from the kids — about the dinner being so filling and rich, about the plum duff being the last straw, about being as full as a bull and not being able to eat any more and probably not eating for a week or a month or a year. But they all happily accepted their serving of plum duff from Grandad after Gramma, at his side, had added her own hot custard and big dobs of thick brandy sauce to order, and whipped cream. I liked plenty of everything and I especially liked the brandy sauce although more for its thick sugary butteriness than its brandy flavour. But best of all was the knowledge that there was money — real silver money — in my pudding. We were warned to be careful, to not bite too hard on the metal coins, and to not swallow them, but the warnings were quite unnecessary; I couldn't imagine how anyone could be so stupid as to swallow anything as valuable as a threepenny or sixpenny bit. To have three or four threepences and three or four sixpences in my hand at one time was to be rich beyond belief. The grown-ups too found money in their puddings which they put aside with a laugh. But the money wasn't for them. It was there for the children and I'll never forget how our excitement and joy — not only at the discovery of the money but about the whole idea of a family Christmas — gave so much pleasure to my Gramma and Grandad.

Grandad served the pudding in small versions of the large serving dish. I liked these dishes because although they were from the same family, being cream with a gold edge, and somewhat crazed, each one had its own old-fashioned coloured scene of the English countryside printed into its inside base. I enjoyed the anticipation of eating my way through my delicious pudding, setting aside the sixpenny and threepenny bits I found in the process, to eventually reveal which of the wonderful pictures lay at the bottom of my plate. I especially liked the one of the big, hairy-footed draft horses like Robbie ploughing a sloping field with dark, stormy-looking clouds on the horizon. But there were others: of hay making in a sunny field; a man standing with a broken gun, staring into the distance, while his reddish-brown setter sat patiently at his side; and huntsmen on horses outside a village pub with traces of snow on the ground. I liked them all. Sometimes, during a visit to Sandringham, I would ask Gramma to let me look at them all at once. So she put them on the carpet for me in a long row — there must have been a dozen or more — and I lay out on the floor, on my tummy and elbows, resting my chin in my hands, and studied each picture for as long as I could, imagining what might lie behind that English hedgerow, beyond that hill, at the other side of that common, beyond the pond and the geese that were there, on the other side of that leaning and broken gate, at the end of that white and winding lane, or inside that thatched cottage which had such a beautiful garden.

'What are those flowers there, Gramma?' I asked, pointing to the row of tall and stately flowers standing against the old garden wall.

Gramma kneeled down, picked up the plate and looked carefully at the details of the cottage garden.

'Oh, they're foxgloves, dear,' she said. 'They're beautiful, but quite poisonous.'

They were beautiful and I've loved them ever since.

I don't know how long we sat at the table after that big dinner but it wasn't long enough for me. Although usually bored by grown-ups' conversation I was on this Christmas day happy and relieved that the tensions which had once existed in our little family were gone forever. Despite Grandad Little's deceit, the police raid on our house, the smashed in front door and the loss of our telephone, it seems all had been forgiven. Gramma and Grandad Little were Catholics again and the grown-ups' conversation was so jolly and happy that I sat quietly in my place listening to every word, watching every expression, and catching every nuance, finally convinced that we really were one big happy family and that perhaps Mum's prayers, saying the rosary every night of the Marian year as the pope had demanded, had really been answered.

At last though the formal Christmas dinner in Sandringham was over and despite Mum's enjoyment of the occasion, and the satisfaction she had from knowing that Grandad Little had reformed and that he and Gramma had returned to the church, her heart and thoughts were now reaching up Dominion Road. And so Tessa and I were ordered to collect our presents and make our thanks to Gramma and Grandad. Everyone hugged everyone good bye. Gramma Little squeezed me so tight it actually hurt. And then, as Gramma and Grandad stood at the gate with Aunty May and Sandra, and everyone waved at everyone, we set off in Uncle Cliff's Vanguard on the next stage of our Christmas day, the short journey to Gramma Fahey's in Mount Roskill.

By the time Uncle Cliff dropped us off, with full tummies and armloads of presents, Gramma Fahey's Christmas day family party was well under way. It was a hot and sunny day but the festivities were held as usual in the room that served as a kitchen and dining room. It had once been dominated by a black coal range but that had been removed and its space, a deep cavity set into the kitchen's outside wall, had been filled by a modern electric stove in the oven of which Gramma Fahey and Aunty Irene baked the cakes and biscuits the family enjoyed so much and which today had been used to cook Christmas dinner. A large table, usually set against the opposite wall, was pulled out for visitors who sat on the long form which was always there, under the table. By the time we arrived the table and the adjacent sink and bench were littered with the recognisable remains of a Christmas dinner not unlike that which we had just finished at Gramma and Grandad Little's: the skeleton of a couple of chooks, large dinner plates smeared with fatty gravy and stray peas, and empty pudding plates showing the dark and smudgy evidence of a Christmas pudding mixed with the sticky residue of custard and cream. And of course everybody was wearing a silly paper hat. Mum and Dad were warmly welcomed by a roomful of grown-ups — who were no doubt slightly intoxicated by the atmosphere as much as by alcohol — who quickly absorbed them into the body of the party. Tessa and I were welcomed equally but were glad to escape the confines of the smoky stuffy room to join our cousins who were playing outside. But first we had to go to the bathroom to change into some old clothes which Mum had brought with her knowing that we would spend the rest of the day in rough and tumble games.

There was Christmas gift giving at Gramma Fahey's but it was a haphazard process; Tessa and I received our presents, something from each of our aunts, at random and quite unpredictable moments in the course of the afternoon. Indeed, the whole Christmas celebration at Gramma Fahey's was an altogether chaotic affair which bore no resemblance to the quiet orderliness of the morning at Gramma and Grandad Little's. At Gramma Fahey's the grown-ups stayed inside doing I know not what while I was free to play away the entire afternoon and evening with the cousins I loved so much.

At first we played our games in Gramma Fahey's small front yard but soon moved to the bigger back yard, and into the old wood-shed that stood there, somewhat crookedly, and served as a hut or a fort or a hideout although Tessa and the other girls didn't like it because of the spiders and wetas which were there or which they imagined were there. And then, later in the day, as the boundaries of Gramma Fahey's property seemed to shrink, we extended our play into the street and then up the street to include the boundless open spaces, winding paths and giant trees of the Big King reserve.

What did we play? Kingaseeny was especially popular with the boys. It was a game even now I don't know how to spell — I have never seen it written down and so it must be spelled here as it sounded to me then — but which we all knew exactly how to play. In kingaseeny someone was first elected he — an election which was made quickly and without dispute — and the he or she so elected was required to stand in the middle of the allotted playing area, Gramma Fahey's front yard was chosen because it was an open space free of trees or shrubs, while everyone else stood together at one side of the yard, an 'end' for the purposes of the game. The person who was he would then make his choice from the cousins ranged in a line at the side of the yard and the chosen one — usually the youngest, weakest or smallest and therefore thought the easiest to catch — would have to use speed and agility to dash across to the other side of the yard without being caught or tagged. Sometimes, when only the boy cousins were playing, we were required to tackle the runner, rugby style, employing a ruthless gang tackle, in imitation of a rugby defence, when there was more than one of us in the middle. But most times it was enough to touch or tag a runner to effect a catch and even then the bigger boys were lenient in their treatment of the girls and downright kind and indulgent to the younger ones who so enjoyed playing with their big cousins. Whichever way the runner was caught he or she would join the person in the middle and, having chosen the next runner, help in his or her pursuit and capture and so increase the size and effectiveness of the team in the middle and decrease the chances of the next runner making it to the other side. If any runner did reach the other side of the yard without being caught then all those waiting to run would whoop out the call kingaseeny and make a mad and mass dash to the other side — called a bull rush — and so confuse those in the middle and minimise the chances of being caught. The winner was the last uncaught player and if the game were to continue it would restart with the first player caught becoming the new he. But kingaseeny required so much energy, leaving most of us puffed out and ready for a rest, that once a winner had been found the game rarely started again. Instead, after a rest on the cool grass in the shade of Gramma's hedge, and a talk, and perhaps a visit inside for a drink, we would all move on to another less vigorous game.

Chasie was of course another standard game and once again there was never any delay or dispute in electing the first person to go he. Could there be a simpler kid's game than chasie? The he (or she) who was he had merely to chase and tag — that is simply touch — someone else to transfer to him or her the quality of being he. It was therefore a game without end but it soon evolved into go home stay home in which the person who was he couldn't transfer being he but had to tag *all* the players; as they were tagged they had to go to a prearranged place — called 'home' — and wait there until all the other players were also tagged. But as well as having to roam the playing area, chasing and tagging, the player who was he also had to guard home because any player not yet tagged was able to free those players at home if he could manage to get there and tag the prisoners himself without being caught. Finally, when all the players were caught and therefore at home the player who was first tagged became he and the game started again.

In the matter of children's games, being he was used by all the kids I knew although I was aware, from books and the pictures, that kids in England called the person who was he the neuter it. I don't know why but it always sounded strange to be it. Immigrant pommy kids using it for he sounded posh and effeminate to Kiwi kids and so were soon bullied into saying he like everyone else although being he must have sounded equally strange to them especially when a girl was he. But being he was devoid of any other meaning than that given it in the context of the game. This use and meaning of 'he' must have been well-established as New Zealand idiom as Dad and other men frequently used the term 'Well, I'll go he' to mean 'Well, I'm surprised' (about some event or outcome). But 'I'll go he' is never heard now and seems to have passed quietly out of use as have other common sayings with the same meaning (such as 'I'll be a monkey's uncle' or 'I'll eat my hat') and exclamations like 'By Jove!', 'What the deuce!', 'What the Dickens!'. The description of something difficult to do being 'a Dickens of a job' was common and 'billy-oh' was an all-purpose word used frequently in phrases such as 'What the billy-oh's going on?' or 'He's feeling as sick as billy-oh'. The all-purpose word 'doings' was used for the petty ingredients or makings or components or fixings of just about anything. 'I've got the doings' meant having all those things necessary to do anything from making a cup of tea to mending a puncture. 'Doings' was also used, as in 'Where's the doings?', like 'thingamabob' and 'thingamajig', for any item whose actual name was apparently or temporarily forgotten. Other commonly used terms not now heard include being 'a box of birds' (for being bright and cheerful), feeling 'like a ball of muscle' (for feeling healthy, strong and well) or, on the other hand, feeling 'a bit crook' (for feeling a little unwell), or just 'crook' (for being ill), or being 'really crook' (for being seriously ill). Indeed 'crook' was a remarkably versatile word and the term 'going crook' (meaning reprimanding someone about something) was then used, heard and understood by all men, women and children.

Another popular game in which someone had to be he was hide

and seek which we called simply hidey. This game required the person who was he to hide his eyes — usually by putting a bent arm up against a wall and burying his head in the inner crook of his elbow — and count aloud to a prearranged number, usually a hundred although more if the agreed playing area were particularly expansive, while the players ran away to find a hiding place. Boundaries were defined in advance — 'you've got to stay in Gramma's place' perhaps, or 'only in the park' — but otherwise there were no rules about exactly where one could hide. Indeed there were few rules in any of these simple games, and never a dispute.

But there was one rule — actually more of a convention than a rule — which applied equally and universally to all people and all games. Called 'gates' it could be used by any player, but only judiciously, to confer a temporary immunity while he or she did something that must be done and couldn't be delayed. Having to go inside to the toilet was an acceptable use of gates; so was being physically hurt although there had to be a decent and obvious wound, and preferably some blood, which made it hard to plead a sprained ankle. Being tired — puffed out was the term used — was acceptable from one of the younger cousins, especially a girl, but was never grounds for gates for boys although having the stitch — a sharp pain in the side from overexertion — was. And if one of the girl cousin's hair ribbons came loose and had to be retied by her mother then gates was granted only reluctantly by the boys and not without some gentle and friendly derision.

We invoked the protective power of gates by crossing the middle finger of each hand over the top of its neighbouring index finger, drawing the other two fingers into the palm of the hand and locking them there with the thumb, and holding up both hands so configured, forward of and a little above our head, and saying the word 'gates' aloud. But the granting of gates was never given without the demand for some sort of proof even if it were just the other players' judgement of sincerity.

An afternoon of such play — and Christmas day was typical, not unusual — was interrupted only when Aunty Irene, with the kindest of intentions, emerged from the house with something to drink: a jug of orange cordial perhaps, or a tray of her delicious cakes and biscuits. But, sadly, such an interruption broke the spell which had charmed us all day. Now the younger kids, especially the girls, including Tessa —

unused to such continuously vigorous play with big boys — discovered how tired and sleepy they were and went inside to find their mother's knee where they knew they could lean, and rest quietly, a thumb in their mouth, and listen to the droning talk of the grown-ups. But the older cousins and I, boys and girls, saw this break as an opportunity. We sensed that the day was drawing to a close, that Christmas would soon be over for another year. And while we knew we would see each other again frequently during the coming holidays it would never be quite the same — quite as magical — as it was on Christmas day. And so now, without the smaller kids to worry about — and we were all and always considerate of our small cousins — we could seek more space to play games more grown-up than chasie. With our tummies full again we left Gramma's place for the first time that day and wandered up the street, talking and laughing incessantly, with the infectious joy of childhood. Sometimes one of us would break into a run, and the others would follow, imitating the galloping lope of cowboys on horseback in pursuit of fleeing Indians, clicking our tongues on our teeth to make a galloping noise. And with one hand gripping the invisible reins in front we whacked our own backsides with the flat of the other hand and galloped up the street to the Big King reserve. There were winding paths and fields of grass and tall trees there where we, a gang of bright, healthy and happy kids, unaware of our parents and the troubles of the world, could become cowboys of the wild west, hiding behind trees and shooting at each other with Colt forty-fives shaped by our hands and fingers. The cracking sounds of the shooting were made at the back of our throats and sometimes we made a zing noise when a bullet ricocheted off one of the rocks in the badlands where we played. Or in a moment, without notice, but in perfect synchronicity, we could transport ourselves across time and space to Sherwood Forest and become Merrie Men supporting Robin Hood, who was always cousin Robert, the oldest cousin, and Maid Marion, who was always cousin Margaret who I thought was the most beautiful girl in the world and the only person I would ever marry if ever I married which I doubted. Together, that early summer evening so long ago, we few children, lost in the boundless world of our shared imaginations, became what we imagined and were without doubt quite prepared to rob from the rich, if only someone rich should pass by, to give to the poor.

At last though it was time to leave the Big King. Now even we were tired and although it was still light we all knew it was early evening and that, sadly, the day — Christmas day — was almost over.

Can children be melancholy? That's how I felt as I walked backed down the volcanic slope to Gramma Fahey's with my cousins, slowly and reluctantly, our heads bowed, our narrow shoulders stooped, chatting idly, fiddling with a stick or a stone. And although we talked quietly of everything, we didn't mention the sadness I'm sure we all felt; the familiar cosmic sadness I knew so well, experienced so often, with which all kids are familiar but which, because grown-ups never mention it, they can never name, explain or even acknowledge.

Back at Gramma's it was time for tea; a make-do meal of Christmas day left-overs spread out on the kitchen table from which we kids, young and old — the grown-ups having made their choice — were free to take whatever we wished. And so we did, greedily, putting it all on paper plates which we took outside. There we sat together, cross-legged, in a big circle, on the hard dry lawn under Gramma's lemon tree, being careful to avoid the patches of prickly Onehunga weed. When we were finished we took our empty plates inside and helped ourselves from big crystal dishes of jelly, of all possible flavours and bright colours, and fruit salad, and a big glass dish of vanilla ice cream, this time using china pudding bowls. We could also help ourselves from the tins of Aunty Irene's little queen cakes, iced with bright red or green Christmas icing, made especially for the occasion.

That I could take and eat what I liked, and as much as I liked, was a rare treat. Despite the deliciousness of Gramma Little's Christmas lunch of roast chicken and stuffing and gravy, and the hot, rich plum duff with custard and cream and brandy sauce, I was hungry again. And the informality and freedom of Christmas tea at Gramma Fahey's made it the best Christmas meal of all especially as I and my cousins sat cross-legged together, under Gramma's huge and thorny lemon tree, laughing and talking quietly, somewhat subdued, but with no grown-up supervision or interference, as day became dusk and dusk became evening and parents began bustling about, turning on lights, tidying up, collecting presents and making ready for the journey home.

A taxi was called for us and our presents but I slept during the whole journey home. I woke early the next morning, Boxing day, wholly renewed by sleep, and sat on the floor of my bedroom in my pyjamas surrounded by all my new toys. Unfortunately the joy of the new day was spoiled because Boxing day was a Sunday which meant we would soon have to get dressed and go to mass. But Mum and Dad were tired and slept late and so instead of rushing, as we usually did on Sunday mornings, Mum made us all breakfast — which meant no communion that Sunday — which we had together before walking leisurely through the burning heat of the morning to attend nine o'clock mass.

Christmas day — presents in the morning, Christmas dinner at Gramma and Grandad Little's, and the afternoon and evening at Gramma Fahey's — was the very best and most wonderful day of my entire Marian year. The joy came mostly from having been left alone for hours to play with my cousins with whom I shared so many opinions about our strange grown-up relations, and an intimate knowledge of family matters and history which I could share with nobody else in the world. And all the fun of Christmas — the pure joy and sheer childish pleasure of that special day, and the possession of so many new presents — was enhanced by the knowledge that once I got home from mass that Sunday morning, Boxing day, I had the entire and seemingly endless summer holiday ahead of me. Time to play with my new toys as much as I liked without worrying about school and its trials. Time to enjoy the long days and evenings and to play at the beach for hours and hours, with all my cousins again, at one of the all-day family picnics Mum and her sisters managed to arrange during those magical six weeks of summer.

It was a wonderful thought and a lovely way to end my Marian year.

Epilogue

A PAINTER CANNOT PAINT PAST THE EDGE OF HIS canvas and nor should I write past the end of my Marian year. But many people have asked for at least a glimpse into the future.

One week after Christmas day it was new year's day, nineteen fifty-five, the feast of the circumcision again, a holy day of obligation. My Marian year was truly over. In late January of that new year, before the end of the summer holidays, Mum took me to George Courts in Karangahape Road to buy the school uniform required by my new school, Marist Brothers' in Vermont Street, Ponsonby. It wasn't especially different from the uniform I was used to wearing except there was a compulsory cap, an unpleasant and old-fashioned thing in navy-blue with horizontal stripes of pale blue and maroon, a rigid peak covered in matching fabric, and a hard button at the very top, where the cap's segments came together, which was the target of bullies who delighted in hitting it with a hard flat book so hurting and badly bruising the top of the victim's head. That was only one of the lessons I was to learn quickly, within hours of my first day at Marist. Another was the rigid almost military discipline of the brothers applied to all matters including the demand that a boy's cap should be worn at all times on the way to and from school and should be raised as a sign of respect to teachers or any adult who might require a greeting. This absurd hat training was wasted on a generation of boys who would soon abandon hat wearing for the rest of their lives.

Mum took me to Taylor's to buy the stationery, required by the new school, from a long list, familiar enough to the shopkeepers, printed in smudged purple ink on coarse paper, including more exercise books (some with special rulings) and note books than I had ever owned, a set of black pencils, a red pencil, and a plastic pencil sharpener and rubber each of which fitted into its own partition in my new pencil case, and, most important of all, a long, slender, varnished wooden pen complete with a sharp steel nib. At Marist I would learn to scratch an ink-laden nib across paper, without tearing the surface or making a forbidden blot, and then, when it was empty and dry, to dip it in the white china reservoir of dull blue ink which was set into the top of every desk. There were standard text books to be bought including a dictionary, and a world atlas in which New Zealand and all the countries of the British Empire were coloured red; and tools too including a wooden ruler inlaid with native New Zealand woods, a semi-circular clear plastic thing with angles printed on it, a set of dividers one leg of which was dangerously pointed while the other had an adjustable pencil grip, and other such unremembered things all of which I would have to carry to school on the first day in the large, stiff and embarrassingly new schoolbag I had received somewhat ungraciously for Christmas.

But despite the new school uniform in my tallboy, and the new schoolbag full of exercise books, newly covered by Mum in spare wallpaper, a new pencil case, freshly sharpened pencils (on the unsharpened end of which Mum had printed my name on a flat plane she had shaved from the round wood), and a set of mysterious metal tools for an unknown discipline called geometry, I had to wait a few more weeks before I could set out on the road I knew, without being told, was leading me not only out of the familiar streets of home but out of the security and innocence of childhood. In the meantime, while I should have been enjoying the summer holidays, and especially the family picnics at the beach, I was burdened by nervous anticipation and the not childish fear of the unknown. For the first time in my life I had worries — secret doubts and fears I could share with nobody — to keep me awake at night and spoil the enjoyment of my summer holiday. I knew by then that Saint Michael's was a school for children and that when I went to Marist I would be a child no more. But what, I worried, would Marist be like? And the brothers? What would it be like to be taught by a man and to have only boys in the class and in the school? Would I be able to find my way to Ponsonby on the new electric trolley bus? How would I know when to get off and change buses? What if I lost the bus concession tickets Mum had bought me? I knew there would be examinations, much harder tests than those I was used to at Saint Michael's; I knew I wasn't clever so I worried about how I would manage against so many new boys when I was so bad at tests. I heard stories about what happens to new boys at Marist. Would there be bullies? Would there be fights? Would Rangi and Tommy be going to Marist and would they still help me?

Often during those few but long weeks of waiting I secretly wished I could stay in the little world I knew so well. I longed to stay with my beautiful, wonderful, kind, thoughtful and loving mother who for some reason now seemed worried, fretful and preoccupied — I didn't know it then but a new baby was on the way — and my remote but not unkind father of whom I was quietly proud; with Tessa the nuisance who had announced in the new year that she now wanted to be called Theresa; with all my cousins and friends in Winstone Street and Milton Street who were not going to Marist but to the local intermediate, or were staying behind in the world I was leaving.

I knew I couldn't stay, and I didn't. Instead, at the end of January, I passed silently and timidly, without protest, through an opening in the heavy but invisible curtain which surrounded my little world, taking my first steps on the road to adolescence and manhood. The curtain closed softly behind me, sealing forever the gap that was so briefly opened, meaning I could never return to the safety and security of the familiar world in which I had learned so much and which had protected and sheltered me so well for more than ten years.

I'm sure those who remained hardly missed me. They were, after all, busy creating and enjoying their own world. And when their turn came to leave they would each take with them their own versions of that which I had taken with me. Incomplete and imperfect as they surely are my memories belong only to me. They are the *only* possessions which are mine alone and which can never be taken from me. Even shared willingly with many others, for many years into the unknown future, they will always remain uniquely mine.

THE END